MW00973907

KASHMIR
The Wounded Valley

KASHMIR

The Wounded Valley

Ajit Bhattacharjea

UBSPD

UBS Publishers' Distributors Ltd.

New Delhi ● Bombay ● Bangalore ● Madras ●
Calcutta ● Patna ● Kanpur ● London

UBS Publishers' Distributors Ltd.
5 Ansari Road, New Delhi-110 002
Bombay Bangalore Madras
Calcutta Patna Kanpur London

First Published 1994

Published in association with the Indian Institute of Advanced Study, Shimla.

ISBN 81-86112-36-7

Cover Design :   UBS Art Studio

Typeset at UBSPD in 10½ pt New Century Schoolbook
Printed at Rajkamal Electric Press, Delhi

To
my daughter
SUMAN
for making it possible

Acknowledgements

A fellowship at the Indian Institute of Advanced Study, Shimla, enabled me to complete this work in the undisturbed scenic setting of the former Viceregal Lodge, with all the necessary academic and research facilities. I am particularly grateful to the Director, staff and Fellows of the Institute for their advice and comments, though they are not responsible for my views.

My thanks are also due to the India International Centre, New Delhi, for its comfortable library and helpful staff. I should like to thank the Nehru Memorial Museum and Library, New Delhi, for allowing me to use its reference library. At the same time, I must express my regret that permission to consult the Nehru papers was denied, though they have been made available to foreign scholars. As a result, my research depended primarily on British and American documents.

For information on current developments, I thank my many fellow-journalists who have covered and interpreted the Kashmir scene and New Delhi's policies. Thanks are also due to Penguin (India) for enabling me to go through the manuscript of the English translation (by Khushwant Singh) of Sheikh Abdullah's autobiography before it was published. I am grateful to the noted historian, Professor Mushirul Hasan, for going through the manuscript before publication.

Finally, I recall with gratitude the opportunity provided by Captain J.C. Kathpalia, of the former Indian National Airways, for flying me into the Kashmir valley in those crucial days of October 1947.

Ajit Bhattacharjea

Preface

*T*owards the end of October 1947, Delhi was still in the grip of communal frenzy after the killings of the previous month. The Muslims who remained in the capital were no longer hunted down by groups eager to wreak revenge for the atrocities on Hindus and Sikhs in the recently created nation-state of Pakistan; they took refuge in protected localities; most of them were sheltered behind the medieval walls of the Purana Qila (Old Fort), guarded by the army. On 2 October, his birthday, even Mahatma Gandhi accepted defeat: in his agony, he called upon his Maker to take him away; he could not stand such barbarism any longer.

On the last day of the month, a friend, a pilot in a private airline, invited me to accompany him on a flight to Srinagar, still threatened by Pathan tribal hordes let through by Pakistan, as reported in *The Hindustan Times*, the paper in which I was starting my career. Civil aircraft had been requisitioned to fly in troops and supplies. My friend's Dakota had been converted into a fuel tanker. The seats had been ripped out and replaced by a huge tank. I was the only passenger.

Heavy with petrol, the plane barely cleared the Banihal Pass. The contrast from the dry, dun-coloured approach from Jammu as we entered the valley was incredible. The prospect before us – fields of delicate shades of green, pellucid blue lakes, majestic trees, rippling streams, enclosed in a frame of the highest mountain ranges in the world – looked as if scissored from some celestial spot. The

Dakota flew low and and Kashmir unrolled slowly before
us with a graduated deliberateness not available in the jet
age.

Only when we circled to land at Srinagar could we see
that all was not well in paradise. Columns of smoke were
rising from the villages beyond. We landed on the dirt
airstrip to find several other aircraft already there,
unloading men and their weapons. The raiders, we were
informed, had been pushed back five miles from the
outskirts of the airfield which they had threatened to seize
three days earlier. Troops were still being ferried directly
to the front.

Bearded men, unmistakably Muslim, who in Delhi
would have been regarded with suspicion as possible agents
of Pakistan, were gathered round the buses and trucks that
lined the approach to the airfield. They were the men who
ferried the troops forward and were loading trucks from the
piles of military supplies left by departing aircraft. And
when we hopped a jeep ride into the city, we found volunteer
groups, organised by the National Conference, patrolling the
roads and guarding the bridges. The Maharaja's police had
fled with him. Even so, many shops were open and traffic
was moving. There was no question of insecurity. The people
around us – mostly Muslim but with many Hindus and
Sikhs among them – were obviously friendly.

At the old Nedou's Hotel, a group of correspondents was
gathered on the lawn, drinking beer under the mild autumn
afternoon sun, recovering from writing about a war being
fought not ten miles away. I envied them but nothing
seemed more unlikely than for a fledgling journalist to get
such an assignment. But the photographs I took of the
scenes in Srinagar possibly impressed the Editor. I was
posted to Srinagar in the summer of 1948, when the
Pakistan army was openly engaged in the war.

By then, the threat to Srinagar had receded, for the
enemy had been pushed back towards the edges of the
valley. Kashmiri Muslims were being trained to fight – an
opportunity not given to them before – beside the Indian

soldiers. There were no tourists; lights were dim; only a few
policemen had returned to work. But, again, there was no
sense of insecurity. Soldiers held their weapons loosely; they
were not loaded until near the front. Two other Indian
correspondents and I shared a houseboat; walked along the
lonely Jhelum bund for briefings and to the club in the
evenings, returning well after dark, without ever having
cause for unease.

The magic of *shikara* rides on the Dal in the moonlight
could be savoured till late at night. The cascading Mughal
gardens were crowded, with fountains playing. One could
imagine the Emperor Jahangir, who created them more
than three hundred years ago, being inspired to write:

The garden nymphs (flowers) were brilliant,
Their cheeks shone like lamps;
There were fragrant buds on their stems
Like dark amulets on the arms of the beloved.
The wakeful, ode-rehearsing nightingale
Whetted the desires of wine-drinkers;
At each fountain the duck dipped his beak
Like golden scissors cutting silk;
There were flower-carpets and fresh rosebuds,
The wind fanned the lamps of the roses,
The violet braided her locks,
The buds tied a knot in the heart.

There were no security guards for Sheikh Abdullah
when the divisional commander, Major General K.S.
Thimmayya, drove him on a barely 'jeepable' track to the
upland valley of Gurez, that had been just retaken. They
were accompanied only by the General's ADC and a
correspondent. Though the Sheikh was Prime Minister of
Kashmir, no guards escorted him on a tour of the valley. He
travelled in a single car with Begum Abdullah and the
writer. He was welcomed in every village. Not every
Kashmiri may have supported the National Conference, but
disagreement never extended to violence within the valley.

But when I suggested in Delhi, on the basis of this

experience, that Kashmiris were unlikely to vote for Pakistan in a referendum, few believed me. The distrust of Muslims, magnified by partition, was too deep. Over the years, tension with Pakistan and communal politics in India drove this doubt deeper, enhancing reverse doubts in Kashmir. Yet, diplomatic observers, at least in the early years, did not share Indian doubts. US State Department files reveal that Chester Bowles, US Ambassador in the early fifties, cabled Washington on 16 November 1951, that he had asked all the chiefs of diplomatic missions in New Delhi as to who would win a plebiscite in Kashmir. Their response: "Each without exception stated India would win; margin varied from three to two to four to one. Many of these mission chiefs or their staffs visited Kashmir recently. American press here, several of whom have recently visited Kashmir, also agree with this analysis."

*L*anding in Srinagar in May 1993 was like entering hostile territory. No bearded locals, except for one or two policemen, were visible at the airport. Everyone was frisked and the place was ringed with para-military troops, their automatic weapons at the ready. The road into town was studded with sandbagged concrete bunkers, with light machineguns poking out from slits. It was patrolled by soldiers in jeeps and squads on the road with fingers always near their triggers. In town, the familiar road on the Jhelum bund was interrupted by security force encampments; entry into several stretches was prohibited; the club was the Central Reserve Police headquarters.

The men of the security forces, from the army as well as para-military units, were under strain. They came from distant parts of the country and knew nothing of the Kashmiri language or culture, or the freezing cold of winter. Their tours of duty were repeatedly extended. They were aware of colleagues being killed or wounded by shots from unexpected directions or by hand grenades pulled out of the

long *phirans* worn by men and women alike. They often
spent hours within the confines of bunkers in which they
could barely stand. In the circumstances, they could hardly
be expected to like the locals, who reciprocated the distrust.
They were no longer seen as protectors.

The row of houseboats on the Dal was empty; so were
the *shikaras*: visitors were advised against rides on the lake
and against venturing out to the Mughal gardens. Hotels
on the lakeside boulevard were occupied by security forces.
Government officials were ferried to and from the
secretariat in guarded convoys. They were not permitted to
venture out of their guarded hostels on their own, lest they
be kidnapped. No official revenues were being collected.
Politicians were noticeable by their absence. They were on
the militant hit list.

Yet Srinagar had survived more than three years of
militant terror and State counter-terror. Children walked
to and from school, several games of cricket were in
progress. Some shops catering to tourists were open. The
bazaars in the old city were crowded as ever. Sikh-owned
shops were wide open and numerous Sikhs, so easily
identifiable, were on the roads. Life was normal wherever
the militants and security forces were absent.

Everyone was willing to talk, ranging from pavement
vendors to a carpet millionaire. As I walked freely through
the old city, I received no hostile glances, even in the famous
Lal Chowk, scene of so many eventful political gatherings,
where now the gutted remains of buildings recalled a recent
encounter with the security forces. Antagonism was targeted
on the security forces and the Government behind them.
Almost everyone I met wanted *azaadi*. They or their
families had fallen foul of the security forces; they were all
full of stories of torture and repression, horrifying even if
one-tenth were true, and some were. There was evidence
even in the few days that I was there.

The local police had recently struck work and
demonstrated after one of them had died under
interrogation. For the second time, several buildings in the

apple town of Sopore had been burnt by the security forces in retaliation for a militant attack. And this excerpt is taken from a report I read on 6 May, in the *Kashmir Times*, a well-established paper:

> Zahoor [a tailor] alleged that during his detention, he was given electric shocks [in addition to other forms of torture] repeatedly.... He started vomiting blood. But the securitymen went ahead with the torture. However, when his condition became very critical, the BSF [Border Security Force] men dropped him in the police control room from where he was handed over to his family members. He was taken to SMHS hospital but later shifted to Soura Institute where he is struggling for life now....

*T*his book is an attempt to understand the causes of the contrast between 1947 and 1993. It focusses on the valley, not the entire State of Jammu and Kashmir, for it is the valley that represents the most serious challenge to India's secular and democratic credentials that it has known since independence. It deals mainly with the political relationship between Kashmir and the Indian Union. It does not delve into the involvement of Pakistan and other foreign countries in Kashmir, including the long debates in the UN Security Council, except to the extent that they directly affect this relationship.

However, one must delve into the long history of Kashmir to comprehend the positive and negative aspects of the relationship. For it is deeply rooted in the cultural and political forces that have influenced the valley over the centuries; and in the native resistance to them. And these forces have been guided by the unique geographic situation of the valley at the northern extremity of the land mass of the Indian subcontinent. While the surrounding mountain ranges induced insularity, passes in them enabled Kashmir to interact positively with surrounding cultures. But the passes also became routes of foreign domination and subjection, leaving a deep impress on folk memory. This, in turn, promoted a sense of *Kashmiryat*: of a distinct, common politico-cultural identity, which continues to dominate the people's vision of their future.

Contents

Chapter I

Introduction

*F*ree India's association with Kashmir was not designed as an imperial connection. Indeed, New Delhi went out of its way to stress, and commit itself to, a free and voluntary association very different to imperial dispensations of the past. The right of the people to determine their own future, even after the then princely State of Jammu and Kashmir had acceded to the Union under pressure of the tribal invasion facilitated by Pakistan, was recognised in a letter accompanying the document accepting the State's accession on 27 October 1947 by Maharaja Hari Singh. His signature was not enough; the accession had to be endorsed by the leader of the main political party in Kashmir, the National Conference, before Jawaharlal Nehru accepted it and despatched the Indian army to protect the valley. Otherwise, New Delhi would be seen as propping up a Hindu Maharaja against his Muslim people: the essence of Pakistan's case, which had considerable plausibility abroad after religious strife led to the partitioning of British India. According to the 1941 census, there were 70 per cent more Muslims than Hindus among Jammu's 1,561,580 residents, whereas among Kashmir's 1,728,600 inhabitants, over 90 per cent were Muslim. The essence of India's case was that the people had preferred India because of its commitment to democracy and secularism.

The crucial test on the ground itself was the active popular support received by the first elements of the Indian army who were flown to Srinagar when the tribals were at its gates. The army officers involved later stated that they could not have held the valley if the local volunteers had not maintained law and order, provided transport and guides, and guarded vital installations. Kashmir would not have been part of the Indian Union without the support of the residents of the valley, of whom more than 90 per cent were Muslim.

In effect, accession was a bargain: popular Kashmiri support for joining India in exchange for self-government, with the Centre's powers limited to the items falling under the three subjects listed in the Instrument of Accession: foreign affairs, defence and communications. And the bargain could be rejected if found unsatisfactory, a commitment made explicitly by the Government of India on the occasion and later to the United Nations. Jawaharlal Nehru's statement to this effect, in the Lok Sabha on 7 August 1952, must still haunt New Delhi. Describing the basis of the relationship between India and Kashmir, he said:

> So while the accession was complete in law and in fact, the other fact which has nothing to do with the law remains, namely, our pledge to the people of Kashmir – if you like, to the people of the world – that this matter could be affirmed or cancelled by the people of Kashmir according to their wishes. We do not wish to win people against their will with the help of armed force; and if the people of Kashmir wish to part company with us, they may go their way and we shall go ours. We want no forced marriages, no forced unions.

This has not prevented many who have chronicled developments concerning Kashmir from adopting the style of colonial historians. They are more concerned with the territory than with the people. And for Hindu extremists, Kashmir is a territory that has been reconquered from the

Muslims and must be held by force, as eloquently argued by Balraj Madhok, once President of the Jana Sangh.

Yet it is the unique fact of the willingness of the people of a Muslim majority area to join India – after the partition of British India and the accompanying communal holocaust – that justifies the special treatment promised to Kashmir. Their support was a living denial of the universality of the two-nation theory on which British India had been divided (which is why Pakistan is so emotionally involved on the other side), and which, if unchallenged, would convert residual India also into a theocratic state.

The essential tragedy behind the crisis in the valley of Kashmir is that it originated in positive developments that strengthened the forces of secular democracy at a crucial time in newly independent India and introduced a new level of flexibility in federal relations. These developments were interlinked. The special status given to Jammu and Kashmir and the limitations originally placed on Central intervention in the State enabled Kashmir's most popular leader, Sheikh Mohammad Abdullah, to counter the religious appeal of Pakistan to the State's Muslim majority. He was able to stress a common Kashmiri identity and the promise of radical socio-economic change to end centuries of oppression and exploitation. Since independence appeared impractical, this was more likely to be achieved, he maintained, in partnership with an India pledged to secularism and democracy than a Pakistan using religion as a cloak for autocracy.[1] He was attracted by Mahatma Gandhi and Jawaharlal Nehru, both committed to secularism and socio-economic change, if in different ways. As India's first Prime Minister and a Kashmiri by descent, Nehru played a crucial role in determining Kashmir's future.

The valley itself, its long history, and the unique social and religious practices of its people, gave promise of their following their own eclectic path if given the opportunity. Kashmir's haunting beauty, shielded by the highest mountain ranges in the world, has no equal. The blend of Sanskrit, Buddhist, Tibetan, Sufi, Persian and Arabic cultural and religious influences is also unique; as is the language. The evolution of Kashmir Shaivism, with its emphasis on monism and egalitarianism, minimised friction with the teachings of Islam when Islam first entered the valley.

Unlike most of the subcontinent, where Islam came through conquest, it came to Kashmir largely through conversion, through the influence of the gentle, meditative order of Sufis, escaping from Persia in the fourteenth century, led by Saiyyid Ali Hamdani. The valley still resonates with the songs of the wandering mystic Lal Ded and verses of Sheikh Noor-ud-Din or Nund Rishi, founder of the Rishi order, who spread their message of universal love soon after. They were revered by both Hindus and Muslims and took inspiration from both religions. The iconoclastic excesses of a local despot, Sultan Sikandar, reduced the number of Brahmins who had resisted conversion to a handful. But his successor, the great Zainul Abidin (1420-70), made up for his excesses. He invited many back from exile, rebuilt their temples and participated in their festivities.

The four million Kashmiris seemed ideally suited to resist the pull of religious fundamentalism, though they were good Muslims in their own fashion. Kashmir also became a test case for India, of its ability to nurture the allegiance of an Islamic people who joined a Hindu-majority nation in October 1947 believing in its commitment to the values of democracy and secularism, despite the communal carnage preceding and following the partition of the subcontinent. Natural linkages of terrain, too, favoured Pakistan. Even so those wanting to join Pakistan were in a minority. But in the 1980s and 1990s, Kashmir's liberal tradition came under severe pressure from the forces of Islamic fundamentalism, financed by oil-rich Gulf countries and sponsored by Pakistan, and as a reaction to the threat perceived from resurgent Hindu nationalism in India and enhanced imposition of Central authority. Kashmir has gone through many dark periods in its long history, which have left their impact on its people. Over the centuries, the biggest problem faced by residents of the valley has been how to keep outsiders out. That is the price they have paid for its beauty. The price has been high, for the valley has attracted the most rapacious neighbours in the region. The intoxication of ruling such an envied spot has gone to the heads of many, even of native rulers, some of whom exceeded outsiders in the privation and suffering they visited on the valley.

Fortunately, that has not been the whole story. Kashmir has had the occasional good fortune to be governed by kings known for their vision and magnanimity. It was better known for the artists, poets, musicians, philosophers, religious divines and other notables that it attracted and inspired. Kashmir is unique in south Asia, indeed in much of the world, in having a recorded history going back three thousand years or more. It was recorded in Sanskrit by Kalhana in the twelfth century, in the heroic style of the times, in his *Rajatarangini* (River of Kings). The first king to figure in it, Gonanda I, was of Mahabharat vintage and was killed on the field of battle by no less than Krishna himself.[2]

History has left its mark on the Kashmiri temperament. To a large extent, it is a mark of suffering. Only the thin layer of the nobility escaped feudal privation. Over the centuries, the Kashmiri learned to bow before authority. He had no other option. The first Dogra ruler, Gulab Singh, bought the valley and its inhabitants from the British in 1846 for as little as seventy-five lakhs of rupees coupled, of course, with a pledge of allegiance to the new imperial power. The barbarity with which he established his dynasty was vividly described by a contemporary British traveller, G.T. Vigne.[3] Prisoners were flayed alive, their skins filled with straw and planted by the wayside for the instruction

of all who passed by. That was the object lesson he gave his
son and successor, Ranbir Singh, in the art of governing.
Economically, too, the Kashmiri was cruelly mulcted by an
array of taxes.[4] Surviving under such pressures became an
exercise in adjustment. The Kashmiri became known for
docility and timidity. Late in the 1930s he began to insist
on his democratic rights and, half a century later, a restive
youth went further to alter this image.

*T*he uncertainty that has haunted Kashmir's post-
independence ties with India is traceable to the overlapping
but not identical motivations of, and countervailing pulls
on, Nehru and Abdullah. They were both charismatic,
dominating, emotional personalities whose visions of the
future, often of the present, did not match realities on the
ground. They shared commitments to secularism and socio-
economic change; they detested feudal rule and were
obsessed with Kashmir, but not entirely for the same
reasons.

Nehru was anxious to fit Jammu and Kashmir into the
framework of a secular nation, which it would strengthen.
Abdullah was a Kashmiri nationalist driven by socialist
rather than religious concerns. His primary concern was to
end the centuries of oppression and exploitation that
Kashmiris had suffered at the hands of rulers from outside
the valley, especially the latest, the Jammu-based Dogra
dynasty. He sought to involve Muslims, Hindus and Sikhs
in his political mission, but could not entirely obliterate
Muslim resentment against the miniscule Brahmin Pandit
community for the preference it received in education and
government office. He resented external dominance and
would have preferred independence for his people, but
realised that it was not feasible in the setting in which the
valley was placed. Kashmir was claimed by both India and
Pakistan, abutted China and Afghanistan and was
separated by a narrow strip of land from the Soviet Union.

Nehru had given evidence of his concern for the plight of the Kashmiris before India became independent. He was arrested by the vacillating last Dogra Maharaja, Hari Singh, for entering the valley to defend the imprisoned Abdullah in June 1946, when it was known that he would be Prime Minister of independent India. In contrast, Mohammad Ali Jinnah, President of the Muslim League and prospective founder of Pakistan, sided with the Maharaja and criticised the movement for democratic rights for which Abdullah had been imprisoned as an agitation carried out by a few malcontents out to create disorderly conditions in the State. That and the Congress party's commitment to democracy, secularism, egalitarianism and a measure of federalism, tipped the balance in India's favour despite the Islamic attraction of Pakistan.

Much has been made of sentiment in assessing Nehru's concern for Kashmir. He was certainly aware that his forbears came from the valley and was proud to proclaim its long historical and cultural links with the rest of India. Long before partition, he stressed his Kashmiri descent and extolled the scenic attractions of the valley in his autobiography written in 1936.[5] In later writings, too, Kashmir evoked glowing prose. His study of Kashmir's history and of its cultural links with India was used to buttress modern India's claim in a lengthy note to the last British Viceroy, Lord Louis Mountbatten, on 17 June 1947, before the Viceroy met Hari Singh who was then faced with the options of joining India or Pakistan or attempting independence.[6]

However, it was Nehru's desire to establish a strong Centre, which he believed would hold the country together as well as direct economic planning, that underlay his differences with Abdullah. This was the same approach that had led to the failure of the British Cabinet Mission plan in 1946, the last effort to avoid partition by conceding considerable autonomy to provincial units. Maulana Abul Kalam Azad, who conducted the talks with the Cabinet Mission in his capacity of President of the Indian National

Congress, regretted Nehru's role in his autobiography
entitled *India Wins Freedom.*[7]

Another concern for Nehru was India's security. This
was spelt out in the letter telegraphed to British Prime
Minister Clement Attlee on 26 October 1947 informing him
of the tribal attack on Kashmir and justifying the decision
to rush military assistance:

> Kashmir's northern frontiers, as you are aware, run in
> common with those of three countries, Afghanistan, the
> USSR and China. Security of Kashmir... is vital to
> security of India especially since part of the southern
> boundary of Kashmir and India are common. Helping
> Kashmir, therefore, is an obligation of national interest
> to India.[8]

At the same time, he did not mind parading sentiment
even on the most serious occasions. Recalling the first
crucial days of the struggle to prevent the tribal raiders
from overrunning the valley, he told the Lok Sabha on
7 September 1948:

> I was so exercised over Kashmir that if anything had
> happened or was likely to happen in Kashmir which,
> according to me might have been disastrous for
> Kashmir, I would have been heartbroken. I was
> intensely interested, apart from the larger reasons that
> government have, for emotional and personal reasons
> – I do not want to hide this – I am interested in
> Kashmir.

Nehru proved to be naïve in referring the Kashmir issue
to the UN Security Council and expecting a decision in
India's favour, given Britain's involvement and the rival
interests of the great powers in the Indian subcontinent. His
grasp of military strategy was also wanting. The decision
to divert forces to the relief of Poonch, when his
commanders were planning to advance beyond Uri to the
bridge at Domel, spoilt an opportunity to take Muzaffarabad
(now capital of Pakistan-occupied Kashmir) and seal off the

valley.[9] Acceptance of the UN-sponsored cease-fire on
1 January 1949, when the army was again poised to retake
the territory, proved similarly expensive. It has been argued
that Nehru had political considerations in mind. The
influence of the National Conference did not extend into this
area. In the event of a plebiscite, or even general elections,
it would not endorse accession to India. But that, except for
the refugees immured in the town, was also true of the
Poonch area which contributed the bulk of the 'Azad'
Kashmir forces.

That Nehru could be ruthless as well emerged in August
1953 when his friend and comrade, Sheikh Mohammad
Abdullah, Prime Minister of Jammu and Kashmir, was
arrested. The Prime Minister of India denied responsibility
for the act, though his chief of intelligence, B.N. Mullik, who
masterminded the operation, later claimed that he was
consulted and kept informed.

*F*or the first few weeks after achieving independence on
15 August 1947, the prospects of India becoming the secular,
democratic nation its leaders had promised seemed bleak.
The promise that every citizen, irrespective of religion or
caste, would enjoy equal and full democratic rights had been
held out by the Indian National Congress during the long
struggle for freedom and was already inscribed in the
Constitution being drafted for the country. But the creation
of Pakistan from the Muslim-majority areas of British India
and the communal massacres and savagery in both
countries that followed partition strengthened support for
the Jana Sangh, the Hindu Mahasabha and other parties
that wanted India to be declared a Hindu State, or at least
a country in which minorities accepted the superiority of
Hindu tradition and culture and did not expect equal status.

This was the thesis advanced, among others, by Balraj
Madhok, who had lived in Kashmir. Since it would be self-
contradictory to maintain that this approach to nationhood

would get popular support in a Muslim-majority State, he argued that India's claim to Kashmir was "not only based on the Instrument of Accession (signed by Maharaja Hari Singh) but also on the right of conquest".[10] The doctrine of Hindutva, was defined in a book of that name by Vinayak Damodar (Veer) Savarkar (1870-1957), ideologue of the Hindu Mahasabha, and continues to inspire communal Hindu parties.[11]

The protagonists of the secular ideal were on the defensive against such primeval passions. Mohandas Karamchand Gandhi, who had faced so many reverses in the struggle for independence without losing hope for the future and had consistently campaigned for communal harmony, was agonised. On 2 October 1947, his birthday, he said in Delhi: "... I invoke the aid of the all-embracing Power to take me away from this 'vale of tears' rather than make me a helpless witness of the butchery by man become savage, whether he dares call himself a Musalman or Hindu or what not."[12]

Prime Minister Jawaharlal Nehru condemned attacks on innocent Muslims who wished to stay on in India, in retaliation for what was happening in Pakistan, but the gory accounts brought by the tide of Hindu and Sikh refugees flooding in from across the newly created border evoked similar barbarity in his own capital. More than 50,000 Muslims had to be protected by the army in the 500-year-old Purana Qila (Old Fort). The Congress leadership was divided on the degree of protection that Muslims deserved, with the reputedly Gandhian future first President of India, Rajendra Prasad, not only questioning the need but also suggesting that Hindus be armed.[13] Home Minister Vallabhbhai Patel, the "iron man" of the Congress party, spoke of evicting all the forty million Muslims still in India if Pakistan threw out the Hindus in its territory and of extending the non-Muslim zone from Punjab to Delhi and western UP.[14]

But the accession to India of the princely State of Jammu and Kashmir, virtually independent after the withdrawal of British paramountcy, on 27 October 1947, had a countervailing impact on domestic politics[15] and a lasting influence on foreign relations. The State had a Muslim majority, with a Hindu ruler whose domain was contiguous to both India and Pakistan. Not until it was invaded by several thousand Pathan tribesmen, encouraged and given access by Pakistan, did he turn to New Delhi for help. In democratic terms, the crucial significance of the accession did not lie in the fact that it was signed by Maharaja Hari Singh but that it was endorsed by Sheikh Abdullah, the recognised leader of the most popular political party in the State and who had been released from jail by Hari Singh only a month earlier. He was to become the first popular Prime Minister of the State.

In fact, as Mehr Chand Mahajan, the last State Prime Minister appointed by Hari Singh before Abdullah, confirmed in his memoirs, it was not until Abdullah supported accession that it was accepted by Nehru and troops were airlifted to save Srinagar.[16] This was consistent with the Congress line that the views of the people of the princely States must be taken into account in deciding their future, and was the reason given by New Delhi for taking over the princely State of Junagadh in Kathiawar though its Muslim ruler decided to accede to Pakistan. The Indian Government maintained that since the vast majority of the population were Hindus, there was no question of them agreeing to be part of an avowedly Islamic country. Even so, a plebiscite was held on 20 February 1948 in Junagadh and in some areas over which the ruler claimed feudal overlordship to establish the point.[17] This created a precedent for the State of Jammu and Kashmir.

The contest for Junagadh was a prelude to the struggle for Kashmir. Pakistan lost the territory but gained the principle of plebiscite, though this went against the stand that Jinnah had taken so far that it was the exclusive privilege of the princes to decide which Dominion to accede to. Mountbatten's hurry to pull out left the future of the princely States somewhat imprecise after the end of British

paramountcy.[18] Hari Singh's belief that some sort of direct
link with Britain could survive was not scotched,[19] contributing to the delay in accession with its tragic consequences.

No attempt was made to evolve an arrangement
acceptable to both India and Pakistan before passions were
inflamed and national pride aroused. Something on the
model of Anglo-Egyptian Sudan or Trieste on the French-
Italian border, whose autonomy both signatories pledged to
respect, could have been envisaged. Or with the autonomous
status of border microstates like Andorra and Liechtenstein.

In the event, Mountbatten's ten-week withdrawal and
partition operation (3 June to 14/15 August 1947) left no
time to consider any such advance mediatory initiatives.
Once it became a subject of claims and counter-claims by
India and Pakistan, Kashmir's very uniqueness made the
dispute insoluble. The dispute was not so much over
territory as over principles basic to their nationhood: to the
two-nation theory (that Hindus and Muslims are different
nationalities) that constitutes the justification for the birth
of Pakistan; to secularism, without which, conflicting ethnic
pulls could split India further. It remains a gut issue for
both.

Abdullah's endorsement of accession was the first
objective sign after partition that Muslims could have
confidence in India's secular credentials. As a result the
anti-Muslim wave was checked in India and faith in
secularism revived. Secularism was further strengthened
when it became known that Kashmiri Muslims helped
transport and guide Indian troops against the raiders, and
formed volunteer groups to patrol and keep order in the city
when the Maharaja and his police had fled to Jammu.

In his first broadcast to the nation on these momentous
events on 2 November 1947, a revitalised Nehru said:

It would be well if this lesson was understood by the
whole of India which has been poisoned by communal
strife. Under the inspiration of a great leader, Sheikh

Abdullah, the people of the valley, Muslim and Hindu and Sikh, were together for the defence of their common country against the invader. Our troops could have done little without this popular support and cooperation.[20]

At a prayer meeting on 29 December, Gandhi, who had supported the airlift of troops to Srinagar, said:

My sole hope and prayer is that Kashmir would become a beacon light in this benighted subcontinent.[21]

A bdullah became the hero and symbol of secularism. He had established his reputation already by converting the Muslim Conference, Kashmir's first political party which he helped organise in the early 1930s, into the National Conference, open to all communities, in June 1938. Thus his political development was the reverse of that of Mohammed Ali Jinnah, founder of Pakistan, who changed from a nationalist into a communal leader, and claimed Kashmir on that basis. Abdullah was inspired by socialist rather than communal aspirations. Yet he was a devout Muslim and his inspiring oratory was tinged with quotations from the holy Quran. Six feet four inches in height, he literally towered over his people. But the uncritical adulation he received induced a flaw usual among such historic personalities: he equated Kashmir with himself, became autocratic in his behaviour and failed to establish democratic procedures.

Abdullah was essentially a Kashmiri patriot who would have preferred independence had it been feasible. He was anxious to secure maximum autonomy and freedom from the Dogra dynasty that had oppressed and impoverished his people. This was reflected in the comprehensive Naya Kashmir manifesto of the National Conference that he sought to implement when he came to office. He saw the relationship with India as the best available option in the circumstances; as a partnership inspired by common ideals of democracy, autonomy, secularism and socio-political reform; not one of subservience. He was disturbed by any development that he interpreted as emanating from pressure exerted by New Delhi or as inspired by Hindutva.

The key to Abdullah's success in countering Pakistan's religious appeal to Muslims lay in fostering the sense of a common, separate Kashmiri identity with deep roots in the past. But to maintain lasting, popular links and keep Pakistan at a distance, the sense of *Kashmiryat* needed to be nurtured and respected by India as well. Any move that seemed to alter the terms on which Kashmir acceded to India was seen as impinging on this sense of identity and promoting religious fundamentalism – an explanation for later developments. The National Conference was designed as a vehicle to express and safeguard the secular Kashmiri identity: it lost its *raison d'être* and its following when attempts were made to merge or ally it with the Congress, the representative of Central power and authority. This led to a drift towards communal organisations.

Due to his association with, and respect for, Gandhi and Nehru, Abdullah distinguished between his hatred for the Dogra dynasty for cruelly exploiting Kashmir and the leadership of secular Hindus. But this did not mean that he was not sensitive to communal tensions. He was wary of the rise of Hindu communalism which was promoted by the Maharaja and his court as a means to protect their lands and feudal rights against Abdullah's socialist zeal, of which Muslims were the main beneficiaries. The latest crime that he held against the Dogras was the killing of Muslims in Jammu.[22] After he shifted from Srinagar to Jammu, Hari Singh, the last Dogra Maharaja, supported the communal Praja Parishad campaign against Abdullah. In a letter to Patel, dated 17 April 1949, Nehru stated that he had information that Hari Singh was financing the Parishad.[23]

Despite their mutual dislike, the Maharaja shared with Abdullah the desire for independence. Although urged by Britain's last Viceroy, Lord Louis Mountbatten, to accede either to India or Pakistan before 15 August 1947, he avoided doing so in the hope of working out a *modus vivendi*

with both; but the Pakistan-sponsored tribal invasion two
months later forced him to seek military support from India,
which Nehru provided only after the Maharaja agreed to
accede and also appoint Sheikh Abdullah as head of an
emergency administration for the State.

Relations between Srinagar and New Delhi were cordial
initially. Jammu and Kashmir was given a special status
that no other State in India enjoyed, including the right to
frame its own Constitution, under Article 370 of the Indian
Constitution. Abdullah, however, became disenchanted with,
and suspicious of, the rise of Hindu communalism in Jammu
and the campaign for ending the State's special status by
the Praja Parishad, which was taken up at the national level
by the Jana Sangh and Hindu Mahasabha. Continuing
communal clashes in various parts of India were also a
source of both concern and embarrassment. Kashmiri
Muslims felt threatened.

Abdullah also complained of what he saw as efforts by
the Union Home Ministry, headed by Patel, who distrusted
him,[24] to extend its role in the State. He began openly to
doubt the permanence of accession to India without
honouring the pledge of a plebiscite made when Hari Singh
signed the Instrument of Accession, and to question whether
secularism would survive Gandhi and Nehru. At the same
time, he began to discuss with US and other foreign
diplomats the possibility of support for an independent
Kashmir, as confirmed by US State Department papers of
the period and diplomatic memoirs.[25]

These events led to Abdullah's dismissal and arrest on
9 August 1953 since when the special status of Jammu and
Kashmir has been steadily eroded. Crores of rupees were
poured into the valley in the hope of maintaining the
support of its people, but much of it was cornered by a
handful of politicians on good terms with New Delhi, and
their affluence antagonised the less fortunate. The impact
of the radical land reform measures undertaken under the
Naya Kashmir programme was eroded by favouritism.[26] It
was also only too evident that the Chief Ministers of Jammu

and Kashmir who succeeded Abdullah owed their office to
New Delhi.

*B*ut while the demand for plebiscite gathered support, as
indicated by the popularity of the Plebiscite Front, set up
after Abdullah's arrest, Pakistan did not benefit. A second
attempt to infiltrate hundreds of saboteurs into the valley
in 1965, code-named Operation Gibraltar by its Pakistani
planners, failed due to lack of local support. It also got no
diversionary assistance during the Bangladesh operations
in 1971. In Pakistan, however, this shattering experience
fuelled the desire for revenge since Indian assistance to the
rebel Mukti Bahini in former East Pakistan was no secret
even before open war erupted.

Popular sentiment in Kashmir found chance of
expression in the enthusiasm with which Abdullah's return
to power in the State was greeted in 1975. The creation of
Bangladesh had demonstrated that the pull of a common
ethnicity could be stronger than that of a common religion.
He had given up the demand for plebiscite after protracted
negotiations, thereby accepting New Delhi's stance that
accession was irrevocable, in return for the assurance that
Article 370 would be respected. This was the essence of the
agreement with New Delhi that enabled his return to
office.[27] He laid great emphasis on retrieving the rights
surrendered to the Central Government, but without
success – a defeat that would injure his reputation.

The National Conference was revived and contested the
State Assembly elections in 1977 on this platform. It won
with a handsome majority in the first unrigged poll in the
State supervised by the Janata Government headed by
Morarji Desai, which briefly took office in New Delhi,
breaking the Congress party's monopoly of Central rule
after independence.

But the new generation in Kashmir, that had enjoyed
the benefits of the free education up to university levels,

which was Abdullah's gift after he first came to power, became restive. Few jobs were available for them. Jamiat schools preaching Islamic fundamentalism had spread their poison (a word used by Abdullah) in the valley. Charges of corruption were levelled against him and his family. The huge sorrowing crowds that turned out for his funeral on 9 September 1982, however, reflected the massive following that the Lion of Kashmir had until his death.

This was also reflected by the acceptance of his son, Farooq Abdullah, as his successor. But Farooq antagonised Prime Minister Indira Gandhi by siding with Opposition groups critical of her. When the State Governor, B.K. Nehru (her cousin), refused to topple him, he was replaced by Jagmohan, an efficient, ruthless bureaucrat, who had served her well in Delhi during the emergency that she imposed in 1975. Jagmohan did so by arranging for defections among Farooq's ministers in July 1984.[28] After another six months, he imposed Governor's rule.

Jagmohan utilised the opportunity to make changes in legal and constitutional procedures which were seen as exceeding his powers, though he also ordered and supervised much-needed measures to clean the scenic lakes surrounding Srinagar, improve sanitation and reduce corruption. But he gained a reputation for distrusting Muslims. Jagmohan's objective, it was evident, was to demonstrate that the State would be better off without the protection of Article 370, which he abhorred. His bureaucratic approach of preferring efficiency to democracy won over the few who benefited but eroded popular support.

Elections were delayed until Farooq agreed to an alliance with the Congress (I) which lost the National Conference the support it had regained. Observers found the elections to be rigged and the newly regained confidence in New Delhi's commitment to democratic procedures suffered. Pakistani propaganda now found favour and its agents found more fertile ground. The experience it had gained in training and directing Mujahideen fighters for Afghanistan and their access to sophisticated arms made a quantum

difference, together with the rise of Islamic fundamentalism
financed with oil money from the Gulf. The dissolution of
the Soviet Union and its empire in eastern Europe created
the impression that similar developments were possible in
the Indian Union.
Armed militancy became widespread for the first time.
There were two main currents. Elements of the Jammu and
Kashmir Liberation Front (JKLF), which had been in
existence for some time, took to arms. Originally the
demand was for greater autonomy, but this hardened to
complete independence. Its spokesmen insisted that the
demand was not motivated by Islamic fundamentalism or
directed against Hindus but by the ethnic pull of
Kashmiryat. The fundamentalist current was led mainly by
the Hizbul Mujahideen. Though less popular, it was better
armed and directed, and more ruthless. It stood for uniting
Kashmir with Pakistan and was favoured by that country.
With money and arms available, many other groups also
emerged, some exploiting the opportunity for murder, rape
and pillage. Hindus felt threatened in the valley for the first
time and began to leave the land of their forbears, to which
they had contributed so much; so did an increasing number
of Muslims with friends and relatives elsewhere in India.
    Even so, the dominant demand was for *azaadi*
(independence) rather than for joining Pakistan. The security forces gained a free hand in Jagmohan's second tenure
as Governor in 1990. Repeated curfews and firings increased
Kashmiri alienation. The Hindu Pandit community and
many Muslims fled. Since then the valley has been
dominated by terror and counter-terror. The unhappy
situation was symbolised by the national flag being raised
on Republic Day 1992 by the President of the Bharatiya
Janata Party -- the Hindutva party campaigning for
abolition of Article 370 – in an empty square, guarded by
Indian troops in a Srinagar under total curfew. The site of
the ceremony was the same Lal Chowk where Nehru and
Abdullah had explained the reasons for accession to India
to a packed, cheering audience forty-five years earlier.

Chapter II

Old Kasmira

*K*ashmir, originally called Kasmira,[1] can boast of a recorded history going further back than the Mahabharata, further than that of most peoples of the world; a history that is as precipitously uneven as the high mountains that surround the fertile valley. It is the history of the evolution of a people isolated by geography in a narrow valley that became reputed for its natural beauty throughout the world. Poets in distant countries tried to capture its loveliness, some without having seen it, but moved by the ecstatic descriptions of travellers.

Kashmir has known great rulers who patronised scholars, poets, painters, singers, craftsmen and are still the subject of folk history; who built monumental temples, laid out cities and terraced gardens that cradled its many lakes; who extended their domain deep into India, Afghanistan and Tibet. It has also known cruel despots, religious zealots and pleasure-seeking sensualists under whom the people often starved, were persecuted and forced to seek survival outside. Foreign adventurers laid it waste and seized the throne; even the small valley was sometimes divided into quarrelling principalities. It has been sundered by cruel religious and sectarian conflicts. For long periods, extending up to recent times, the ordinary people were so exploited and oppressed that their harsh, brutish existence contrasted sharply and unhappily with the beauty of their environment.

Yet through this kaleidoscopic mosaic of the past, detailed by great historians, one can glimpse the growth of a common culture, a native pride, a togetherness and mutuality that has been called *Kashmiryat*, something local and indigenous to the valley. In Kashmir's great epochs, this has overcome religious and sectarian divisions and impelled the people to defend their country against foreign invaders. One of its greatest rulers, Sultan Zainul Abidin, though a Muslim, inspired and revitalised Hindu arts and scholarship. Even more pervasive, however, than the vision of enlightened monarchs was the influence of itinerant mendicants, male and female, Hindu and Muslim, who caught the imagination of the people by renouncing the world and singing devotional hymns in their language, Kashmiri, rather than in official Persian or scholarly Sanskrit. Thus it is the memory and compositions of Lal Ded and Noor-ud-Din and Habba Khatoon that continue to inspire Kashmiris, irrespective of class or religion. They are revered by all.

Sir Mark Aurel Stein, a noted scholar who spent many years in Kashmir towards the end of the last century, stressed the geographic features that have determined the valley's history and culture. He wrote:

Kasmir owes its historical unity and isolation to the same facts which gave to its geographic location a distinct, and in some respects almost unique character. We find here a fertile plain embedded among high mountain ranges, a valley large enough to form a kingdom for itself and capable of supporting a highly-developed civilisation.[2]

Kashmir is unique in more ways than one. Its long and eventful history and its beauty – limpid lakes surrounded by some of the highest mountains in the world, crystal-clear rivers and streams, statuesque trees, myriad flowers – have inspired great learning and literature. Nearly four hundred years ago, the Mughal Emperor Jahangir, who laid out the fragrant Shalimar gardens near Srinagar, was moved to eloquence. He wrote in his memoirs, *Tuzuk-i-Jahangiri*:

If one were to take to praise Kashmir, whole books would have to be written.... Kashmir is a garden of eternal spring, or an iron fort to a palace of kings – a delightful flower bed, and a heart-expanding heritage for dervishes. Its pleasant meads and enchanting cascades are beyond all description. There are running streams and fountains beyond count. Wherever the eye reaches, there are verdure and running water. The red rose, the violet and the narcissus grow of themselves; in the fields, there are all kinds of flowers and all sorts of sweet-scented herbs more than can be calculated. In the soul-enchanting spring the hills and plains are filled with blossoms; the gates, the walls, the courts, the roofs are lighted up by the torches of the banquet-adoring tulips.[3]

Francois Bernier, a French physician attached to the Mughal court in Delhi, travelled to Kashmir in 1665. After an extremely hot and dusty journey up to the foothills, he wrote a lyrical description of "The Paradise of the Indies" in a letter to a friend. After describing the scenery in ecstatic detail, he went on:

You have no doubt discovered before this time that I am charmed with Kachemire. In truth, the kingdom surpasses in beauty all that my warm imagination had anticipated. It is probably unequalled by any country of the same extent, and should be, as in former ages,the seat of sovereign authority.... It is not indeed without reason that the Mogols call Kachemire the terrestrial paradise of the Indies, or that Ekbar [Akbar] was so unremitting in his efforts to wrest the sceptre from the hands of its native Princes. His son Jehan-Gyre [Jahangir] became so enamoured of this little kingdom as to make it the place of his favourite abode, and he often declared that he would rather be deprived of every other province of his mighty empire than lose Kachemire.[4]

Bernier found the inhabitants no less attractive than the scénery:

> The Kachemirys are celebrated for wit, and considered much more intelligent than the Indians. In poetry and the sciences they are not inferior to the Persians. They are also very active and industrious.... They perfectly understand the art of varnishing, and are eminently skilful in closely imitating the beautiful veins of a certain wood, by inlaying with gold threads so delicately wrought that I never saw anything more elegant or perfect. But what may be considered peculiar to Kachemire, and the staple commodity, that which particularly promotes the trade of the country and fills it with wealth, is the prodigious quantity of shawls which they manufacture, and which gives occupation even to the little children.... The people of Kachemire are proverbial for their clear complexions and fine forms.[5]

The fame of Kashmiri shawls spread far beyond the subcontinent. They were reputedly discovered by Napoleon when he was campaigning in Egypt and taken back to Paris as a present to the Empress Josephine, since when their fame spread rapidly among the European aristocracy.[6]

A thousand years earlier, the legendary Chinese traveller Huien Tsang spent two years in the valley, his longest stay in any one place. His impressions confirmed the learning of the inhabitants but were otherwise mixed:

> They are light and frivolous, and of a weak, pusillanimous disposition. The people are handsome in appearance, but they are given to cunning. They love learning and are well-instructed.[7]

Shielded by high mountains, the people of the valley have been able to develop their own social customs and language. They can trace their identity much further back than other inhabitants of south Asia for they enjoy the

unique advantage of a recorded history of their rulers going
far back into antiquity, primarily the work of the historian
Kalhana who, writing in the twelfth century, put together,
in a long Sanskrit prose poem, the chronicle of the rulers
of the valley since Gonanda I ascended the throne. Since it
goes back so far in time and depends on manuscripts that
are no longer in existence, historiographers are unable to
confirm the early dates, but the names of the rulers are
listed in order together with the period of their reigns. The
work was fittingly entitled *Rajatarangini*, the River of
Kings.

There are several translations of the *Rajatarangini*
which is in Sanskrit. The most detailed and authentic is
by M.A. Stein.[8] Most students of Kashmir's history have
depended on his monumental work. Elsewhere, Stein lays
stress on the unique nature of Kalhana's chronicles:

> Kashmir can claim the distinction of being the only
> region of India which possesses an uninterrupted series
> of written records of its history, reaching back beyond
> the period of the Muhammadan conquest and deserving
> the name of real chronicles. In other parts of India, the
> historical student is obliged to reconstruct the general
> outlines of the country's history with the help of the
> scanty and frequently uncertain data which a patient
> examination of inscriptions, coins, and occasional
> references in literary works may reveal, and he can
> scarcely ever hope to recover a continued account of the
> leading events even for a couple of centuries. If the
> student of Kashmirian history finds himself in a far
> better position, this is due to the preservation of the
> documents alluded to; they testify to the continued
> existence among the population of the valley of that
> genuine historical sense in which the Indian mind on
> the whole is so conspicuously deficient.... Although
> Kalhana himself mentions several historians as his
> predecessors, none of their works have come down to us.
> The *Rajatarangini* has thus become the most direct
> source of information on the ancient history of Kashmir.[9]

A more recent historian, Dr R.C. Mazumdar, confirms the *Rajatarangini's* unique character:

This is the only work in ancient Indian literature that may be regarded as an historical text in the true sense of the word. The author has not only taken great pains to collect his material from the existing chronicles and other sources, but, at the beginning of his work, he has set down a few general principles for writing history which are remarkably far in advance of his age. Indeed these may be regarded as anticipating, to a large extent,the critical method of historical research which was not fully developed till the nineteenth century A.D.[10]

Kalhana completed his work in the reign of King Jayasimha. Pandit Jonaraja took over and completed the record through the last anarchic days of Hindu rule to the beginnings of Muslim rule, up to the time of the great Sultan Zainul Abidin which is still recalled as the golden age of Kashmir. The historical tradition was carried on by Srivara and Prajyabhatta who continued the chronicles up to the time when Akbar brought the valley under Mughal rule. The language in which history was written then changed from Sanskrit to Persian, but the record continued to be written. Thus, as Stein points out, Kashmir has the unique distinction of enjoying a complete chronicle of its history from the earliest times to the present day.

The era of the earliest ruler named in the *Rajatarangini*, Gonanda I, takes us back to the period preceding the Mahabharata. According to Kalhana, he died besieging the forces of Krishna near Mathura. Gonanda II, his infant grandson, was on the throne when the Mahabharata was waged which was why, writes the historian, he was "taken by neither the Kurus nor the Pandavas to assist them in the war". Then follow thirty-five rulers whose "names and deeds," says Kalhana, "have perished through the destruction of records."[11]

The first major historic name to figure in the *Rajatarangini* is that of Asoka (274 to 237 B.C.), the great

Buddhist ruler who extended his empire up to Kashmir. He was the first outsider to rule the entire valley, but his coming was fortunate. He respected all religions and introduced a regime of tolerance. He is said to have founded the prosperous city of Srinagari, from which the present capital of Kashmir takes its name.[12] Another foreign king to rule Kashmir was the Kushan emperor Kanishka (A.D. 78 to 123), who was also a devout Buddhist and organised the third great Buddhist Council designed to resolve differences between contending sects near Srinagar. When Huien Tsang visited the valley in A.D. 631-633, he was impressed by the community of Buddhist monks, originally settled there by Asoka, that he found there. Another Chinese traveller, Ou-kong, who saw the valley in A.D. 725, also describes the appearance of Buddhism in Kashmir.

Buddhism did not enter Kashmir abruptly by royal fiat or under threat of force. One of the unique features of the valley has been that religious conversion has been largely a gradual, voluntary process, with one system of belief leaving its impress on popular thinking even after giving way to another. Even today, traces of the original Naga cult can be found. The process of conversion has also usually started with the less privileged sections of society who welcome a belief that does not reinforce and justify social injustice, as traditional religions tend to do. And, so, when Vedic Brahmanism, which had replaced animistic Naga worship, allied itself with cruelty and suppression, the humanist, egalitarian message of the Buddha, spread by devoted monks, found ready acceptance. When Buddhism itself became corrupted by ritual and involved doctrines, Brahmanism staged a return, to be followed by Islam. Buddhism was prevalent from the third century B.C. to the twelfth century A.D.[13]

Kalhana continues to chronicle the deeds of Kashmir's rulers, some great, some petty and cruel. His work is a saga of elemental passions, spread over centuries, in which are exposed the noblest and basest passions that move mankind. We have the invasion of the White Huns under the depraved

Mihirgula who slaughtered his subjects on a whim and did not spare even animals. Stein actually travelled to the dangerous pass in the Pir Panjal, where Mihirgula had a hundred elephants thrown down a precipice because he took delight in their screams. The pass has since been called Hastivanj or Elephant Pass. Kalhana graphically describes the terror aroused by the approach of Mihirgula:

> The people knew of his approach by noticing vultures, crows and other [birds] which were flying ahead eager to feed on those being slain within his armies' [reach].
>
> This royal Vetala was day and night surrounded by thousands of murdered human beings, even in his pleasure-houses.
>
> This terrible enemy of mankind had no pity for children, no compassion for women, no respect for the aged.[14]

Reacting to this searing experience, the Kashmiri nobility organised themselves after Mihirgula's death in A.D. 530 to resist oppression and later expelled Yudhisthira I from the throne, replacing him with a prince from outside, Pratapaditya. But to interpret this, as done by Prem Nath Bazaz,[15] as a revolutionary step towards establishing the right of popular rule is perhaps exaggerated. For during the next 1400 years, Kashmir had many occasions to suffer persecution and misrule.

The next ruler to be widely remembered after Kanishka is Lalitaditya, a great indigenous king who ruled from A.D. 724 to 760. He extended his empire well beyond the valley, deep into India and central Asia. He is also remembered as a great builder. His greatest work was the magnificent temple of Martand, now in ruins but still most impressive. After comparing it with the ruins of ancient Egypt and Greece, the British historian and writer, Francis Younghusband, wrote:

> It is a ruin now, but yet, with the other ruins so numerous in the valley and similar in their

characteristics, it denotes the former presence in Kashmir of a people worthy of study. No one without an eye for natural beauty would have chosen that special site for the construction of a temple and no one with an inclination to the ephemeral and transient would have built it on so massive and enduring a scale.[16]

As has happened repeatedly in the long history of Kashmir, Lalitaditya was succeeded by weak kings who lost control of the vast empire he had built up extending far beyond the valley. Not until a century later did another outstanding ruler, Avantivarman (855-883), come to the throne. He, too, was a great builder and town planner, as the ruins of Avantipura, seventeen miles from Srinagar, reveal. It was during his reign, also, that extensive drainage and irrigation schemes were carried out in the valley, with the Jhelum being diverted to create new fields near the place where it flows into the Wular Lake.

Again, however, followed a series of inept rulers; victims of palace intrigue. It was at this unhappy time that the first of the Muslim invaders of the subcontinent, Mahmud of Ghazni, tried to enter the valley. Unlike elsewhere, he was repelled mainly due to the high mountains and the intense cold. He made two infructuous attempts, in 1015 and 1021, but could not cross the Pir Panjal range.

Among the few rulers who merit Kalhana's praise in this period is Ananta (1028-63), who repelled an invasion from the north, Harsha (1089-1101), who was a great patron of art and learning but had disastrous streaks of insanity, and Uccala (1101-11), who proved a capable and resourceful successor to Harsha until he was murdered. Then followed an era of unrest and insecurity, with Jayasimha (1128-49) able to survive for an extended reign, but only by playing off one feudal baron against another. The inadequacy of the rulers had tragic consequences. Sahadeva ran away and made no attempt to defend the valley against the Mongol hordes led by Dulacha who laid it waste in 1320. An era was ending. Hindu society in Kashmir had degenerated and the land was ripe for the coming of Islam.

In the centuries that had passed since Gonanda I, however, Kashmir knew periods of intellectual and cultural excellence unequalled in the region. Women were not confined to household chores. They went about freely unveiled and enjoyed equal civic rights. They owned immovable property, managed their own estates and even fought at the head of their troops.[17]

Literature and philosophy flourished. Kashmir lays claim to the great Sanskrit poet Kalidasa on the basis of several references in his works, including Shakuntala, which show an intimate knowledge of, and partiality for, the valley. Many other outstanding works, on a variety of subjects, originated in Kashmir. Among them, Kshemendra (990-1065) was one of the most versatile figures of his period and is known to have left at least thirty-four books, including descriptions of current affairs, satire, and philosophical and poetical works. According to Kalhana, Ashvoghosha, author of Buddhacharita and a well-known poet, musician and Buddhist scholar of his times, lived in Kashmir. He was honoured and given the facilities that he required by Kanishka. Some remarkable works on medicine by Charaka and Narhari have been traced to the same period – the first century A.D.

One of the greatest Buddhist philosophers, Nagarjuna, though not born in the valley, chose to make it his home in the first century before Christ. Founder of the Madhyamika or Middle Way of Buddhism, he was responsible for popularising the religion and its spread through much of Asia. It was Nagarjuna's philosophy that persuaded the people of Kashmir to relinquish their earlier primitive religious rites, comments Kalhana. Nagarjuna was also renowned as a chemist and for prescribing a wide range of drugs and medicines and is regarded as the father of Indian chemistry.

The period following Nagarjuna saw the evolution of a religious philosophy which embodied the fusion of the ancient Vedic with the Buddhist belief. It has come to be known as Kashmir Shaivism or simply as Trikha. It was founded in the eighth century by Vasugupta, who was followed by a succession of scholars who elaborated on the theme and have left erudite works and commentaries on Shaivism. The greatest and most prolific of them was Abhinavagupta whose monumental *Tantralokha* is even today regarded as a profound encyclopaedia on the subject. Abhinavagupta was born in the tenth century, before the advent of Islam in the valley. But with its strong emphasis on monism and egalitarianism, Trikha eased the passage from one religion to another which was to take place with less friction and bloodshed than in other parts of the subcontinent.[18]

Chapter III

Peaceful Conversion

*T*hat Islam came to Kashmir initially by peaceful rather than enforced conversion was of considerable significance to its future history. The form in which it made its first impact on the valley also eased its passage. Escaping from the cruel intolerance of Timur, who conquered Persia in the second half of the fourteenth century, seven hundred followers of Saiyyid Ali Hamdani[1] left the Persian city of Hamadan for Kashmir. Theirs was the gentle, meditative, eclectic order of Sufis, originating in Bukhara, whose way of life evoked admiration rather than fear. The Sufis emphasised meditation and contemplation in common with Hindu and Buddhist practice. They also emphasised the universality of all religions,[2] which did not endear them to conservative Muslims.

Another Sufi divine from Turkestan, Sayyid Bilal Shah, was to leave an indelible mark on Kashmiri history. He was soon revered in the valley and made several converts, the most eminent of whom was the young Balti chieftain, Rinchin, from the high country beyond the Zojila pass, who captured power in the valley in 1320 to become its first Muslim ruler.

Then there were the great mystics, teaching all who would listen in a mixture of verse and song. They were both Hindu and Muslim in origin, but their beliefs had much in common. The first and best known of them was Lalla, born in 1335 into a Hindu Pandit family. Like the Hindu saint Mira in India, she abandoned her family and worldly duties and wandered through the valley, dressed in rags, singing her verses and depending on local hospitality to survive. In the course of these wanderings, she is said to have met a Shaivite teacher, Sidh Bayu, who introduced her to the philosophy of Trikha. Lalla also held discussions with Shah Hamadani, when he came to Kashmir with his followers, and learnt the philosophy of Islam from that renowned spiritual teacher.[3] Thus her personal philosophy was a blend of the best of both religions and she was revered by Muslim and Hindu equally. Hindus remember her as Laleshwari or Lalla Yogeshwari, while to Muslims she is Lalla Maji. But the most popular name by which she is known throughout the valley is Lal Ded or mother Lalla.

The valley still resounds with Lal Ded's verses. Typical of those preaching religious integration is:

Shiva lives everywhere. Do not divide Hindu from Muslim. Use your sense to recognise yourself; that is the true way to God.

And:

Truth is not a prisoner of mosques and temples and is all-pervading.
Idol is of stone, temple is of stone;
Above and below are one;
Which of them wilt thou worship, O foolish pandit,
Cause thou the union of mind and soul?

Lal Ded did not limit her preaching to Hindu-Muslim unity; she was also concerned with caste:

The time is coming when seven generations will sink to hell,
When ultimately showers of rain and dust will fall,
When plates of flesh and wine cups,
Brahmins and sweepers will take together.

Although a hermit and mystic, she was not given to
extremes. She believed in moderation and typical of her
advice to her followers was:

> By overeating you will not achieve anything and by not
> eating at all you will become conceited by considering
> yourself an ascetic.

Lal Ded had considerable influence on a Muslim divine
who attained equal fame. Sheikh Noor-ud-Din was born in
1377 and disdained the orthodox Islamic schooling and
religious formalities. He spent his time in contemplation
and was filled with self-doubt until he learnt from Lal Ded
to have faith in himself and his own destiny and not to
depend upon the mercy of the higher powers on whom the
mullahs and priests preached reliance. According to popular
legend, he suckled at her breast as an infant, thus imbibing
both mysticism and religious harmony.

The Sheikh was popularly known as Nund Rishi,
founder of the austere, tolerant Sufi order of Rishis, and his
mystical teachings spread almost as widely as his mentor's.
Like Lal Ded, he is revered by Muslims and Hindus alike.
His teachings are virtually untranslatable because of their
devotional fervour. The following is an attempt:

> The love is he who burns with love,
> Whose self doth shine like gold;
> When man's heart lights up with the flame of love,
> Then shall he reach the infinite.

Or more simply and humanely:

> Sow thou the seed of friendship for me everywhere,
> And slay not even my enemies.

Nund Rishi was no admirer of the priestly class and
drew attention to their greed:

> Thy rosary is like a snake;
> Thou bendest it on seeing the disciples;
> Thou hast eaten six platefuls, one like another;
> If thou art a priest, then who are the robbers?

And he advised his disciples:

Do not go to the sheikh and priest and mullah;
Do not feed the cattle on ankhor leaves;
Do not shut thyself up in mosques or forests;
Enter thine own body with breath controlled in
communion with God.

The great Sultan Zainul Abidin was the chief mourner at the Sheikh's funeral. His grave at Tsrar Sharif continues to be a place of pilgrimage for followers of all religions.

*T*he possibility of becoming a Muslim without being forced or evoking public ostracism came to be the hinge on which the change from Hindu to Muslim rulers turned smoothly. The architect of the change was a Buddhist chieftain named Rinchin from Baltistan who captured power in the valley in a palace coup in 1320, after he, Shah Mir, a Muslim adventurer from Swat, and Kota Rani, daughter of king Ramachandra (who had fled into the safety of his castle), organised a limited resistance to Dulacha's hordes. Rinchin killed Ramachandra and married Kota, a talented, brave, hard-headed princess. He turned out to be an effective and popular king.

Since by then Buddhism had a limited following in Kashmir and a new ruler needed as much popular support as he could get, Rinchin decided to change his religion. His first choice was Hinduism, but the head priest ordained that conversion was not permissible, thus paving the way for a turning point in history. According to local legend, the first person he saw next morning at prayer was the Sufi divine, Bulbul Shah. Impressed by his austerity, he decided to become a Muslim. The fact that his friend and comrade, Shah Mir, was already a Muslim, was probably an additional factor. He took the title of Sultan Sadruddin, the first of Kashmir's Muslim rulers.

More than Rinchin, it was his pragmatic queen, Kota Rani, who provided the physical link in the battles for succession in those turbulent times. After the death of Rinchin three years later, she retained power and briefly put a Hindu back on the throne, by marrying Udayanandeva, son of a previous ruler, and arranging that he occupy the throne instead of her own infant son, Haider. But he, too, proved inadequate and ran away to Ladakh when a Turkish adventurer attacked the valley. A popular and effective defence was organised by Kota Rani and Shah Mir, who had become an influential noble.

After Udayanandeva's death in 1338, the gallant queen made a bid for the throne herself and ruled briefly, making Bhikshana her chief minister, thus antagonising Shah Mir who had become too powerful to be overlooked. He besieged the queen and she was forced to surrender. He offered to marry her and thus continue the link with the past. But within twenty-four hours of the ceremony, she was dead. According to local legend, she killed herself. It is equally possible that Shah Mir did away with her. Either way, the only remaining link with the past was removed, together with the career of a remarkable woman. Shah Mir crowned himself Sultan Shamsuddin in 1339, the first of an uninterrupted chain of Muslim rulers until Maharaja Ranjit Singh annexed Kashmir nearly five hundred years later.

*S*tein provides the following description of the virtually painless transition from Hindu to Muslim rule, in contrast to what happened in areas where Islam was imposed by force:

> Islam made its way into Kasmir not by forcible conquest but by gradual conversion, for which the influx of foreign adventurers both from the south and from Central Asia had prepared the ground. The adoption of Islam by the great mass of the population which became

an accomplished fact during the latter half of the
fourteenth century but which probably began already
towards the close of Hindu rule, did neither affect the
independence of the country nor at first change its
political and cultural conditions. The administration
remained as before in the hands of the traditional official
class, the Brahmans, for whom a change of religion
presented no advantage and who accordingly retained
their inherited status, together with its literary
traditions.[4]

Traditional architecture in Kashmir is also a happy
blend of Hindu, Buddhist and Islamic influences which is
found nowhere else. The mosques, especially, are unique,
with their wooden spires raised on the pattern of Buddhist
structures. Again, many shrines are revered by Hindus and
Muslims alike. Even otherwise, as Sir Walter Lawrence,
who was appointed Kashmir's first Settlement Commissioner
in the 1890s, notes in his definitive *The Valley of Kashmir*:

> Generally speaking it may be said that when one finds
> the Musalman shrine with its shady chinars and lofty
> poplars and elms, a little search will discover some old
> Hindu asthan. It was only natural than Musalmans,
> when they were converted to Islam, should cling with
> tenderness to the old religious places, and should adopt
> sacred spots already familiar to the country-side. I have
> shown in my chapter on Customs how certain ideas are
> common to the Hindus and Musalmans of Kashmir, but
> I attribute much of the delightful tolerance which exists
> between the followers of the two religions to the fact that
> the Kashmir Musalmans never gave up the old Hindu
> religion of the country.

More recently, Prithivi Nath Kaul Bamzai sums up the
positive aspects of the interface between Hinduism and
Islam in the following terms:

> Islam entered the Valley not as a result of foreign
> invasion, but by a coup d'etat from within the country.

Its influence and teachings had penetrated into the Valley long before a Muslim king ascended the throne, being carried thither by Islamic missionaries and military adventurers. Happily for the new religion it found fertile ground there to grow and expand in. The people had been groaning under the misrule of the later Hindu rulers, when trade languished and agriculture was at a standstill. To add to their misery there were crushing burdens of rites and rituals which the dominating Brahmins had laid upon the common man. The shackles of caste had already been broken by the teachings of Buddhism and the general mass of the people did not, therefore, find it difficult to embrace the new faith as preached by the Sufi dervishes who projected its social and religious humanism.[5]

Another Kashmiri historian, Prem Nath Bazaz, lays considerable emphasis not only on the peaceful transition to Islam but also its regenerative impact. Describing social and cultural changes in some detail, he states:

The peaceful and rapid conversion of the large masses of the people in Kashmir to Islam, which has been the source of wonder and astonishment for many students of history and religion, was facilitated and made possible by the spread of the cult of Religious Humanism taught by Lal Ded, Nund Rishi and their followers. Islam as practised in the Valley, though it surely stands on the basis of the cardinal principles taught by the Quran, has been deeply influenced by the ancient Kashmir culture.... A Kashmiri Muslim shares with his Hindu compatriots many inhibitions, superstitions, idolatrous practices as well as social liberties and intellectual freedoms which are unknown to Islam. Of course Islam in turn has not left Hinduism unaffected in the Valley.[6]

Some historians feel that Bazaz overstated the case for peaceful conversion and the positive aspects of Muslim rule. Certainly, the coming centuries were not entirely as orderly or fruitful as he suggests. In fact, one of the early Sultans,

Sikandar (1389-1413), equalled the most bloodthirsty and iconoclastic Muslim conquerers anywhere in his zeal to obliterate all traces of the Hindu religion and convert its followers to Islam on pain of death. Temples were levelled and some of the grandest monuments of old damaged and disfigured. Archaeologists agree that the scale of destruction wreaked on the monumental structures at Martand and Avantipura suggest the use of gunpowder. Thousands of Hindus escaped across the borders of Kashmir; others were massacred.

In his *Kings of Kasmira*, the historian Jonaraja recalled:

There was no city, no town, no village, no wood, where the temples of the gods were unbroken. When Sureshwan, Varaha and others were broken, the world trembled but not so the mind of the wicked king. He forgot his kingly duties and took delight day and night in breaking images.

Sikandar is still known in the valley as 'Butshikan' (idol-breaker). That this title is reserved for him, however, suggests that his Muslim predecessors and successors did not fully share his iconoclastic zeal, although some like Mirza Haider Dughlat, Yaqub Shah Chak, some Mughal Governors and the Afghan rulers were also religious zealots.

B y one of those unpredictable quirks of fortune that history rather than fiction provides, Sikandar's second son, Shahi Khan, who succeeded to the throne after his elder brother's brief seven-year rule, gave Kashmir its most glorious era since that of Lalitaditya. He took the title of Zainul Abidin (1420-1470). The word "Zain" before innumerable public structures like rest houses, palaces, gardens, monasteries, even temples, in the valley, shows how much he was loved. The first bridge in Srinagar is still named after him. But the local name by which he is fondly remembered throughout the valley is Bud Shah.

Only eleven Hindu families are said to have been left
in Kashmir when Sikandar's rule ended. But Zainul Abidin
persuaded many to return. He rebuilt their temples, visited
their shrines and joined their cultural festivities. He went
on pilgrimage to Amarnath and even forbade the killing of
cows. The new ruler, who was also a scholar of Sanskrit and
Persian, set up schools and colleges and gave scholarships
to oustanding students to study in the great universities of
India. He balanced the interest he showed in reviving
Hinduism and Sanskrit by inviting noted Islamic scholars
from abroad to settle in Kashmir. It is no wonder that the
arts and sciences flourished under Zainul Abidin, whose rule
lasted for half a century. He was particularly interested in
poetry and drama and revived shawl weaving, pottery, wood
carving and all the home industries for which Kashmir was
and is famous. He introduced papier-mâché for which the
valley's artisans have become equally known. For the
common man, there was justice, which had been a rare
commodity. Only the orthodox were dissatisfied.[7]

Bazaz obviously had Zainul Abidin's reign in mind when
he wrote of the revitalising impact of Islam. In fact, like
Akbar the Great, the Kashmiri ruler was one of the rare
medieval monarchs who were able to appreciate the philoso-
phic essence of religious teaching and surmount the cruder
antagonisms cultivated in its name. He did not try to evolve
a distinct religious faith like Akbar's Din-i-Ilahi, but represented a distillation of the two religions and cultures.
Bazaz writes:

> As a matter of fact, while Muslims have owned Zainul
> Abidin as a co-religionist, Hindus have always believed
> that he was Bhat Shah (the Brahmin King), a tapasvi
> of a very high order who had taken birth as Sultan of
> Kashmir merely to restore the Hindu Dharma to its
> deserved place. A modern-minded patriot might contend
> that the very name Bud Shah and his works are ample
> proof that he was neither a Hindu nor a Muslim but

essentially a Kashmiri who built a progressive and
secular State on the foundations of the composite
Kashmir culture which had been evolved through
thousands of years till his own day.[8]

When it became known that Bud Shah was dead, the
court historian Srivara noted:

No one cooked his food on the day; no smoke arose from
the houses; all were dumb with grief. They lamented and
said the king was the greatest among the sovereigns.

Jonaraja reviewed the reign in its historical perspective,
with an eye to the uncertain future:

He possessed courage and a will to perform what was
beyond the power of past kings, and what may be beyond
the ability of future rulers.

It did not take long for Jonaraja's apprehensions to be
fulfilled. Zainul Abidin's son Haji Khan, also known as
Haider Shah, proved to be a transformation in reverse.
Kashmir was back to the unhappy times of despotic rule.
Without institutions to maintain administrative continuity,
there was no protection against the uncertainties of dynastic
succession.

The concluding years of local Muslim rule in Kashmir
were as unsettled and unhappy for the people as the last
years of the Hindu period. Different groups fought to wrest
the throne from each other. Shias and Sunnis frequently
came to blows. Somewhat surprisingly, there was enough
local patriotism for Kashmiris to unite in repelling the
forces of Babar, the founder of the Mughal dynasty, who
tried more than once to add the valley to his dominions after
occupying the throne of Delhi. The last attempt was in 1529.

Kashmir, however, continued to fascinate the Mughals.
Babar's cousin, Mirza Haider Dughlat, tried to persuade
Babar's son, Humayun, to rest and consolidate his forces in
the valley when he was on the run before Sher Shah Suri.

But Humayun preferred to withdraw all the way to Iran.
On his first attempt to conquer the valley in 1532, Dughlat
had to retire when the Kashmiri nobles united against him.
Eight years later, however, they were divided. When
Dughlat tried again in 1540, he met no resistance. He
placed Nazuk Shah, a descendant of Shah Mir, on the throne
and gave Kashmir a stable administration. But in course
of time he injured Kashmiri sentiment by placing Mughals
in all senior posts. The locals were further upset when he
minted coins in the name of Humayun, who was back in
Delhi, and treated him as emperor. He also persecuted the
Shias and the Sufis. Eventually, there was a widespread
uprising and he was killed on the battlefield.[9]

One of the last Sultans of Kashmir to merit notice was
Yusuf Shah Chak, but more for romantic than kingly
qualities. His queen, the rustic singer Zoon or Habba
Khatoon, made a far deeper impact on the valley. Their
trysts in its loveliest spots, like Gulmarg and Sonmarg, are
part of Kashmiri lore. He was also a liberal ruler, promoting
music and the arts and not discriminating between his
subjects for reasons of religion or sect.

But Yusuf neglected administration. His conservative
nobles revolted and drove him out of Srinagar. He invited
the Emperor Akbar to help him regain his throne; then
realised that this was inviting annexation and changed his
mind. But Akbar was affronted and ordered a force
commanded by Raja Bhagwan Das to march into Kashmir.
At this point, Yusuf led the Kashmiri army against the
invaders in the best romantic tradition, halted them and
forced Bhagwan Das to negotiate a treaty in which he would
retain the throne but coins would be struck bearing Akbar's
name and various concessions would be made to the Mughal
emperor.

Yusuf was not destined to end his life on a heroic note.
Raja Bhagwan Das persuaded Yusuf to accompany him to

Attock, where Akbar was encamped. Akbar promptly imprisoned him, which the Raja regarded as a slight on his honour since he had assured Yusuf his safety, and committed suicide in accordance with the best Rajput tradition. Yusuf was eventually banished to Bihar; he died in Patna district in 1592. In Kashmir, Habba Khatoon composed her most poignant songs as she pined for his return:

> Say, friend, when will fate smile on me,
> And my love come to me again? Say when?
> I've waited long and patiently,
> My heart is numb and idle and empty of hope.
> Sweet is the ritual of love;
> I would deck my love with ornament,
> And in henna dye his hands.
> I would anoint his body with fragrant kisses
> And offer wine in golden goblets.
> The lotus of love which blooms in the lake of my heart;
> Say, friend, when will fate smile on me...

Yusuf was succeeded by his son, Yaqub Shah Chak, who, in a last show of defiance, repudiated the treaty between Yusuf and Bhagwan Das (which had not been ratified). This provoked Akbar to order another attack on Kashmir, which was successful. Yaqub, the last ruler of an independent valley, fled on 10 October 1586.

Chapter IV

Foreign Domination

*I*f Kashmir had to come under foreign domination, it was fortunate that it was Akbar the Great who ended the sad chapter of the last days of the valley's independent Sultans by annexing it to the expanding Mughal empire ruled from Delhi and Agra in 1586. Like Zainul Abidin, he ended discrimination between Hindu and Muslim and his viceroys introduced a uniform administrative and tax structure. Steps were taken to revive the shawl industry and generate employment, thus mitigating the chronic poverty of the valley. Mughal troops were ordered to keep to their barracks outside Srinagar to avoid friction with the people. The Emperor first visited Kashmir in 1589. His second visit came three years later in the month of October. Diwali was being celebrated and Akbar joined in the festivities after ordering illuminations along the Jhelum. He put his imprimatur on the houseboat, which was to become one of Srinagar's tourist attractions.[1] It was also the season to savour the spectacle and perfume of the famed saffron fields of Pampur.

Akbar's last visit in 1597 took place in less auspicious circumstances. The valley was in the grip of such a severe famine that a Jesuit priest, Father Hierosme Xavier, who accompanied him, wrote that parents were forced to try to sell their children on the roadside. The Emperor ordered public works where men and women were employed in large numbers. Grain was also rushed to the valley from Punjab. Kashmiri resentment was mitigated but not effaced. They paid for better administration with higher levies. Revolts continued, especially by the warlike Chaks, and were put down with medieval cruelty. It took time for the valley to accept foreign rule.

When Jahangir succeeded Akbar, the romantic poet in him was infatuated with Kashmir, and its beauty infuses his memoirs. He paid as many as eight visits to the valley, two in the company of his father and six as Emperor. His wanderings there, together with Nur Mahal, his search for the most beautiful and secluded spots to adorn with gardens and pavilions, most of all the Shalimar and Nishat gardens on the outskirts of Srinagar, are part of popular lore. When travellers' accounts and translations of local works reached Europe, distant Kashmir became the most romantic place in popular imagination.

An English poet, Thomas Moore, made a fortune with his rhapsodic descriptions of the scene in a long poem, *Lalla Rookh*, for which he was paid as much as three thousand guineas without ever going there. The poem is of unequal texture; a few lines are enough to taste the atmosphere sought to be created:

Oh! best of delights as it everywhere is
To be near the loved One, what a rapture is his
Who in moonlight and music thus sweetly may glide
O'er the Lake of Cashmere with the One by his side!
If woman can make the worst wilderness dear,
Think, what a Heaven she must make of Cashmere!
So felt the magnificent son of Ackbar,
When from the power and pomp and the trophies of war
He flew to that Valley, forgetting them all
With the Light of the Haram, his young Nourmahal...[2]

Jahangir's unforgettable tribute to Kashmir is the widely quoted Persian stanza:

Gar firdaus bar rue zamin ast
Hamin ast, hamin ast, hamin ast!

(If there be a paradise on earth,
It is this, it is this, it is this.)

[To which a contemporary, anonymous Kashmiri poet has responded:

Ferishte agar ayen to ijazat se ayen.
Yeh mera watan hai, koi jannat nahin.

(Even if angels come, they should come with permission. This is my land, not paradise.)][3]

Jahangir's successor, Shah Jahan, also visited the valley, which had become a popular retreat for the nobility to escape the heat of the plains in summer. The settled administrative pattern and peaceful conditions and general improvement in the economy were reflected in a substantial increase in revenue. The court journeyed to Kashmir four times in his reign. It was still a long and tortuous route. But, as the present-day visitor can testify, the contrast between the searing, dusty plains and the cool, verdant valley is an unbelievable relief. However, the imperial visit was not just a holiday. When complaints of unjust levies and other exactions were placed before Shah Jahan, he had them annulled.

Then, as now, the Governors appointed by Delhi were of varying character. Jahangir discovered that one of them had gone far beyond his legitimate powers in exacting taxes. Thereupon, to ensure that his instructions were known and obeyed, a royal edict was engraved in stone on the gate of the Jami Masjid in Srinagar that gives us an inkling of the detailed and comprehensive imposts that could be levied and ways in which unpaid labour could be extorted. It also reflects the anxiety of the Emperor to let his subjects know that he was concerned with their welfare.[4]

Many poets were attracted to Kashmir during the rule of Jahangir and Shah Jahan. Most of them had emigrated from Persia, but the valley also spawned local genius. By now, Persian was the language of literature as well as that of the court. Altogether, it was a fruitful time for Kashmir; it had never known such a long period of settled government before.

Although a better administrator than the preceding Mughal emperors, Aurangzeb's stern religious temperament began the undoing of what his predecessors had achieved in terms of winning the loyalty of their subjects, irrespective of religion or sect. In Kashmir, it was not only the Hindus who found themselves again subjected to unfair laws, but the Shia community was also persecuted by Aurangzeb's Governors. The Emperor was a rigid Sunni. He was not given to enjoyment and visited the valley only once. He changed his Governors frequently, but the people became increasingly restive. Once again there was civil disorder. One of the longest periods of peace and order known by the valley was coming to an end.

A long night descended on Kashmir as the lesser Mughals followed, each more inept than the next. As a distant outpost of the empire, the valley suffered greatly. There was nobody in Delhi capable of checking the brutality and greed of its provincial Governors. Not unnaturally, the locals began to look to other rulers in the vicinity for help. In 1752, two Kashmiri nobles travelled to Lahore where the Afghan ruler, Ahmad Shah Durrani, was preparing for one of his many invasions of India. He despatched a force to Kashmir. The Mughal troops stationed there attempted resistance but were overcome and Kashmir came under Afghan rule.

However, if the people thought they would be better off, they were soon disappointed. The Afghan Governors proved to be even more exacting and tyrannical than their predecessors. Within six months one Governor extorted one

crore of rupees from his charge and presented it to Kabul.
The economy was soon at a standstill. Temples were
desecrated and women molested. Pandits were disallowed
from wearing the sacred thread and from teaching Sanskrit.
Kashmiri slaves were sent to Afghanistan. The remaining
years under Afghan rule were much the same, with each
Governor trying to improve on the other in mulcting the
people. Hindus and Shias were the main victims but
everyone suffered.

There were a few attempts to fight oppression. One of
the Governors, Raja Sukh Jiwan Mal, was a Hindu, which
is evidence that social relations in the valley were not as
sharply divided on communal lines as a superficial reading
of the darker aspects of history may suggest. Sukh Jiwan
and his closest adviser, Abdul Hassan Bande, a Muslim,
jointly asserted independence when Kabul's demands for
additional revenues became too exorbitant. The new regime
started well and tried to restore some of the scholarly
pursuits for which Kashmir was known. A contemporary
chronicler, Ghulam Ali Azad Bilgrami, wrote:

> He [Bande] bestowed favours on every visitor to the
> court, whether he was poor or not. Once in every week
> he held a poetical conversazione. It was attended by all
> the well-known poets. At the end of it he gave a dinner.
> He engaged five of the best scholars to complete a
> history of Kashmir from the earliest habitation to his
> own time. Each writer was provided with ten assistants.
> The head of these historians was Muhammad Taufiq,
> with Taufiq as his nom de plume, and was known as
> Lalaju in Kashmiri. He is a poet unrivalled in Kashmir
> today.[5]

Meanwhile, Bande briefly brought back earlier times by
his exertions to alleviate the impact of one of the periodic
famines that devastated the valley. But he and Sukh Jiwan
fell out and finally troops despatched by Ahmad Shah
Durrani were able to reoccupy Kashmir in 1762. Sukh Jiwan
was captured, taken to Durrani in Lahore, where he was
blinded and trampled to death by an elephant.

Another Governor who tried to become independent and win popular support was Ata Mohammed Khan. He went to the extent of striking coins in the name of Nund Rishi, whose memory was revered by Hindu and Muslim alike. His rule was brief but it was also notable for introducing Kashmir's next rulers to the valley. In 1813, Sikh soldiers, despatched by Maharaja Ranjit Singh, joined Afghan troops in attacking the valley. The Afghans got in first and installed Sardar Mohammed Azim Khan as Governor. Ata Mohammed's brief liberal tenure was over. The next year, Ranjit Singh tried again to enter Kashmir on the excuse that the Afghans had not paid him the eight lakh rupees promised for aiding them the previous year. He did not personally go beyond Poonch. Intense cold and heavy rain helped the Afghans to repel his forces.

The last Afghan Governors of Kashmir proved to be even more cruel than their predecessors. Azim Khan took revenge against leading members of the Hindu and Muslim communities on a charge of inviting the Sikhs. He discharged all Kashmiris from the army. The last Afghan Governor, Jabbar Khan, was no better and by this time the entire populace had been antagonised. Nothing, it seemed, could be worse than Afghan rule. Birbal Dar, an influential Pandit landowner, secretly travelled to Ranjit Singh's court to convey the desire of all those he knew that the Maharaja make another attempt to take Kashmir. After some hesitation, Ranjit Singh agreed and this time there was hardly any opposition. Lahore was illuminated for three days to celebrate the Sikh annexation of Kashmir. The year was 1819; it marked the end of Muslim rule in the valley after nearly five hundred years.

*K*ashmiris who hoped that the change from Afghan to Sikh rule would be an improvement, however, were soon disappointed. Their new rulers were no less cruel and anxious to mulct them. An English traveller, William

Moorcroft, who entered the valley in 1824, after securing the permission of Maharaja Ranjit Singh, wrote:

> Everywhere the people are in the most abject condition, exorbitantly taxed by the Sikh Government and subjected to every kind of extortion and oppression.... Not more than about one-sixteenth of the cultivable land is in cultivation, and the inhabitants, starving at home, are driven in great numbers to the plains of Hindustan.... Butchers, bakers, boatmen, vendors of fuel, public notaries, scavengers, prostitutes, all paid a sort of corporation tax.[6]

(Virtually the same complaint was made about the oppressive, wide-ranging taxes imposed by the first Dogra ruler, Raja Gulab Singh, by Francis Younghusband.)

Easier communications with Europe brought in a number of adventurous travellers anxious to see the remoter parts of the British Empire and adjoining areas. The British Government was becoming concerned with the proximity of the Czarist empire to its borders and some of the travellers doubled as intelligence agents. William Moorcroft was one of them. Godfrey Vigne was another traveller who wrote extensively on Kashmir. He found conditions had deteriorated when he was there in 1835:

> The villages were fallen into decay. In the time of the Moghuls, Kashmir was said to produce not less than sixty laks of kirwahs [or karwahs] of rice, which was there grown wherever a system of irrigation was practicable; but such is the state to which this beautiful but unfortunate province is now reduced, and so many inhabitants have fled the country that a vast proportion of the rice-ground is uncultivated for want of labour and irrigation.[7]

Lahore was no less exacting than Kabul had been; nor did the change in the religion of the rulers make them less brutal. The valley continued to be an exploited colony. But there were individual exceptions to the succession of rapacious Governors. According to Vigne:

> Kupar (Kirpa) Ram was four years governor of the valley and the kindest and best of all. He attended to the wishes and rapacity of Runjit (Maharaja Ranjit Singh) and was luxurious without being tyrannical. The dancing girls were his constant companions and his state barge was always paddled by women.

Baron Schonberg confirms Vigne's view, as also the thesis that enlightened rule can also be profitable. But the mere fact that they were so impressed by Kirpa Ram shows how unusual good government was. Schonberg wrote:

> The Sikh governor who enjoys the best reputation amongst the inhabitants of Kashmir is Kapar Rham. The term of his viceroyalty is compared by the people of the valley to those pleasant days when Jehangir used to make an annual visit there. Kapar Rham remitted to the government every year forty-two lacs of rupees, and the country was at that time happy, in comparison to what it now is: and yet for many years after the rule of Kapar Rham, the tribute amounted to only twenty lacs, and at the present time Gulam Muhyddin returns but six lacs of rupees yearly, while the country, so far from being benefited by the decrease in the tribute, is become still more wretched.[8]

Visitors testified to the gulf between the affluent aristocracy, who lived in palatial splendour, and most of the populace who were clothed in rags and had barely enough to eat. Agriculture and the shawl and carpet industry had been ruined by a confiscatory rate of taxation. Fields were left untended because most of the produce was taken away. The valley's economy had been ruined. A succession of famines, partly caused by maladministration, floods, fires and the plague made things worse. All this was vividly described by the English travellers: part of the motivation could have been to make a case for British intervention.

Sikh rule lasted just twenty-seven years. A new power
was extending its grip on India. The British employed
various strategies ranging from occupation of territory to
propping up complaisant rulers who were willing to accept
their overlordship. The death of Ranjit Singh in 1839 was
the beginning of the end. His successors inherited neither
his guile nor his valour and were defeated in the Battle of
Sobraon after which the British captured Lahore. Kashmir
awaited another change of masters. The British found a
convenient tool in an ambitious, wily local ruler. The well-
being of the Kashmiri people was irrelevant; their feelings
were ignored.

Chapter V

Dogra Rule

*T*he collapse of the Sikh empire left a vacuum in Kashmir. The British were not willing to govern it directly. The bitterly fought and narrowly won Sikh wars had drained the resources of the East India Company, preceded as they were by the Afghan wars, which had been even more expensive in blood and treasure. The distance to the valley, over mountainous paths, was another disincentive. The Governor-General, Lord Hardinge, explained in a letter: "To keep a British force three hundred miles from any possibility of support would have been an undertaking that merited a strait-waistcoat and not a peerage."[1]

So Hardinge preferred to place Kashmir under a local boss of proven reliability; the Dogra Raja, Gulab Singh, was ready and willing. He had been working for this opportunity for a long time, using every occasion to show the British that he knew they were the coming power and that they could rely on him, even when he was on the other side. It was then, in fact, that he proved his value. He was Prime Minister of the Sikh Government in Lahore when the crucial Battle of Sobraon was fought in 1846 and betrayed his charge by disposing his forces in such a way as to help the British. Since it was a closely fought engagement, his betrayal may well have tilted the scales. William Edwards, in his *Reminiscences of a Bengal Civilian*, testified:

> Gulab Singh urged the army not to attempt attacking the British until he joined them and this he avoided doing on one pretext or another knowing full well that in due time the British would attack and capture the position of Sobraon.

Gulab Singh's career was that of a soldier of fortune par excellence. Starting as a common soldier, he worked his way up through intelligence and hard work, coupled with the sense of timing and opportunism required to realise when to switch sides. At one point, he took service under a local feudatory, Sultan Khan of Bhimbar, but left him to join the forces of Maharaja Ranjit Singh, who was rapidly becoming head of the strongest power in the region. Soon afterwards, the Sikh forces captured Sultan Khan and he was placed in the custody of Gulab Singh, who had learnt the art of joining the winning side in good time.

He served Maharaja Ranjit Singh well enough to be rewarded with the *jagir* of Jammu and adjoining territories. In 1841, the now Raja Gulab Singh was sent to neighbouring Kashmir to restore order which had been disturbed by a local revolt of the Sikh soldiery after the death of Ranjit Singh in 1839. He put it down successfully and, as instructed by Lahore, appointed Shaikh Mohiuddin as Governor. It may well have been this experience that instilled the ambition to rule the valley, with its lakes and gardens, so near and yet so much more attractive than his own dusty *jagir* in the plains.

After the death of Ranjit Singh, the British, now masters of most of the subcontinent, were clearly destined to influence the future, if not take over, the Punjab and north India. Gulab Singh, the ace opportunist, began to send out feelers. He helped them during the Afghan wars, their hour of need, with rights of passage and supplies to the army. When, eventually, the British clashed with the Sikhs, he kept in touch with them, even though trusted with high office by the Lahore court. By now he had also learnt the diplomatic arts of suggestion and circumlocution, of which his letter of 15 January 1846 to the assistant agent to the Governor-General, Lieutenant E. Lake (quoted by Khushwant Singh in *A History of the Sikhs*) is an oustanding example. He clearly had his eyes on Kashmir in this disguised offer of timely collaboration:

> He who wishes to climb the summit of a lofty mountain, must start at daybreak; should he delay, night may close over him ere he has gained the desire of his heart; the treasure which is buried in the depths of the mountain will become the prize of that man who is first to reach the summit.

The summit was near. Writing, as was customary, to his monarch, Queen Victoria, Sir Henry Hardinge, in a letter dated 18 February 1846, explained his plans to establish British influence on north India before actually putting them into effect in the Treaties of Lahore and Amritsar. At that time, it would seem that, owing to the financial and administrative constraints on the East India Company, the British were hesitant even to take over the Punjab (they did; three years later). Hardinge wrote that it was desirable:

> To weaken the Sikh State which has proved itself too strong – and show to all Asia that, although the British Government has not deemed it expedient to annex the immense territory of the Punjab, making the Indus the British boundary, it has punished the treachery and violence of the Sikh nation, and exhibited its power in a manner which cannot be misunderstood.... For the same political and military reasons, the Governor-General hopes to be able, before the negotiations are closed, to make arrangements by which Cashmere may be added to the possessions of Gulab Singh, declaring the Rajput Hill State with Cashmere independent of the Sikhs of the plains.

In a minute, Hardinge also made it clear that this

generosity was a reward for Gulab Singh's duplicity in
offering to help the British while still holding office with
the Sikhs:

> Raja Golab Singh, on being installed as Minister (in the
> Sikh Durbar), put himself in communication with us,
> proffering every assistance in his power for the
> furtherance of any ends in regard to the State of Lahore
> which we might have in view.

Younghusband later explained:

> In 1846, the East India Company had no thoughts or
> inclinations whatever to extend their possessions. All
> they wished was to curb their powerful and aggressive
> neighbours, and they thought they would best do this,
> and at the same time reward a man who had shown his
> favourable disposition towards them, by depriving the
> Sikhs of a hilly country and handing it over to a ruler
> of a different race.

The outcome of these designs was the Treaty of Amritsar
of 16 March 1846, which handed over Kashmir and
adjoining territories, ceded after their defeat by the Sikhs,
to Gulab Singh, now titled Maharaja, while asserting
Britain's overarching supremacy, for the absurd sum of
seventy-five lakhs of rupees. The summit had been attained.
At the age of fifty-four, Gulab Singh had established a new
Dogra dynasty. For the people of Kashmir, who had not been
consulted in any way, the deal meant another century of
exploitation by alien rulers.

The first article of the treaty gave Gulab Singh his
heart's desire:

> The British Government transfers and makes over, for
> ever, in independent possession, to Maharaja Gulab
> Singh, and the heirs male of his body, all the hilly or
> mountainous country, with its dependencies, situated to
> the eastward of the river Indus, and westward of the
> river Ravi, including Chamba and excluding Lahul,

being part of the territory ceded to the British Government by the Lahore State, according to the provisions of Article Four of the Treaty of Lahore dated March 9, 1846.

In addition, he was promised British aid in protecting his territories from external enemies. Article Ten of the treaty, the last, however, clarified his subordinate role:

Maharaja Gulab Singh acknowledges the supremacy of the British Government, and will, in token of such supremacy, present annually to the British Government one horse, twelve perfect shawl goats of approved breed (six male and six female), and three pairs of Cashmere shawls.

The cynical deal attracted some criticism, even at a time when the rights of the people were not given priority, in England as well as in India. "The transaction," wrote Captain Joseph Davy Cunningham, "scarcely seems worthy of the British name and greatness."[2] Those in Kashmir who may have hoped that the British would deliver them from Sikh oppression were intensely disappointed on finding themselves handed over to another oppressor. The great Urdu poet Mohammed Iqbal later expressed their sentiments in verse:

Their fields, their crops, their streams,
Even the peasants in the vale
They sold, they sold all, alas!
How cheap was the sale.

It was easy enough for the British to sell Kashmir to Gulab Singh in a paper transaction. But they were not ruling it and Governor Imamuddin, though placed in office by Gulab Singh, resisted the take-over under instructions from Lahore. The new Maharaja had to seek the assistance of his new British allies and it was only on 9 November 1846, that he entered Srinagar. The Kashmiris did not favour either side. According to a contemporary report, "not a single Kashmiri took up arms on either side. To the

Kashmiris both armies were alike odious, for they disturbed the peace of the Valley, destroyed trade and made rice dear."

For the once common soldier, however, it was a moment of supreme triumph. Step by step he had increased his domain, by timely opportunism as much as by the force of arms, until he now ruled over a vast territory stretching up to Ladakh and Baltistan, not to speak of such nearby principalities as Kishtwar, Bhimbar, Rajouri and Poonch, which had been added to Jammu. It became the biggest princely State in British India.

Jammu and Kashmir had become a medieval mini-empire, with variations of religion, language, race, custom, status and economic advancement as diverse as its land-scape, stretching from the plains to the highest mountains, from the fragrant valley to the bare high-altitude plateaus bordering Tibet. But this expansion brought with it the seeds of future unrest, as soon as people began to question the right of distant rulers to govern them.

No such heresies were allowed to flourish, however, when Gulab Singh took over Kashmir. He was as autocratic as any of his predecessors and his methods of imposing authority no less barbarous, as noted by Vigne. Besides, Gulab Singh was in a hurry to make up the seventy-five lakhs of rupees that he had given the British for Kashmir. Another contemporary visitor, Lieutenant-Colonel H.D. Torrens, wrote:

> Goolab Singh went far beyond his predecessors in the gentle acts of undue taxation and extortion. They had taxed heavily, it is true, but he sucked the very life-blood of the people; they had laid violent hands on a large proportion of the fruits of the earth, the profits of the loom, and the work of men's hands, but he skinned the very flints to fill his coffers.[3]

Another glimpse of Gulab Singh's greed was provided by yet another traveller, Frederic Drew. He recalled how it was known that one way to ensure that the Maharaja would receive a petition was to hold up a rupee as he passed by.

Then, "he would pounce down like a hawk on the money, and having appropriated it would patiently hear out the petition."[4]

Apart from his personal cupidity, however, Gulab Singh was an able, intelligent and energetic ruler. After the uncertainties of Afghan and Sikh rule, the valley came under firm administration, with controlled rice prices and a reorganised tax system. But its residents continued to be discriminated against in comparison to those of Jammu. This began to take a communal complexion because the Maharaja was an orthodox Hindu, as were most of the people of Jammu, whereas Kashmir was almost entirely Muslim.

Gulab Singh was succeeded by his son, Ranbir Singh, in 1857, the year of the greatest and last armed revolt against British rule in India. The new ruler hastened to follow his father's policy of retaining their favour by despatching two thousand State troops, two hundred cavalry and six guns to help them retake Delhi. He was duly rewarded with a *sanad* from the Viceroy, Lord Canning, amending the Treaty of Amritsar to authorise him to adopt a male heir not being born to him. His position in the princely pecking order was raised by adding two guns to the salute of nineteen fired in his honour on ceremonial occasions. He was also showered with honours by Queen Victoria. In due course, his full title was: His Highness Maharaja Sir Ranbir Singh, Indar Mahindar, Sipar-i-Saltanat, General, Asakir-i-Inglishia, Mushir-i-Khas-i-Qaisara-i-Hind, Grand Commander of the Star of India, Grand Commander of the Indian Empire.

Ranbir Singh outdid his father as an orthodox Hindu. It was said that his ambition was to build as many temples in Jammu as there were in Varanasi. He was not successful, but spent substantial amounts on the project as well as on promoting religious education, ceremonies and publications. He held literary conferences to which scholars from distant parts of India were invited. Dogri was promoted in the army, with Dogras gradually taking over as officers.

All this was of little benefit to Kashmir, reeling at the time under the impact of repeated famines, epidemics and earthquakes. The famine of 1877 was the severest of all. As much as one-third of the population is estimated to have died, entire villages were deserted, as were even some parts of Srinagar. An anonymous memorandum was submitted to the Viceroy alleging that the Maharaja was drowning his Muslim subjects by the boatload to avoid the responsibility of feeding them. It was actually inquired into by a commission before the allegation was dismissed for lack of evidence. Several other charges were also made against the administration. The burden of taxation was increased further. "There were almost prohibitive duties levied on all merchandise, imported or exported," wrote Younghusband, in a passage quoted earlier.

While the allegations against Ranbir Singh indicated mounting dissatisfaction in the valley, they were also seized upon by the Viceroy to increase pressure on him to fall in line with British imperial policies. The Punjab had been annexed and British territory now abutted Jammu and Kashmir. Hardinge's reasons for avoiding direct responsibility for the State were no longer valid. And the threat from Czarist Russia, which had expanded its Asian empire until it bordered Afghanistan, was a favourite Victorian bugbear.

One of Ranbir Singh's achievements was to retake Gilgit on the northern border of the State, which the British regarded as a vital outpost to keep an eye on movements across the border and for the defence of the subcontinent. But despite the eagerness he had shown to retain British support by sending troops to help them put down the Mutiny, the Maharaja had resisted moves to interfere in the internal administration of the State, including the suggestion that he appoint a British Resident.

British pressures mounted after the death of Ranbir

Singh in 1885. A British Resident was forced on the State
before his son, Pratap Singh, could master the reins of office.
The young Maharaja was further unsettled by charges that
he was conspiring to murder the Resident, Trevor Chichele
Plowden, and was in league with Russia. Plowden also
reported that the Maharaja was an imbecile and could not
supervise the administration (he later proved the opposite).
Then newspapers reported that he was indulging in
treasonable activities. This was all a plot to prepare the way
to annex the State. Fortunately, for Pratap Singh, an Indian
paper, the *Amrita Bazar Patrika* of Calcutta, took up his
cause and published a secret official note, thus disclosing
the plot. The British had to scale down their ambitions.
Pratap Singh was required to step down in favour of a
council of regency, over which the Resident had control, in
1889.[5]

In classic manner, the Viceroy was now able to interfere
in the State administration whenever he chose without
taking the responsibility of direct rule. Even after the
Maharaja had handed over powers to the Council of
Regency, the Viceroy justified intervention with a message,
its language reflecting the harsh fact of British
paramountcy. It stated:

> Notwithstanding the ample resources of your State, your
> treasury was empty; corruption and disorder prevailed
> in every department and every office; Your Highness was
> still surrounded by low and unworthy favourites, and
> the continued misgovernment of your State was
> becoming, every day, a more serious source of anxiety.

As in other areas of the subcontinent, historians and
political analysts differ on the benefits or otherwise of the
extension of British rule and influence. Indirect rule or rule
by proxy in the princely States was perhaps the worst, for
British backing provided the ruler a buffer to protect

himself against the pressures for self-rule that were
beginning to mount. On the other hand, some reforms and
changes were the outcome of British influence. Kashmir had
its share of both. The Dogra dynasty owed its existence to
British power and, as Bazaz wrote:

> The Dogras have always considered Jammu as their
> home and Kashmir as the conquered country. As we
> shall presently see they established a sort of Dogra
> imperialism in the State in which all non-Dogra
> communities and classes were given the humble places
> of inferiors. The people of the valley were thus brought
> under the imperialism of the Dogras which itself was
> functioning as a vassal of the super-imperialism of the
> British. But though Dogra imperialism brought nothing
> but misery, thraldom, physical and mental deterioration
> in its wake, the other imperialism did not come without
> some blessing. By coming under the British suzerainty
> the valley began to have the impact of western ideas and
> modern civilisation which finally awakened the people
> to demand their birthright of independence and
> freedom.[6]

One of the beneficial results of British influence was the
appointment in 1889 of a settlement commission for
Kashmir to establish a uniform basis for the payment of
land revenue. There was considerable opposition from
landlords and city-dwellers who benefited from the arbitrary
procedures in force and the control it gave them over the
peasantry. In addition to levies in cash and kind, the poor
farmer could be whisked away from home for *begar*, or
forced labour, which could mean long periods of hacking
paths out of the mountainous terrain between the valley and
Gilgit, from which many did not return.

In spite of local opposition, Sir Walter Lawrence of the
Indian Civil Service was able to complete his labours and
the much-persecuted cultivator, mulcted for generations,
was able to pay a known, fixed amount in cash. This was
still 30 per cent of his gross produce, but less than the half

or more exacted before. Perhaps the biggest boon was that
begar was abolished. The Maharaja contributed his share
by writing off land revenue arrears amounting to thirty-one
lakhs of rupees.

It is to Lawrence, too, that we owe a detailed account
of the valley on the lines of the provincial gazetteers of
India, as well as the most readable descriptions of his
experiences. We get a graphic picture of conditions in
Kashmir when he arrived there in *The India We Served*:

> When I started my work, everything was taxed. Fruit
> trees, birch-bark, violets, hides, silk, saffron, hemp,
> tobacco, water-nuts and paper were treated as State
> monopolies and farmed out to the Pandits. The right to
> legalise marriage was farmed out, and office of grave-
> digger was taxed. Prostitutes were taxed, and
> everything save air and water was brought under
> taxation. Meanwhile, agriculture, the only stable source
> of revenue, languished, and the treasury was empty. The
> land revenue was, as a rule, extorted from villagers by
> violent methods. I once caught a revenue officer using
> the thumb-screw on an unfortunate peasant who had
> paid his land revenue in full, but declined to pay an
> equal amount as a bribe to the officer. But the revenue
> thus collected did not reach the State treasury. Fully a
> half was intercepted by the officials, and this was
> debited against the helpless cultivator as arrears of
> revenue [p. 134].[7]

Lawrence had mixed opinions about the Pandits.
"Nowhere had he met a body of men so clever and courteous,
but they also exploited the Muslims and resented their
emancipation," he wrote.

Land settlement was not the only achievement of the
Pratap Singh regime. Land reclamation, model farms,
sericulture, cooperative banks and other projects to improve
the economy were initiated. New roads were constructed.
Srinagar was linked with Rawalpindi in 1890 by the first
road capable of taking wheeled traffic. The road over the

Banihal Pass from Jammu was completed in 1915. Hospitals
were opened, electricity introduced and the first municipal
act placed on the books. By 1905, the Viceroy, Lord Curzon,
had agreed to abolish the Council of Regency; Pratap Singh
regained his powers.

Efforts to improve and strengthen the administrative
services, however, created resentment among the Pandits
of the valley who had dominated the few jobs available. The
court language was changed from Persian to Urdu to attract
qualified people from India. But the flood of outsiders, some
of whom got the best jobs, led to friction between Kashmiris
and non-Kashmiris. Tension mounted as more and more
Kashmiris secured education in the colleges just opened in
the State. Following a representation to the Government of
India, instructions were issued that locals be given
preference to outsiders, but the phrasing was too loose to
be an effective check.

In any case, the valley's Muslims lagged far behind in
education and now they began to demand better facilities.
By 1916, the pressure was strong enough to persuade the
Maharaja to invite the Educational Commissioner to the
Government of India to constitute a commission to look into
their complaints. This he did, but little was done to
implement his recommendations. Eight years later, leading
Muslims submitted a memorial on Muslim grievances to the
Viceroy, Lord Reading, when he visited Kashmir. Their
demands were far from excessive. Among them: proprietary
rights for peasants (almost all of whom were Muslims), more
representation in State services, more education facilities
and effective abolition of *begar*, some forms of which
survived. But the Maharaja was annoyed that the Viceroy
had been approached directly. After an official committee
had gone through the formality of examining the memorial,
the complaints were dismissed and its signatories punished.

*D*espite his inadequacies, Pratap Singh's reign is

remembered for bringing Kashmir into the modern era. He died in 1925 and was succeeded by his nephew, Hari Singh, who began his career with a sensational law suit in London. Caught in bed with a woman, he was blackmailed for a large amount. A court case ensued. Although thinly disguised as "Mr A", wide publicity was inevitable because the central figure was a fabled Maharaja. At home, he permitted court favourites to pack senior appointments in the administration with Dogra Rajputs, thus further antagonising the valley's Muslims.

Sir Albion Bannerji, who had been invited to be the Maharaja's Foreign and Political Adviser, became disgusted with the continuing misrule. Resigning after two years, he issued a statement to the press in 1929, which received wide publicity:

Jammu and Kashmir State is labouring under many disadvantages, with a large Mahommedan population absolutely illiterate, labouring under poverty and very low economic conditions of living in the villages and practically governed like dumb driven cattle. There is no touch between the Government and the people, no suitable machinery for representing grievances and the administrative machinery itself required overhauling from top to bottom to bring it up to the modern conditions of efficiency. It has at present no sympathy with the people's wants and grievances.

Kashmiris felt even more victimised when Hari Singh stopped the practice of shifting the State capital to Srinagar in summer, keeping it in Jammu throughout the year. No Kashmiris were recruited to the army. Only Rajputs were allowed to retain firearms. The Pandits launched a "Kashmir for Kashmiris" movement against discrimination in 1925. They demanded not only their share of jobs in the public services, but also freedom of the press and to form associations, and the establishment of a representative legislature. They were partially successful. A law was passed defining hereditary State subjects and an order issued forbidding employment of non-State subjects in the public services. Outsiders were also banned from buying agricultural land.

The primary beneficiaries of this change were the Dogra Rajputs, with the Pandits getting more clerical appointments. The Muslims of the valley were no better off than before. But they were no longer willing to accept their subservient status. A higher number of Muslims had been educated, many in Indian universities which were then seething with nationalist fervour. They could not remain unaffected. Some went to the Aligarh Muslim University, where the special problems of their community were discussed and talk about a separate nation began.

As the 1920s drew to a close, Kashmir was headed for a confrontation. After centuries of subjection, the people were aware of their rights. And in Hari Singh they had a ruler who continued to live in the past. All that was needed was a spark, and a leader capable of mobilising mass discontent.

Chapter VI

Mass Awakening

*T*he dawn of political awakening in Kashmir can be traced back to the 1930s. For the first time in its long history, the people began to realise their rights and put pressure on the regime. After initial attempts at repression had inflamed public sentiment further, the Maharaja realised that he would have to make some gestures towards popular rule. But they proved belated.

The man who was to be the architect of change was twenty-five years of age when the decade of the thirties began. The talents which contributed to Sheikh Mohammad Abdullah's charismatic leadership were visible early. Born on 5 December 1905, his early education in a traditional Muslim *maktab* (religious school) inculcated a love of the *Quran* which lasted till the end. He was still at the *maktab* when, as he recalled in his autobiography *Aatish-e-Chinar*[1] (written in Urdu and completed in 1982 with assistance from friends), he discovered that he was unusually talented in reciting passages from the holy book and could move listeners to joy and to tears.[2] This was a gift that developed into a capacity to enthuse the thousands who flocked to hear his politico-religious sermons at the great Hazratbal mosque.

Abdullah regarded himself primarily as the spokesman of the Kashmiris, more than 90 per cent of whom were Muslims, and did not hesitate to arouse their passions from the mosque. Yet, after he matured, he saw himself as the leader of all the impoverished people of the valley, irrespective of their religion, and he gloried in its ancient history.[3] His autobiography begins with two quotations, significant in content and origin. One is ascribed to Pandit Kalhana's *Rajatarangini*:

> Kashmir.... By the power of the spirit... yes;
> By the power of the sword... never.

The other to Nund Rishi:

> I broke my sword and fashioned a sickle.

Although Kashmiri Muslim children were seldom educated beyond the *maktab* level, Abdullah showed early signs of his determination to secure higher education by resisting family pressures to start working and gained admission to a government high school, though it meant a ten-mile walk each way.

The young Abdullah wanted to be a doctor. He managed to gain admission to college and do well enough in the qualifying F.Sc. examination to hope to receive State support for admission to the medical school. But now he encountered his first experience of discrimination. Not a single Muslim figured in the list of those recommended for scholarships. He switched over to science, got his B.Sc. from the Islamia College in Lahore and then went over to the Aligarh Muslim University for his Master's degree. It was while he was at Aligarh that the statement issued by Sir Albion Bannerji, condemning the ill-treatment of the Muslim majority of Jammu and Kashmir, hit the headlines.

In *Aatish* Abdullah recalled that when some Muslims loyal to Hari Singh issued a counter-statement, he was provoked to write a letter to the *Muslim Outlook* describing the plight of the Muslims in the valley. He was overjoyed when it appeared. "I had finally found my voice," he wrote; "I was now prepared to face whatever challenges came my way."[4] It was also at Aligarh that he saw Mahatma Gandhi

for the first time. This proved to be an early counter to the
forces of Muslim fundamentalism that were pressing on
him. Even then he was filled with admiration for the
Mahatma's simplicity and informality;[5] the admiration
increased over the years and was a major factor in his belief
in Indian secularism.

As the first Kashmiri Muslim to obtain an M.A., second
division, from Aligarh, he hoped to get a scholarship to study
abroad, but was unsuccessful, which he ascribed to
discrimination. On returning home, he also found that the
highly educated Pandit community monopolised Government jobs and the majority community was marginalised.
He was angered by instances of ill-treatment of Muslims
and then, as he related in his autobiography:

> I started to question why Muslims were being singled
> out for such treatment. We constituted the majority and
> contributed the most towards the State's revenues, still
> we were continuously oppressed. Why? How long would
> we put up with it? Was it because a majority of
> Government servants were non-Muslims? Or because
> most of the lower grade officers who dealt with the
> public were Kashmiri Pandits? I concluded that the ill-
> treatment of Muslims was an outcome of religious
> prejudice.[6]

Abdullah decided to campaign for improving the
conditions in which the Muslim majority lived and also for
removing the handicaps that they suffered. In an extended
interview in 1968, published under the title of *The
Testament of Sheikh Abdullah*, he recalled:

> I had decided when I was still a student that I wanted
> to enter politics, but before doing so I wanted to prepare
> myself thoroughly for the hard life of a politician. It
> became my firm conviction that my people have the
> right to live an honourable life and until they achieved
> their freedom, I could not sit in peace. My mind had
> already reacted strongly against political conditions in

Kashmir: the Kashmiris were hated everywhere and looked upon as liars and cowards. The condition of the Kashmiri labourers was the worst as they had been very badly exploited. Whenever I think of their poverty I boil within. I want to bring about a revolution in the life of every Kashmiri – I want to change his entire life. If I cannot do that I shall prefer death for myself because I feel it is better to die than to live in disgrace.[7]

Under the circumstances, it was only to be expected that Abdullah would react on communal lines. Although they constituted the bulk of the population of the valley, it was the Muslims, who, as we have seen, were the poorest and the most discriminated against. Since political associations were banned, the new group of educated young men formed the Kashmir Muslim Reading Room. At that stage, their ambitions did not go much beyond securing a fair proportion of jobs for Muslims in the administration. Abdullah's independence of thought and outstanding powers of oratory, coupled with his tall, commanding presence, brought him to the forefront. He was picked to be one of a two-man deputation who conveyed their problems and requirements to the State Government. Their request for reservation of jobs for Muslims, who were unable to compete on equal terms with others owing to their handicapped background, was promptly turned down.

Frustration mounted against the State Government. It also turned, to some extent, against the Hindus. The Maharaja was a devout Hindu and the Pandits, who had so far virtually monopolised the valley's share of administrative jobs, did not sympathise with the Muslims' plight. At the same time, communal newspapers published in Lahore launched a campaign vilifying the Maharaja and urging Muslims to rise against his regime. It needed only a spark to ignite a conflagration.

Some incidents occurred, which were interpreted as an insult to Islam and protest meetings were held at which the State's Hindu Government was openly condemned. Sheikh

Abdullah was one of the seven prominent Muslims elected at a meeting in Srinagar in June 1931 to submit grievances to the Maharaja. Jammu Muslims also elected four representatives, of which one was Chaudhri Ghulam Abbas who was to become Abdullah's rival and play a prominent role in partitioning the State. The spark was lit when the police arrested one Abdul Qadir for urging the general massacre of Hindus at the meeting.

The crucial day was 13 July 1931, later observed as Martyrs' Day, when Abdul Qadir's trial began and a large crowd gathered outside the prison. Some were arrested; stones were thrown; and the police fired; not an unusual scenario in British India at the time, when nationalist fervour was mounting. But, in Kashmir, it was the first occasion that Dogra authority had been challenged spontaneously by the common people and as many as twenty-one had died in the firing. Prem Nath Bazaz, who was then personally involved in political activity, recounts the outcome:

> Public opinion among the Muslims had by this time crystallised on the point that the government and the Hindus were inseparable and one stood for the other. Almost all the officials were Hindus and the Maharaja was a Hindu. So the responsibility for the actions of the government must be shared by the Hindus. The jail firing which killed several Muslims created great resentment in the mob mind against the Hindus. So when the procession reached Maharaj Ganj, a busy trade centre of the city, Hindu shops which had been closed owing to panic after hearing of the jail incident, were broken open and looted.[8]

Serious communal rioting followed, for the first time in the valley. Three Hindus were killed, many more wounded, and hundreds of shops looted. There was more firing and many arrests. But a watershed had been crossed; repression would not be accepted quiescently again. Among those arrested were Abdullah and Abbas, who were to be incarcerated in the Hari Parbat fort. They had to be released before order was restored.

Communal conflict, perhaps, was inevitable. But what was different from the rest of the subcontinent was that communal politics did not gather strength. *Kashmiryat* and Abdullah's personality made the valley reject Muslim fundamentalism and set an example of religious tolerance. The Hindus were not untouched by communalism. As it became evident that the Maharaja was being forced to give a fairer deal to the majority, a section resolved to resist under the banner of the Kashmiri Pandits' Conference. But another section, led by Bazaz, saw the writing on the wall and helped the rise of secular politics by getting together with Muslim leaders who had a similar approach.

Demonstrations and protests continued. Abdullah was in and out of jail. The movement spread to other parts of the State. In Jammu, it was joined by Muslim groups from neighbouring Punjab and the Maharaja had to seek the assistance of British troops to put it down. In Mirpur, the peasantry utilised the occasion to destroy the property of Hindu moneylenders, but the reaction was to exploitation rather than to religious differences. Here, again, British assistance had to be sought.

The Maharaja's administration reacted alternately with repression and concession, but was eventually forced, in November 1931, to appoint a commission headed by a senior English official, Bertrand Glancy, from the Foreign and Political Department of the Government of India. He was assisted by four citizens of the State: a Muslim and a Hindu from Kashmir and the same representation from Jammu. One Hindu later resigned under pressure from conservatives who saw the commission as a concession to the Muslims. The other, the historian Bazaz, however, did not.

Many of the legitimate grievances of the Muslim community were recognised and sought to be allayed by the commission. Their religious buildings, taken over by the State Government, were restored. Special administrative arrangements were suggested to improve their education and widen employment opportunities. The commission also tried to mitigate the condition of peasants and, once more, to abolish *begar* and insist that proper payment be made for requisitioned labour. Obviously, this was a practice that had continued in spite of previous bans, indicating the plight of the people, even in the 1930s.

The participation of Bazaz in the Glancy Commission corrected the impression that all Hindus were opposed to giving Muslims the rights that they had been denied. Those in senior positions, however, feared that the process would inevitably lead to popular government, which meant majority rule, and did their best to oppose it. But a meeting between Bazaz and Sheikh Abdullah in July 1932 led them to cooperate in seeking full democratic rights for all. The campaign gathered force and Ghulam Abbas, who had been appointed 'dictator' of the Muslim Conference movement, was arrested. The Maharaja was obliged to announce a constitution providing for a legislative assembly. It had severely attenuated powers; nevertheless, the process of democratisation had begun.

In October 1933, Abdullah married Akbar Jahan, daughter of Harry Nedou, the eldest son of the proprietor of Srinagar's well-known Nedou's Hotel. Harry had converted to Islam and married a Gujjar girl. She gave birth to Akbar Jahan, who in spite of her mixed parentage, was a devout Muslim. In course of time, she participated in her husband's political work and began to campaign on her own. Gandhiji invited her to read the *Quran* at his prayer meetings. (Among their progeny was Farooq, who was to later succeed the Sheikh.)

In August 1935, another step was taken towards uniting Muslims and Hindus in the struggle for democratic rights with the appearance of a political weekly in Urdu, *The Hamdard*, edited jointly by Abdullah and Bazaz. The following year, the Muslim Conference launched a Responsible

Government Day throughout the State. Its President, Sheikh Abdullah, appealed to the minorities to participate. Many leading Hindus and Sikhs responded, paving the way for the next big step, which proved unique in reversing the trend in the rest of the subcontinent, to convert a religious organisation into a secular, political one.

Abdullah's presidential address to the sixth annual session of the Muslim Conference in March 1938 was to transform its character. He declared:

> Like us the large majority of Hindus and Sikhs in the State have immensely suffered at the hands of the irresponsible government. They are also steeped in deep ignorance, have to pay large taxes and are in debt and are starving. Establishment of responsible government is [as] much a necessity for them as for us. Sooner or later these people are bound to join our ranks. No amount of propaganda can keep them away from us....
>
> The main problem therefore now before us is to organise joint action and a united front against the forces that stand in our way in the achievement of our goal. This will require rechristening our organisation as a non-communal political body. Firstly, we must end communalism by ceasing to think in terms of Muslims and non-Muslims when discussing political problems. Secondly, there must be universal suffrage on the basis of joint electroates. [9]

In June, the working committee of the Muslim Conference adopted a resolution urging its general council to amend the name and the constitution of the Conference so that "all such people who desire to participate in this political struggle may easily become members of the Conference irrespective of their caste, creed or religion". It took all of Abdullah's powers of persuasion to push the resolution through after a discussion lasting fifty-two hours.

Since it appeals to reason rather than emotion, the process of secularisation was far more difficult to sustain than the appeal to religious fervour that was persuading

Muslims in many parts of British India to join the Muslim League. 'Islam in danger' has always been a potent slogan. The fact that Muslims were in a majority in Jammu and Kashmir, and more so in the valley, perhaps also made it possible for them to feel less threatened than they did in other parts of the subcontinent where they were in a minority, despite their unhappy experience with the Dogras. In any event, without Abdullah's consistency of approach and persuasive eloquence, comparable to the oratory of the Muslim League President, Mohammad Ali Jinnah, the transformation of the Muslim Conference into the National Conference may never have been achieved.

Such a transformation was delayed when a frightened State Government went in for another wave of repression and jailed hundreds of people of all communities, including Abdullah, Bazaz and Abbas. But the process could not be reversed and they had to be released by February 1939. A special session of what was then the Jammu and Kashmir Muslim Conference was called, with 176 delegates attending it from all parts of the State. The historic resolution replacing 'Muslim' with 'National' was adopted on the morning of 11 June 1939, after a night-long debate.

This development proved to be the high-water mark of united nationalist fervour in Kashmir. Differences soon began to appear. Of particular interest, in view of its unexpectedness, if seen in communal terms, was the rift between Abdullah and Bazaz. The politics of the subcontinent was having its inevitable impact on the State, with the Muslim League moving towards the demand for partition on the basis of the 'two-nation theory', that Hindus and Muslims constituted separate nations, in opposition to the Indian National Congress' commitment to unity.

It was not quite so unusual for Abdullah to veer towards the Congress. Several prominent Muslims in the subcontinent, including the similarly placed Pathan leader, Khan Abdul Ghaffar Khan, whose following was entirely Muslim, felt the same way. But Bazaz was the rare Hindu who insisted that since Muslims constituted the majority in the State, they should join Pakistan. He took this stand in spite of the fact that his own historical research showed that if any ethnic nationality could boast of a distinct history and culture that overrode religious differences, it was the Kashmiri.

At the Anantnag session of the National Conference (NC) in 1939, the Abdullah line emerged clearly. The session ratified what was called the 'National Demand', a document issued earlier by the leadership. One of the clauses read:

> The election of the Legislature shall be made on the basis of joint electorates; seats should be reserved for the minorities and all safeguards and weightages should be guaranteed to them in the Constitution for the protection of their linguistic, religious, cultural, political and economic rights according to the principles enunciated, accepted or acted upon by the Indian National Congress from time to time.

Abdullah first met Jawaharlal Nehru in 1938 and accompanied him on a tour of the North-West Frontier Province, where they were joined by Ghaffar Khan. He was charmed by Nehru and impressed by Ghaffar Khan's confidence in Mahatma Gandhi. In the extended interview he gave thirty years later, he clearly recalled the meeting. Even though, by then he had been ejected from office and imprisoned by Nehru's Government, he fondly admitted Nehru's influence on him:

> He [Nehru] suggested opening the Kashmir Muslim Conference to non-Muslims as well. When I expressed doubt about it, he explained that by opening the membership to all, any campaign against the ruler would gain more strength. Each time we met thereafter our friendship grew stronger but it was the first meeting that I remember most vividly.

As for Gandhiji, Abdullah stated:

When I first met Mahatma Gandhi, I judged him to be a leader of the highest ideals and very clear in his objectives. I was drawn to him by his honesty and his love of the truth. He accepted his errors openly and never asked anyone to do something he himself would not do.[10]

Nehru, too, was impressed by Abdullah. He was just the kind of Muslim leader whom Nehru wanted to promote; his commitment to socialism and his anti-feudal record could counter the canker of communalism. For more than ten years, he sang Abdullah's praises. In fact, at the very next meeting of the All India States People's Conference (the organisation sponsored by the Congress to promote people's movements in the princely States), he took the opportunity to condemn the frequent incarceration of such popular leaders as Abdullah. Nehru involved Abdullah in the activities of the States People's Conference, of which he eventually became President. At the same time, Abdullah was invited to take interest in Congress affairs, and he attended the Tripura session in 1939. Nehru responded with a visit to the valley the same year, together with Khan Abdul Ghaffar Khan. The ties between the Jammu and Kashmir National Conference and the Indian National Congress were being strengthened.

Abdullah did not seem concerned that his political mentors were mainly Hindu. But as he drew closer to the Congress, some of his colleagues felt he was going against the policy of equidistance between the NC and the Muslim League that had been accepted when the NC had been inaugurated. As a result, they resigned from the organisation. One of the resignations would have far-reaching repercussions. It was by the Jammu leader, Ghulam Abbas, who went on to reconstitute the Muslim Conference from pro-Pakistan elements in the State when they revolted against the Maharaja in 1947 and went on to form 'Azad'

Kashmir. Bazaz also resigned to form his own Kashmir
Socialist Party, mainly a gathering of leftist academics,
leaving Abdullah more vulnerable to charges of authorit-
arianism.

The President of the Indian Muslim League, Mohammad
Ali Jinnah, spent two months in Srinagar in 1944 trying to
bring Kashmiris back into the Muslim Conference fold.
Although the initial meetings were cordial, a clash between
Jinnah and Abdullah was inevitable. They represented
opposite trends: Jinnah had moved from secular to
communal politics and Abdullah in the other direction. The
exchanges began politely enough, with Jinnah stressing the
need for Muslim unity and Abdullah for uniting Kashmiris
of all religious persuasions. But soon one was calling the
National Conference a band of gangsters and the other
harshly warning the Muslim League President not to
interfere in State politics. In the course of his farewell
statement, Jinnah said:

> When I, after careful consideration, suggested that the
> Mussalmans should organise themselves under one flag
> and on one platform, not only was my advice not
> acceptable to Sheikh Abdullah but, as is his habit, which
> has become a second nature to him, he indulged in all
> sorts of language of a most offensive and vituperative
> character in attacking me.[11]

Abdullah gave his estimate of the Westernised Jinnah
in *Aatish*:

> He emerged as the undisputed leader of the
> fundamentalist Muslims who were campaigning for a
> separate homeland for themselves, although his
> background and upbringing had nothing in common
> with the people he was supporting. Neither was he
> conversant with Arabic, Persian or Urdu, nor was he
> prepared to mould his life according to the tenets
> prescribed by Islam. Although he even found it difficult
> to offer *namaaz*, he became the beacon light of the quest
> for Pakistan.[12]

Having rejected the appeal of communalism, the National Conference went on to commit itself to a programme of radical reform. At the annual session in Sopore in September 1944, it adopted the 'Naya Kashmir' manifesto, an ambitious document touching on every aspect of public life, that showed the impact of socialist ideology and democratic values on Abdullah and his colleagues. The first part guaranteed human rights, including free universal education (which was implemented when the National Conference came to power); the right to work (which could not be, leaving a growing volatile body of educated unemployed); equality of opportunity; and popular democratic institutions at all levels. Unusual, especially for an organisation whose members were mostly Muslims, was the emphasis on equal rights for women.

The section dealing with economic justice was even more radical, going beyond the pledges made by the Indian National Congress. Landlordism would be abolished and the land distributed to the tiller (it was; leading to communal problems because most of the landlords were Hindus) and key industries nationalised.

I n the early 1940s, the map of the subcontinent had yet to be redrawn. Britain was involved in a protracted war with Nazi Germany that drained its resources. As a result of the Quit India Movement of 1942, the Congress leaders were in jail, leaving the Muslim League unopposed. The princely States demonstrated their loyalty to the British Crown by aiding the war effort. Maharaja Hari Singh sent a detachment of his troops to the front. As the war progressed, it became evident that Britain was too exhausted to retain its empire much longer and the United States of America, its affluent ally, began pressing for self-rule for colonies.

The war was nearly over when the Congress leaders, who had been imprisoned during the Quit India Movement in 1942, were released in June 1945 for talks on the transfer of power. In August, Jawaharlal Nehru, Maulana Abul Kalam Azad (then Congress President), and Khan Abdul Ghaffar Khan attended the annual session of the National Conference in Srinagar to strengthen Abdullah and reverse the impact of Jinnah's foray into the valley. They received a warm public welcome, with the presence of two senior Muslim leaders impressing a largely Muslim audience with the secular character of the Congress. They publicly endorsed Abdullah's leadership, while Nehru advised his fellow-Pandits to realise that their future lay in cooperating with the majority.

Meanwhile, Hari Singh seemed to realise that he would have to make some gestures towards meeting the demand for popular government. In October 1944, he accepted a measure of popular representation in the Government. One of his new ministers was Abdullah's colleague, Afzal Beg, who became Minister for Public Works. Thus, another milestone was reached: the National Conference had now too much clout to be ignored. However, there was some surprise in the valley that a party with such a radical programme had agreed to participate in a regime that was still dominated by the Maharaja.

The reconciliation did not last long. Afzal Beg found it difficult to function and resigned in March 1946. The British Cabinet Mission arrived in India in the same month and its pronouncements on the return of full ruling powers to the rulers of the princely States increased the tension between the rulers and ruled. The princes, especially of the larger States (and Jammu and Kashmir was the largest), began to dream of full independence, with no fetters on their authority. Their people, aware that the process of transferring power to popular regimes had begun in British India, wanted the same. The Congress had encouraged people's movements in the princely States through the States People's Conference, of which Sheikh Abdullah was the President in 1946. He submitted a memorandum to the Cabinet Mission, on behalf of the National Conference, demanding that power be transferred to the people, not to the Maharaja, when the British withdrew, because the Dogras had only bought Kashmir by sale-deed in the Treaty of Amritsar and had no legitimate rights to it.[13]

A clash with the Maharaja was now inevitable. The National Conference launched the Quit Kashmir movement, modelled on the Congress movement of 1942; but here the target of expulsion was the ruling family rather than the British. In one respect, however, Abdullah and Hari Singh thought on similar lines: both preferred independence, if feasible, or the maximum autonomy available, to becoming full part of the Dominions of India or Pakistan, now that partition seemed near.

The Quit Kashmir movement followed predictable lines. Like the Muslim League in British India, the Muslim Conference kept aloof, as did many Hindus. Even so, the National Conference was too well entrenched to be overawed. But the current Prime Minister of the State, Ram Chandra Kak, a Pandit, had been handpicked to be tough and he proudly told the press: "We shall be ruthlessly firm and we make no apology about it." Repression began. In May, Abdullah was arrested and Dogra soldiers were let loose on Srinagar. Instead of being cowed, citizens responded with the sabotage of communication facilities. One of Abdullah's lieutenants, Bakshi Ghulam Mohammad, escaped to Delhi and briefed Jawaharlal Nehru, who issued an exaggerated version of the situation in the valley in a statement which dramatically announced: "Srinagar: Almost a City of the Dead".[14] Nehru went on to promise full support to his friend:

> Everyone who knows Kashmir knows also the position of Sheikh Mohammed Abdullah there. He is the Sher-e-Kashmir, beloved of the remotest valleys of Kashmir. Numerous legends and popular songs have grown around his personality.... Does anybody think we are going to desert him or his comrades in Kashmir because the Kashmir State authorities have a few guns at their disposal? We shall stand by the people of Kashmir and their leaders in this heavy trial they are going through.

Not content with a statement, Nehru decided to go to
the valley. Although decades had passed since his stint at
the Inner Temple in London, he could still claim to be a
lawyer. He announced that he would defend Abdullah whose
trial had been fixed for 21 June. Nehru persisted even
though he was refused permission to enter the State. After
a five-hour confrontation with bayoneted police at the
border, he was allowed to enter the State and then detained.
This evoked headlines throughout India: negotiations for the
transfer of power were at an advanced stage and Nehru was
expected to lead the Interim Government to be set up in
August. Since the princes were being treated as virtually
independent, some of Nehru's senior colleagues felt he was
being rash in challenging their authority and facing a
possible denigration of his own prestige. Abul Kalam Azad
summoned him to return; which he did.

In his autobiography, *India Wins Freedom*, Maulana
Azad recalled:

> I was not very happy about the developments. While I
> resented the action of the Kashmir Government, I
> thought that this was not the proper occasion to start a
> new quarrel over Kashmir. I spoke to the Viceroy and
> said that the Government of India should arrange that
> I should speak over the telephone to Jawaharlal. He had
> been detained in a dak bungalow and I got the
> connection after some time. I told Jawaharlal that I was
> of the view that he should return to Delhi as soon as
> possible. It would not be proper for him to insist on
> entering Kashmir at the present stage. So far as the
> question of Kashmir was concerned, I assured him that
> as Congress President I would take up the matter
> myself. I would also work for the release of Sheikh
> Abdullah and his colleagues but Jawaharlal should
> immediately return.

Nehru treated the episode, serious as it was, as high
adventure. During his face-off with the Kashmir authorities,
he wrote daily to his daughter, Indira Gandhi. The tone was

set in his first letter from Domel on 19 June:

> I had hoped that this very brief Kashmir visit would
> prove a diversion. My hopes have been amply justified.
> This is only the first day and do not know yet what
> tomorrow will bring. So we must offer thanks to the
> Kashmir Govt. for the astonishing folly with which it
> conducts its affairs. It tried to stop me at Kohala. It did
> not succeed. I spent five hours there getting more and
> more bored. Then we sallied out and faced the Kashmir
> police and pushed forward. I felt in my element as I
> always do when there is a question of forcing a
> barricade.... What an odd mixture is my life. There is
> talk of a Provisional Govt. and at the same time I am
> functioning as a law-breaker!

The next day, he assured Indira that he had not been
injured by the Maharaja's bayonets, as widely reported: "I
am quite well and unhurt. It is true that it was touch-and-
go last night and a bayonet might easily have hurt." Though
his colleagues were embarrassed by his impetuosity, he
sounded far from regretful:

> I imagine I have managed to upset many an applecart.
> Well, what am I to do about it? If the Kashmir Govt.
> wants to behave with crass stupidity and discourtesy,
> things will happen. I offered them an opportunity to
> adopt a correct course gracefully and without loss of
> dignity. They were too conceited to accept my suggestion
> which was merely to allow me to go to Srinagar for a
> day or two. I expressed my desire to meet the Maharaja.
> But no, they took a different course and now they will
> have to face the consequences.[15]

There were no visible consequences, except that Nehru
was permitted to visit Srinagar the following month and
spent four days there. Abdullah did not benefit. He was
sentenced to three years in jail, where he would remain
until the climactic days preceding the State's accession to
India

*T*he portraits that Abdullah drew in *Aatish-e-Chinar* of
national leaders are perceptive as well as revealing of his
relationship with them and their impact on events in
Kashmir. He had this to say of the leading three:
On Mahatma Gandhi:

> The only individual with a national perspective and
> point of view was Gandhi. He stood like a human
> barricade in the path of hate.... To protest against
> communal killings, he started a fast unto death.
> Regardless of the fragmentation of India, he still
> considered Pakistan a part of his spiritual territory....
> During his last days, Gandhiji was wedged between two
> extremes. One extreme was the fire-spitting hatred of
> the Muslim League.... Since the Muslim League was
> primarily represented by these powerful landlords, it
> was concerned with protecting their rights, rather than
> safeguarding the interests of the common man. Gandhi's
> words to the votaries of this extreme were wasted
> effort.[16]

The other extreme was Mahatma Gandhi's own
Congress Party which had talked itself into accepting
partition. The old Congress leaders were, by this time,
eager for power so that at the end of their lives they
could leave their impact on history. They presented deaf
ears to Mahatma Gandhi. The Hindu bourgeoisie were
anxious to replace the British in government, but more
so in the wealth and power which they saw within easy
reach. In working towards this goal, adherence to
Gandhian principles was increasingly viewed as an
impediment.

On Sardar Patel:

He was influenced by Hindu fundamentalism and
wished to secure the interests of Hindu revivalists. From
the social and political standpoint he was a staunch
reactionary; he shunned progressive politics. During the

communal clashes he encouraged the Hindu
communalists to combat the Muslims. Once, while
talking to me, he said that the one way to destroy
Pakistan was to drive more and more Muslims there so
that it may burst at the seams and be forced to come to
terms with India.[17]

On the contrast between Nehru and Patel:

There was a vast difference between the ideologies of
Sardar Patel and Jawaharlal Nehru. Jawaharlal was
born and brought up in a family which recognised no
communal barriers.... On the contrary, Sardar Patel was
brought up in a fundamentalist Hindu environment. He
regarded himself as the representative of the Hindu
masses and the rightful claimant of Prime Ministership
.... One must concede the fact that Jawaharlal was a
dreamer and an idealist whereas Sardar Patel was an
adroit administrator and a realist.... Since Nehru and I
were ideologically close to one another, Sardar disliked
my friendship with Nehru and counted me among his
opponents.[18]

Chapter VII

Communal Politics

*K*ashmir could not be isolated from the rise of communal politics in British India. But the process began later. Hindus and Muslims had coexisted in the subcontinent since the coming of Islam. It was the personal convictions of the ruler that determined whether one community or the other was given preference or discriminated against, or whether both were given equal opportunities in the administration and the army and wherever else imperial power could reach: whether someone like Akbar or Aurangzeb ruled in Delhi; or Zainul Abidin or Sikandar, in Srinagar. Only when the goal of popular rule and regular elections was accepted, did numbers become important and the concept of majority and minority community became meaningful in politics, as did the factors of religion, caste and ethnicity.

As we have seen, because of the medieval conditions prevailing in Kashmir until the 1930s, the possibility of representative government seemed remote. At the turn of the century, however, this right was conceded to the parts of the subcontinent ruled directly by the British in response to the rise of nationalist opinion. The spread of English education, the visits of eminent Indians to England, the projection of Westminster as the ideal system of government, had all made popular franchise, party politics and majority rule the accepted goal. Consequently, some Muslim intellectuals began to worry about the future of their community in an India dominated numerically by Hindus and to seek reservations and constitutional guarantees to protect themselves.[1]

Muslim separatism was fuelled by Hindu revivalism. Western scholars, like Sir William Jones (founder of the Asiatic Society in 1784) and Max Muller, had researched and written glowingly about the glory that was India long before Islam came to the subcontinent.[2] Beginning with Major General Alexander Cunningham in the mid-1850s, British archaeologists dated historic structures and unearthed shards of ancient civilisations. Independence began to be interpreted in terms of going back to a pre-Islamic age, a vision Muslims could not share. Their revivalism was of more recent vintage: they recalled that the last occupant of the throne in Delhi, before the British, was a Muslim, that they had entered India as conquerers (though, in fact, the majority were converts from Hinduism). The *mullahs* (clerics) and *madrassas* (Muslim schools) maintained the orthodox social distinction between believers and heretics.

The intellectual centre of Muslim aspirations was the Aligarh Muslim University. Like many other eminent Indian Muslims, its founder, Sir Syed Ahmed Khan, started his career as a nationalist concerned with improving the educational and economic conditions of his community, but gradually came to believe that the interests of the two communities were divergent, and that the Muslims were safer under British rule than they would be in a democratic India with a Hindu majority. Since the possibility of independence was still very remote when he died in 1898, the idea of partition had yet to be conceived. His main worry was the birth of the Indian National Congress in 1895, even though it then pressed for no more than representation of Indians in the administration.

The partition of Bengal in 1905 and its repeal, six years later, transformed a largely academic debate into communal politics. A precursor to developments forty years later, the British Government sanctioned the partition because the province of Bengal, which then included Assam, was regarded as too unwieldy for efficient administration. It was welcomed by Muslim politicians because it created a Muslim-majority province and Muslims had occupied a subordinate position in the economy and administration of the undivided province. But it was strongly opposed by the Congress and Hindu opinion as 'vivisecting' the Bengali homeland. By the time the partition ended in response to a country-wide Congress agitation, the thesis of Hindu-Muslim divergence had taken popular root and contributed to the founding of the Muslim League.[3]

The Muslim League was formed in 1906 to counter the Congress and with the explicit objectives of supporting the British and looking after the rights and interests of Muslims. From then on, the divergence widened as the quantum of Indian representation in the legislative councils increased. Although many notable Muslim leaders opposed it, the idea of separation gathered momentum, especially in the United Provinces (later Uttar Pradesh), where Muslims, though privileged in the past, were in a minority. It was in the English university town of Cambridge, in 1933, that a student, Rahmat Ali, formally suggested that a separate nation named Pakistan, which would include Kashmir, be created in north-west India exclusively for Muslims.

Originally, the concept was vague and the separate units seen as part of a federal or confederal structure. The demand for two completely separate countries emerged later. It became a serious political objective when taken up by Mohammad Ali Jinnah in the communally surcharged atmosphere of the forties when it became clear that the British were actually preparing to quit. Although Gandhi strove hard to persuade Muslims that they would not be discriminated against in a Hindu-majority India, his use of Hindu symbols and concepts like Ram Rajya to arouse national sentiment antagonised orthodox Muslims.

*T*he Hindu counter to Sir Syed Ahmed Khan was Pandit Madan Mohan Malaviya who founded the Banaras Hindu University. He laid emphasis on Hindu *sangathan* (social unity) and defended its orthodox practices, which kept the Muslim at a distance. He was succeeded by several political leaders capable of mobilising Hindu sentiment and also influential in the Indian National Congress, among them Bal Gangadhar Tilak and Lala Lajpat Rai. Though the Congress was committed to secularism, its tactical approach of striking deals with representatives of Muslim orthodoxy and treating Muslims as a monolithic community strengthened the forces of separatism.[4]

As mentioned earlier, the actual ideology of Hindutva was defined in a book of that name by Vinayak Damodar (Veer) Savarkar (1870-1957) who had suffered imprisonment in the Andamans for combating British rule. For him, Hindu and Indian were virtually coterminous. As defined by him, "every person is a Hindu who regards this Bharat Bhoomi – this land from the Indus to the seas – as his Fatherland and Holyland – the land of origin of his religion and the cradle of his faith." While this definition included Jains, Buddhists, Sikhs and tribal cults, it left out Muslims and Christians. Their loyalty to the country, especially that of Muslims, he insisted, was divided. "The Muslims remained Muslims first and Muslims last and Indians never."[5]

According to Savarkar, "Hindutva is not a particularly theocratic, religious dogma or creed. It embraces all departments of thought and activity of the whole being of the Hindu race. Forty centuries or more have been at work to mould it as it is." He favoured democracy as an institution and his revivalistic passion did not extend to endorsing the caste system. But his basic vision was exclusivist, as was his political doctrine: "We Hindus must have a country of our own in the solar system and must continue to flourish there as Hindus, descendants of a mighty people." He was first elected President of the Hindu Mahasabha in

December 1940, and charged Gandhi with placating
Muslims and weakening Hindus by preaching non-violence.
As a princely State with a Hindu ruler and Muslim
majority, Savarkar took considerable interest in developments in Jammu and Kashmir. As early as 13 December
1937, he spoke of the need to check anti-Hindu forces in
Kashmir and denounced Gandhi for suggesting that the
Maharaja abdicate. He visited Jammu and Srinagar in July
1942. The possibility of partition was then being debated
and he took the line that though Hindus were in a minority
in Kashmir, they were a part of the national majority from
whom they were not cut off.[6]

The RSS abjured direct involvement in politics and
instead concentrated on building up disciplined cadres. The
daily morning ritual of uniformed drill with sticks, to the
sound of bugles, instilled militancy. Founded in Nagpur in
1925 by Dr Keshav Baliram Hedgewar, whose views
paralleled those of Savarkar, its activities spread rapidly. In
1940, Madhavrao Sadashiv Golwalkar had taken over as the
supreme leader of the RSS. His version of Hindutva
improved on Savarkar's:

> The non-Hindu peoples of Hindustan must either adopt
> the Hindu culture and language, must learn to respect
> and hold in reverence Hindu religion, must entertain no
> idea but those of glorification of the Hindu race and
> culture...in a word they must cease to be foreigners, or
> may stay in this country, wholly subordinated to the
> Indian nation, claiming nothing, deserving no privileges,
> far less any preferential treatment – not even citizen's
> rights.[7]

The despatch of the Cripps mission in early 1942 by the
British Government, when Japanese armies were at the
gates of India, seemed to bring independence nearer. One
of the reasons why the mission failed was that the Congress

could not accept the condition that the provinces be free to opt out of the Indian federation to be formed when independence was gained after the war. This was a concession to the Muslim League, the first time that the possibility of partition was seriously considered. The princely States would also be free to opt out, although Sir Stafford Cripps told their representatives, including the Maharaja of Jammu and Kashmir, that Britain would not come to their aid if they did, according to Maulana Azad, who conducted the negotiations on behalf of the Congress. The Quit India Movement in August put an end to further negotiations until late 1944.

With its leaders in detention, the Congress was politically inert for most of the war. The Muslim League, on the other hand, gave full support to Britain and was given equivalent status to the Congress in return. The Hindu Mahasabha and the RSS functioned freely throughout the war and expanded their activities. Anxious for Hindus to gain military experience, the Mahasabha urged them to join the armed forces and cooperate with the British. The RSS did not approve of this approach, but concentrated on expanding its cadres. Although they both represented Hindu revivalism, the two organisations did not work together. On the eve of partition, the Mahasabha's influence was waning while the RSS was gaining strength. Both organisations, especially the RSS, were seen as threats by the Muslim community.

*T*he Kashmiri Muslim leadership was initially influenced by the communal political theories of Aligarh, as reflected in the Muslim Conference formed by Abdullah and his colleagues. But though the struggle against a Hindu Maharaja and a Hindu ruling elite suggested a superficial similarity between the politics of Kashmir and British India, the numerical superiority of the Muslims, not only in the valley but also in the entire State of Jammu and Kashmir, meant that they had nothing to fear from representative government in the State. In addition, their history and ethnic heritage differed from those of the Muslims of British India. This made it possible for Abdullah to convert the Muslim Conference into the National Conference. Unlike the Muslim League, which essentially represented landowning interests, the National Conference was committed to radical social and economic change.

All this brought Kashmiri intellectuals nearer the leftists in the Indian National Congress and attracted sections of the Communist Party of India. But communal fears were aroused by the rise of Hindu revivalism in the Congress and more so by the emergence of organisations committed explicitly to Hindutva, which attracted an influential following in semi-feudal Jammu, where the Dogra landowning class was antagonised by the egalitarian commitments of the National Conference's Naya Kashmir manifesto.

Even after partition, when Muslim extremism could no longer be regarded as a threat to India, RSS influence continued to spread. The work of its volunteers in the partition riots, where they defended Hindu localities and looked after Hindu refugees, widened its appeal and reputation. One of its primary concerns was to ensure that Jammu and Kashmir came to India in view of its religious, cultural and historical importance in Hindu lore. The ancient Hindu rulers of the valley and its great Sanskrit scholars were recalled with pride and quoted as justification for it being part of India, as also the existence of the holy Hindu shrine at Amarnath in Kashmir.[8]

The RSS connection with Hari Singh was used in October 1947, at Union Home Minister Vallabhbhai Patel's instance, when Golwalkar was sent on a mission to Srinagar to urge the Maharaja to accede to India. Whether prompted to do so by Patel or not, Golwalkar also urged the Maharaja to recruit Punjabi Hindus and Sikhs into his army.[9] Later, some of the arms sent by the Indian army for a militia raised by the National Conference was diverted to the RSS in Jammu, as Nehru complained to Patel.[10]

The RSS, as well as the Hindu Mahasabha, suffered a major reverse when Gandhi was assassinated on 30 January 1948. His assassin, Nathuram Godse, had been a member of the RSS and was editing a pro-Hindu Mahasabha paper in Pune. There was a country-wide reaction against Hindu communal organisations; some of their leaders were attacked and their offices ransacked. The RSS itself was banned for three years and hundreds of its workers arrested. Although Veer Savarkar did not join the RSS due to differences with its leaders, he continued to inspire its workers. In his statement to the court trying him, Godse described Savarkar as "the ablest and most faithful advocate of the Hindu cause".

After the ban on it was lifted, the RSS again became active. Sardar Patel regarded its members at worst as "misguided patriots" and tried to draw them into the Congress, but the move was stymied by Nehru.[11] While officially keeping away from politics, the RSS exerted its influence through affiliated parties and groups, in which its workers manned senior positions. Both the Hindu Maha-sabha and the RSS sponsored the Bharatiya Jana Sangh when it was inaugurated in 1950 by Shyama Prasad Mookerjee. He had resigned from Nehru's Cabinet in protest against the Government's failure to retaliate against Pakistan for the eviction of Hindus from what was then East Pakistan. Mookerjee was a former President of the Mahasabha. Technically, the Jana Sangh was open to all communities but since it espoused Hindutva, it attracted only Hindus.

From its inception, the Jana Sangh focussed on Kashmir. Its first manifesto, published in 1951, set the pattern of insisting on full integration of the State into the Indian Union. It was against special rights being given to any minority. Directly or indirectly, several of its objectives impinged on the State. It condemned secularism, which was described as "only a euphemism for the policy of Muslim appeasement". This was refined in 1957 to the objective of "nationalising all non-Hindus by inculcating in them the idea of Bharatiya culture". In the same year, the Jana Sangh committed itself to "democracy, nationalism, unitary form of government and full integration of Jammu and Kashmir State with the rest of India." Since by unitary form of government, it meant the complete abolition of states, integration would be guaranteed. The emphasis on over-arching central authority was aimed to exploit the deep-rooted fear of disintegration stemming from history and the separation of Pakistan.

Together with the support given by the Jana Sangh to the Praja Parishad campaign in Jammu against the Abdullah Government (described in a later chapter), this began the process of rethinking in the valley on the wisdom of joining India. But though the Jana Sangh campaign may have created doubts there, it secured votes for the party in the Delhi by-elections in 1953, in which integration of Kashmir was a major issue. Its candidates won three out of four seats.[12]

Although the Jana Sangh did not do too well in the first general elections in 1952 (it won only three seats in the Lok Sabha), the party improved its performance later. The RSS maintained its control on the party by evicting leaders who did not conform to its directives, like Mauli Chandra Sharma in 1954 and Balraj Madhok in 1972. The RSS did not limit its activism to politics; the Jana Sangh was only one of its affiliates. Others expanded its influence in other fields. It published newspapers and journals in English and other languages; established private schools; sponsored student organisations; and inducted Hindu religious leaders into the Vishwa Hindu Parishad (VHP), which was to arouse communal passions in the future.

*T*owards the end of the 1960s, elements in the RSS cadre who were anxious to play a more active role in national life, rather than focus exclusively on character-building, became more prominent. The need to attract a wider following, especially among the underprivileged, was also recognised. The liberal shift was exemplified by the choice of Atal Behari Vajpayee as President of the Jana Sangh. He was regarded as a 'leftist' in the party, in contrast to Madhok, who was soon to quit. With Vajpayee came closer links with other Opposition parties, which culminated in the participation by Jana Sangh and RSS workers in the mass movement organised by Jayaprakash Narayan (JP) in Gujarat and Bihar (in 1974-75), and finally against Indira Gandhi's Government at the Centre for "Total Revolution", or a basic change on Gandhian lines in the political structure and in all other areas of public and personal life.

The Prime Minister responded by imposing a harsh state of emergency throughout the country in June 1975. Thousands were jailed, including all the leaders opposing her. But in jail, they met and discovered common ground. When she and the Congress were defeated in the 1977 elections, the togetherness survived; they combined to form the Janata Party under JP's patronage, and formed the first non-Congress Government at the Centre. JP had also won over the liberalised RSS, which supported the Janata Party. Vajpayee became an oustanding Foreign Minister in the Central Government headed by the stern Morarji Desai.

But the liberal phase did not last long. JP died in 1979 after a long disabling illness. Implicit strains became overt. Those in the Janata Party who did not come from the RSS became worried about the prospect of being swamped by them and insisted that dual membership should not be permitted, meaning that those from the RSS must sever their connection with it. This even Vajpayee could not accept. The Janata Party splintered well before Indira Gandhi staged a comeback in January 1980. The old Jana Sangh component then came together as the Bharatiya Janata Party (BJP). Vaypayee tried to give it a more liberal image than its predecessor. Muslims were invited; Sikandar Bakht became a general secretary (and later leader of the

Opposition in the Rajya Sabha). The party philosophy was vaguely described as Gandhian socialism in a bid to claim the Jayaprakash Narayan heritage. But this was soon forgotten: the massive Hindu vote was more attractive.

The conversion of low caste Hindus to Islam in the village of Meenakshipur in Tamil Nadu in 1982 helped the conservatives to capture the BJP. It was used by the VHP to ring alarm bells throughout the country that Hinduism was in danger, which proved to be as potent a slogan as Islam in danger was before. The RSS then threw its weight behind the Assam campaign to drive out 'foreigners', meaning Muslim immigrants from Bangladesh (Hindus were regarded as refugees), leading to riots there.

Then came the occasion provided by the opening of the Ram Janambhoomi/Babri Masjid complex at Ayodhya, which became an issue inspiring Hindu revivalism. Vajpayee's conservative successor as BJP President, Lal Krishna Advani, created country-wide tension with his Rath Yatra from Somnath to Ayodhya in 1990. (He was arrested in Bihar before getting to Ayodhya.) The party was rewarded by being returned as the second largest in Parliament in the 1991 general elections. His successor, Murli Manohar Joshi, went one better with a south-to-north Ekta Yatra, and took the campaign to the Kashmir valley. It ended in a curfewed Srinagar. The VHP proved its might with the erasure of the Babri Masjid on 6 December 1992. And Advani returned to lead the party as well as represent it in Parliament. These developments could not but be of concern to Kashmir.

Chapter VIII

The Last Maharaja

*D*espite his resonant titles, Lieutenant General His Highness Inder Mahander Rajrajeshwar Maharajadhiraj Sir Hari Singh, Jammu and Kashmir Naresh Tatha Tibbet adi Deshadhipathi, Ruler of Jammu and Kashmir savoured the ambience of unfettered sovereignty briefly and for the first time on 15 August 1947. With the British withdrawal from the Indian subcontinent, the combined fetter and protection of imperial paramountcy for the 565 princely States was withdrawn. So far, a British Resident had ensured that they fulfilled their imperial obligations; in return, they were given protection by the imperial forces and, up to a point, were free to run their princedoms as they thought fit, mostly in autocratic fashion. Now they were free to join India or Pakistan or, if they so wished, try to be independent. In fact, the choice was limited. Except for the two largest States, Jammu and Kashmir and Hyderabad, they were not politically or economically viable and, with a combination of pressure and patronage, Sardar Vallabhbhai Patel, Minister for States and Home Affairs, was able to make them accede to India.

Maharaja Hari Singh could not be blamed for wanting to make Jammu and Kashmir fully independent. His princedom was the largest in the subcontinent. He could claim to rule over 80,000 square miles of territory, as large as the British Isles. Jammu and Kashmir abutted not only both India and Pakistan, but also the Tibet region of China and the Chinese province of Sinkiang; Afghanistan as well, with only the narrow Wakhan tract separating it from the Soviet Union. The prospect of independence was tempting, but perilous, as he was to soon find out. He had yielded reluctantly and minimally to pressures for democratic reform, but continued to wield authoritarian powers and lived the luxurious life of a traditional Maharaja.

From the windows of his first floor living room in the new palace he had built on a hill overlooking the Dal Lake, Hari Singh had an enchanting view stretching beyond the Shalimar Gardens laid down by Jahangir. He liked vacationing in Srinagar, for Jammu was still the seat of the Dogra empire carved out by Gulab Singh and his generals. With the British, from whom the valley had been purchased and to whom he owed allegiance, on their way out, he could legally be absolute ruler of a mixture of territory and peoples described vividly by a British officer, Major Arthur Neve, at the turn of the century:

> And so Jammu became the capital of a kingdom larger than England, in fact, about equal to Great Britain, with tributary peoples speaking a dozen different languages and dialects, and at a Darbar, in the olden days, one might have not seen only the Dogra Princes and Sikh generals, with bold Rajput veterans of the many fiercely contested mountain campaigns, but those who had been subjugated, Tibetan chiefs from Leh and Zanskar, Balti Rajahs from Skardo or Shigar, Dard chiefs from Astor or Gilgit, with their picturesque and truculent followers, all clad in the most diverse costumes.[1]

But Hari Singh came into conflict with Jawaharlal Nehru, an outspoken critic of the princes and advocate of popular government who had made his views clear before he became India's first Prime Minister. He was on better terms with Sardar Vallabhbhai Patel, the organisational boss of the Congress Party, who became the Minister responsible for dealing with the princely States and was able to dissolve most of them while treating the Maharajas with respect. But Nehru dealt with Kashmir directly and their approaches differed.

Patel did not share Nehru's regard for Abdullah, nor his concern for secularism. As an outstanding party manager, he was concerned more with getting the job done, less with the means. It has been suggested that left to himself, Patel would have handled the Kashmir issue as conclusively as the other princely States he brought into the Union. This is the view taken by an analyst of Patel's political style, who suggests that Hari Singh, the man in power and Patel's protégé, would have been a more effective ally for India than Nehru's friend Abdullah.[2] But that is to overlook the unique character given to Kashmir by its Muslim majority and proximity to Pakistan, not to speak of its strategic location. The dispute touched upon the basis of partition as well as British assurances to the princes concerning their rights after the lapse of paramountcy. India and Pakistan were Dominions at the time, with limited sovereignty. Both Governments pleaded their case with Prime Minister Clement Attlee.

When it became known that the British had actually decided to quit and that the subcontinent would be partitioned, with the two wings of Pakistan being carved out of India, Hari Singh was placed in a quandary. The majority of his people were Muslims, but to join Pakistan would mean that the substantial number of Hindus in Jammu and Kashmir might have to flee. Also, although the future rulers of Pakistan had taken the stand that it was for the princes, not the people, of the princely States to decide their future and had given personal assurances to Hari Singh, a Hindu prince's future would be uncertain in an avowedly Islamic country.

India's leaders were pledged to secularism and this had enabled the leader of the most popular party in Jammu and

Kashmir, Sheikh Mohammad Abdullah, to evolve close ties with the Indian National Congress and especially with Jawaharlal Nehru. But the stated policy of the Congress was that the people of the princely States should determine their future and Nehru, the Maharaja's arch-critic, was to be Prime Minister. Hari Singh had imprisoned Abdullah and, as we have seen earlier, even detained Nehru when he tried to enter Kashmir to defend Abdullah in June 1946. Both options thus had major impediments.

The third possibility of independence remained. But to achieve this, too, was difficult. It was bound to be opposed by both India and Pakistan; neither wanted a small newly independent country in such a strategic setting. Nor, contrary to much contemporary speculation, did Washington, the only feasible source of foreign assistance. The primary anxiety of the United States Government, as official documents reveal, was that a weak Kashmir might fall victim to communist penetration from the Soviet Union or China.[3] The Maharaja might have pulled off independence with the support of Abdullah, but this was not possible in view of the long-standing enmity between them and the feudal atmosphere of the court. Yet, Abdullah too favoured independence and did not commit himself on the future of the State until the Pathan raiders sent in by Pakistan forced both the Maharaja and him to seek help from India.

Karan Singh, Hari Singh's son and briefly the Maharaja's regent when he was forced to leave Jammu and Kashmir, provides interesting insights into the atmosphere of his father's court in his autobiography. Hari Singh's closest companion was Victor Rosenthal, a White Russian who had fled his homeland after the Russian Revolution in 1917. Official and unofficial local advisers came and went. Among them Swami Sant Dev, who had been banished when Hari Singh took over from Maharaja Pratap Singh but staged a comeback in 1946, was staying in the beautiful Chashmeshahi Guest House overlooking the Dal Lake. Hari Singh became a devout follower of the swami, and it was he, according to Karan Singh, who played on the Maharaja's

feudal ambitions, "planting in my father's mind visions of
an extended kingdom sweeping down to Lahore itself, where
our ancestor Maharaja Gulab Singh and his brothers Raja
Dhyan Singh and Raja Suchet Singh had played such a
crucial role a century earlier".[4]

Another facet of Hari Singh's personality is brought out
by the British writer Leonard Mosley, who had access to
official Indian and British documents: "The Maharajah of
Kashmir was so rich that he bought hundreds of concubines
and dancing girls at 20-50,000 pounds apiece and once paid
150,000 pounds (in blackmail) for one hour with a female
crook in a London hotel bedroom."[5] The contrast with the
poverty-stricken lives of his subjects, heavily taxed to keep
him in luxury, could not have been more striking.

Hari Singh's political ambitions emerged in an
announcement made by him on 15 July 1946, when the
possibility of the entire subcontinent remaining united in
a loose federal relationship was still under discussion: "We
look forward to taking our due place in the new
constitutional structure of India.... But our concern for the
progress of India does not imply acceptance by us of
dictation in our internal affairs." In an obvious reference
to the arrest of Nehru on the State's border in June, the
announcement justified denial of access to Kashmir "if we
are convinced that such access in any case will lead
inevitably to strife, disorder and consequent bloodshed
amongst my people...".[6]

On 11 July, he had written directly to Nehru stating:
"The reason why my Government felt it their duty to
prevent you from proceeding to Srinagar was that they were
convinced, in view of the controversial nature of what you
had stated in the Press, in public and in your
communications to me, that your coming at that juncture
would be certain to result in danger to the public peace."[7]
His Government's approach to Sardar Patel was very
different, as reflected in the warmth of State Prime Minister
Ram Chandra Kak's invitation to him on 25 August: "When
you are in a position to fix a date for your visit to Kashmir,

will you kindly send me a wire? We must insist on the
pleasure of having you as guest of the State or of my wife
and myself."[8]

In Prime Minister Kak, the Maharaja had a tough
conservative exponent of independence who shared his
dislike for Nehru. Kak's response on 12 September 1946 to
letters from Patel urging the release of Abdullah and better
relations between rulers and ruled was typical. Everything
was justified "in the interest of law and order". Rejecting
the thesis that the Interim Government had inherited
Britain's authority, he insisted on his Government's
legitimacy and right to to rule in a response to Patel:

> The analogy you draw between the British Government
> and the Interim Government on the one side and this
> Government on the other is misleading. This
> Government is fundamentally of this country. Its history
> is our history, its hills and valleys were traversed and
> occupied by our forebears countless centuries ago. The
> Government is indigenous and broad-based and its
> members are not drawn from any single section, class
> or community. It contains a substantial popular
> element....[9]

Meanwhile, Abdullah remained in jail, together with
Nehru's secretary, Dwarkanath Kachru. On 16 September,
Nehru wrote to the second last Viceroy, Field Marshal Lord
Archibald Wavell. Condemning the arrests and obstructions
being placed in the way of National Conference candidates
in the Kashmir Assembly elections, he stated: "I cannot
remain a silent spectator of these events when my own
colleagues are concerned and when I believe the State
authorities have functioned in a most objectionable manner.
Nor can the Congress remain silent and impassive."[10]

Meanwhile, Kak's curtness had angered even the more
tolerant Patel, who conveyed an implicit threat when
writing to him on 28 September:

> I tried to arrive at a friendly and honourable
> understanding on the Kashmir question. I had no other

interest in coming to Kashmir at present. I felt that I could render a service to H.H. the Maharaja Sahib and you by placing my services at your disposal. But your reply betrayed a cold, official touch-me-not attitude.... The State can lose nothing by allowing daylight to shine on the doings of Kashmir. No State can treat itself as outside the purview of India or regard Indians outside its boundary as strangers or foreigners.[11]

The parameters of the conflict were now clearly set. When Britain's intention to quit became evident but the decision to partition the country had yet to be taken, Hari Singh's ambitions and anxieties were conveyed to the Viceroy. The British Resident in Kashmir, Lt. Col. Webb, sent a despatch to the Secretary to the Crown Representative (the Viceroy's title in relation to the princes) on 14 November 1946, enclosing a note from Kak. "I am seriously inclined to think that the Maharaja and Kak are seriously considering the possibility of Kashmir not joining the Union if it is formed," warned Webb.

The note from Kak left no room for doubt:

Recent events have...shown that those who are likely to assume the reins of government in India in future are not disposed to show consideration for the security of the State and are prone to interfere and coerce even in regard to purely internal affairs on the flimsiest of grounds. Not only that, agitators inside the State are encouraged if not invited to create trouble.

The State naturally does not feel happy about the future and unless satisfactory assurances are forthcoming that interference in its internal affairs in any shape or form will in future not be made, may even decide to decline to join the Indian Union, should it materialise.

If such a contingency does arise, what would the nature of this State's relations with the Crown be? Would necessary wherewithal be supplied to maintain the integrity of the State for such time as it may be able to stand on its own feet?[12]

On 2 December, Webb was authorised to repeat to Kak the line taken by the British Cabinet Mission on the subject earlier that year. This was "to hope that the States would come into the new constitution and that the Cabinet Mission could not deal at this stage with a hypothetical question [whether princely States that did not want to join the Union would be free to maintain a relationship with Britain]." He was also asked to make two specific points: "(1) that Kashmir is economically so dependent on India [Pakistan had yet to be created] that it cannot afford to alienate India; and (2) that Kashmir is strategically of such importance to India as a whole that India cannot afford to alienate a Kashmir in which Ruler and subjects are united."[13]

Neither Kak nor Hari Singh took the advice. Abdullah and many others remained in jail.

*L*ess than two months before British paramountcy was to end, the last Viceroy, Lord Louis Mountbatten, flew to Srinagar and stayed there from 18 to 23 June. He had met Hari Singh under different circumstances twenty-five years earlier when he visited India with the Prince of Wales. Now he tried to persuade the Maharaja to decide between India and Pakistan, taking with him an assurance that the Indian Government would not object if he chose Pakistan. Karan Singh makes the revealing comment:

A typical feudal reaction to a difficult situation is to avoid facing it, and my father was particularly prone to this. Instead of taking advantage of Mountbatten's visit to discuss the whole situation meaningfully and trying to arrive at a rational decision, he first sent the Viceroy on a prolonged fishing trip to Thricker (where Mountbatten shocked our staff by sunbathing in the nude) and then -- having fixed a meeting just before his departure -- got out of it on the plea that he had suddenly developed a severe attack of colic.... Thus the

last real chance of working out a viable political
settlement was lost.[14]

The Viceroy had to content himself with brief
conversations with the Maharaja during car drives in the
countryside[15] and an interview with Kak in which he made
the case for an early choice between India and Pakistan. The
relevant passages from the official record of the interview
are significant:

> ...in his [Mountbatten's] opinion, Kashmiris would find
> it very difficult to protect themselves against the
> pressure of the Congress unless at the right moment
> they joined one or other of the two Constituent
> Assemblies.... If Kashmir joined the Pakistan
> Constituent Assembly presumably Mr. Jinnah would
> protect them against pressure from the Congress. If they
> joined the Hindustan Assembly it would be inevitable
> that they should be treated with consideration by
> Hindustan. But if they joined neither Assembly they
> would be in a very difficult position.... H.E.
> [Mountbatten] pointed out that Pandit Nehru felt very
> strongly about Kashmir, and it would be very difficult
> for him (H.E.) to do anything to help protect Kashmir
> after the 15th August, when Pandit Nehru would
> become Prime Minister of Hindu India, and H.E., even
> if he remained, would become only a constitutional
> Governor-General. The only protection for Kashmir after
> the 15th August was to join one or other of the
> Constituent Assemblies.[16]

The British historian Alastair Lamb interprets the
difference in the wording of Mountbatten's advice
("presumably Mr Jinnah would protect them" and
"inevitable that they should be treated with consideration
by Hindustan") as evidence that he was trying to push Hari
Singh towards India.[17] But the concluding paragraph, which
he does not mention, could well give the opposite
impression.

The version of the Srinagar meeting that Mountbatten
held with Nehru on 24 June was somewhat different,
according to the Viceregal record of the interview. He said
he had advised Hari Singh (who had avoided a substantial
discussion on the plea of colic, which Nehru said was
feigned) and Kak that Kashmir should not join either the
Indian or Pakistani Constituent Assemblies until the
Pakistani Assembly was set up; that it should enter into
standstill agreements with both new States; that,
eventually, it should join one of them, at least for defence,
communications and external affairs. Nehru is said to have
agreed that the advice was unexceptionable, but insisted
that the Kashmir problem would not be solved until
Abdullah was released and the rights of the people restored.

Nehru is then said to have expressed his anxiety to go
to Kashmir, but Mountbatten dissuaded him, pointing out,
according to his record, that:

> There were four hundred millions in India and only four
> millions in Kashmir. He would soon be Prime Minister
> of an Indian Government ruling at least two hundred
> and fifty millions; and I would consider it highly
> reprehensible of him to desert his most important duties
> at the Centre to interest himself on behalf of four
> millions who might very well be going to join Pakistan
> and have nothing more to do with him. In fact I called
> upon him as a matter of duty not to go running off to
> Kashmir until his new Government was firmly in the
> saddle and could spare his services.

Nehru, again according to Mountbatten (Nehru's
version, if any was recorded, is not available), accepted the
admonition quite tamely. "He reluctantly agreed that I was
right," the Viceregal record states, "and took my advice in
very good part."[18]

But this was not the end of the affair. Nehru, joined by
Gandhi, persisted in the desire to visit Kashmir, with the
Viceroy resisting the move. The importance of Kashmir to
them was not a matter of numbers but in the reverses it

would inflict on Jinnah's two-nation theory if a State with
a Muslim majority joined India with popular support, as
represented by Abdullah's National Conference. Patel did
not go along with this approach and sided with
Mountbatten. It was also evident that the relationship
between Nehru and Mountbatten was not as friction-free
as often assumed. The detailed official *Transfer of Power*
documents, published by the British Government, enable us
to follow the rapid pace of developments as independence
neared and shed light on the personalities involved.

Obviously nettled by the refusal of Nehru and Gandhi
to accept his advice, the Viceroy described them as being
"pathological" on the subject of the princely States in his
next personal report to London dated 27 June. He then
reported on Hari Singh's attack of "Maharaja's colic", but
wrote that he had persuaded him and Kak not to "make any
independence declaration for the present" and to seriously
consider joining either the Indian or Pakistani Constituent
Assemblies. This had pleased Nehru.[19] But he had not
succeeded in his primary mission of securing an assurance
that Hari Singh would opt for either India or Pakistan
before 15 August. Nor did he secure the release of Abdullah,
on which Nehru had laid so much emphasis.

The next day Mountbatten wrote to Hari Singh
reporting on his talks with Gandhi and Nehru and what he
had told them about his talks in Srinagar. A new point to
emerge in the letter (soon to be denied) was his impression
that "you were seriously considering the question of linking
yourself up from the military point of view with one or the
other new Dominion, and might consider sending
representatives to that Constituent Assembly provided that
this did not involve you in closer association than you
desired."

The letter went on to say that Mountbatten had persuaded Gandhi to go to Kashmir in place of Nehru, provided
he made no political speeches or carried out any form of
propaganda.[20] He also wrote to Webb suggesting that he
persuade Hari Singh to agree to Gandhi's visit, adding in a

confidential note:

> For your private information I can tell you that Nehru
> is over-working himself to such a degree that he
> practically is not sleeping at night and is having real
> difficulty in controlling himself at meetings. He is under
> very great strain and I consider that a visit by him to
> Kashmir at this moment could only produce a most
> explosive situation; whereas if His Highness can be
> persuaded to handle Gandhi tactfully, I believe there is
> a good chance that his visit could be passed off without
> any serious incident.[21]

Nehru had sent a lengthy note to Mountbatten before
the Viceroy's visit to Srinagar. It elaborated India's claims
to the State well before the Pathan raiders forced Hari
Singh to accede to India and focussed on the role of Abdullah
and the National Conference. It also stressed the need to
avoid any move to push Kashmir into Pakistan, though this
contradicted the assurance conveyed by Mountbatten that
India would not object to Kashmir joining Pakistan. It also
claimed that the National Conference stood for joining the
Indian Constituent Assembly. Nehru urged the removal of
the Kak regime and its replacement by a democratic
government headed by Abdullah. He pointed to "the great
strategic importance of that frontier State," and went on:
"There is every element present there for rapid and peaceful
progress in cooperation with India. Communalism has not
vitiated the atmosphere as in other parts of India." Other
significant observations were:

> There is no doubt that Sheikh Abdullah himself is [by]
> far the most outstanding leader in Kashmir.... The
> National Conference has stood for and still stands for
> Kashmir joining the Constituent Assembly of India.... If
> any attempt is made to push Kashmir into the Pakistan
> Constituent Assembly there is likely to be much trouble
> because the National Conference is not in favour of it
> and the Maharaja's position would also become very

difficult. The normal and obvious course appears to be
for Kashmir to join the Constituent Assembly of India.
This will satisfy both the popular demand and the
Maharaja's wishes. It is absurd to think that Pakistan
would create trouble if this happens.[22]

Patel depended more on Hari Singh than Abdullah. He
wrote to the Maharaja on 3 July 1947:

I fully appreciate the difficult and delicate situation in
which your State has been placed, but as a sincere friend
and well-wisher of the State, I wish to assure you that
the interest of Kashmir lies in joining the Indian Union
and its Constituent Assembly without any delay. Its past
history and traditions demand it, and all India looks up
to you and expects you to take this decision. Eighty per
cent of India is on this side. The States that have cast
their lot with the Constituent Assembly have been
convinced that their safety lies in standing together with
India.... In Free India you cannot isolate yourself, and
you must make friends with the leaders of Free India
who want to be friends with you.[23]

Nehru's friend and future High Commissioner in
London, Krishna Menon, tried to do his bit in a somewhat
confused personal letter to Mountbatten suggesting that if
Kashmir went to Pakistan it would be seen as an element
of continuing British imperial strategy.[24]

Hari Singh remained intractable. In his reply to
Mountbatten on 8 July, he politely denied that he was
thinking of establishing military links with either new
Dominion and was as reluctant as ever to admit "outside
leaders" into Kashmir. He indicated that Nehru was not
acceptable, but if Gandhi insisted on coming, he should not
do so before the end of autumn (which would be well after
India became independent).[25] On 16 July, however, Gandhi
wrote to Mountbatten desiring to go "at the earliest possible
moment", adding the implicit threat that otherwise Nehru
would probably want to go.[26] The next day the Viceroy

replied that it may be preferable to wait until Kak came to Delhi the following week. Gandhi agreed[27] and met Kak.

The next move came on 27 July when Nehru wrote acidly to Mountbatten: "Your visit to Kashmir from my particular point of view was not a success and things continued as before.... I know very well that the work in Delhi is important and urgent and it is not very easy for me to leave it [referring to the Viceroy's earlier admonition]. But Kashmir has become a first priority for me." Accordingly, he had decided to go to Kashmir on 4 August for four or five days. He made no mention of seeking the Maharaja's permission.[28]

The next day, Mountbatten wrote to Gandhi that Kak regarded him as less of a risk than Nehru and preferred a visit from him. He added once more: "May I therefore urge that you should suggest to Pandit Nehru that your visit at this moment would be better than a visit from him; for I really do not know how the future Prime Minister can be spared from Delhi with only 18 days left for him to take over power."[29] He followed up with a telegram to Webb putting the blame on Kak for Nehru's proposed visit, but saying he would make one more effort to stop him. Rather petulantly, he instructed Webb to inform Hari Singh that:

> ... I warned Kak after he had seen Gandhi that if he had indeed succeeded in preventing Gandhi from going there would almost certainly be a visit from Nehru. I therefore must hold him solely responsible for the visit. Please point out that declaration of adherence to one or other of the two Dominion Governments as soon as possible before the arrival of Nehru is now in the vital interests of His Highness. I need hardly ask His Highness to ensure that Nehru is decently treated and nothing is done to embitter relations between Kashmir and the new Government of India.[30]

Webb responded the next day that: "His Highness says visit of either Gandhi or Nehru [is] not only most inadvisable at this stage but most dangerous from point of view of even India as a whole." There was no ban on entry into the State but public gatherings, processions, etc., were banned. "As for declaration regarding adherence to a Dominion His Highness says no decision has been arrived as yet."[31]

On 28 July, Nehru wrote a letter to Gandhi giving vent to his exasperation with Mountbatten:

> For many months – ever since Mountbatten came – this question of your going or mine has been discussed and postponed. I have had enough of this business. This is not my way of doing anything. I hardly remember anything that has exasperated me as much as this affair.... I shall go ahead with my plans. As between being in Kashmir when my people need me there and being Prime Minister, I prefer the former.[32]

Sardar Patel came into the act on 29 July, when Mountbatten tried again to dissuade Nehru. He called a meeting with Gandhi, Nehru and Patel in which he recalled previous developments and repeated his opposition to Nehru's visit so soon before he became Prime Minister. According to his record of the meeting, he then said:

> I also pointed out that a visit by any Congress leaders [*sic*] could not fail to be badly received in the world press just at the time it was known that Kashmir had the choice of Pakistan or India before its Ruler; but that this effect would be somewhat mitigated if Mr Gandhi went on account of the religious aura that surrounded him, whereas if Pandit Nehru went it would be regarded as a piece of straightforward political lobbying.

However, it was Patel who put paid to Nehru's visit. The Viceroy reported:

> Sardar Patel gave it as his view that neither of them should go, but that in view of Pandit Nehru's great mental distress if his mission in Kashmir were to remain unfulfilled, he agreed that one of them must go. He very bluntly remarked: "It is a choice between two evils and

I consider that Gandhiji's visit would be the lesser evil".[33]

Nehru bowed before this pressure; Gandhi left the following night for Srinagar via Rawalpindi. Giving a resumé of these events to London on 1 August, Mountbatten added a paragraph retailing second-hand gossip that boosted his considerable self-esteem:

I have reason to believe that when Patel had tried to reason with Nehru the night before our meeting, Nehru had broken down and wept, explaining that Kashmir meant more to him at the moment than anything else. Patel found it impossible to deal with him and told a friend after our meeting that I had probably saved Nehru's political career and thus the chance of Congress making good on the transfer of power.[34]

Gandhi made a low-key visit to the valley. In accordance with the assurance to Mountbatten and Kak, there were no public speeches or political propaganda. He informed Nehru and Patel in a note that:

No public prayer was held on the day of arrival but I appeared before them twice or thrice and said that I could not make any public speech, not because there was any prohibition but because I had promised to myself that if I was to make my visit devoid of political significance in so far as it was possible, I must not address public meetings.... Public prayers [which were well-attended] were held during the two days following in Srinagar and the third in Jammu. During the two interviews with the Prime Minister [Kak] I told him about his unpopularity among the people.... He wrote to the Maharaja... that on a sign from him he would gladly resign [which he did soon after]....
I met [the Maharaja and the Maharani]. Both admitted that with the lapse of British Paramountcy the true Paramountcy of the people of Kashmir would commence. However much they might wish to make the join to the

[Indian] Union, they would have to make the choice in
accordance with the wishes of the people....
Bakshi [Ghulam Mohammad, Abdullah's deputy] was
most sanguine that the result of the free vote of the
people, whether on the adult franchise or on the existing
register, would be in favour of Kashmir joining the
Union provided of course that Sheikh Abdullah and his
co-prisoners were released, all bans removed and the
present Prime Minister was not in power. Probably he
echoed the general sentiment.[35]

On 6 August, on his way back from Kashmir, Gandhi
spoke of his visit to Hindu and Sikh refugees gathered at
Wah in what was soon to become Pakistan. They were
fleeing from Muslim League excesses and could not have
been too sympathetic to Muslims. Yet he emphasised the
commonality of Hindus and Muslims in the valley. He had
been unable, Gandhi told the refugees, to see Sheikh
Abdullah, "undoubtedly the leader of the Kashmiris". He
had held no public meetings in Srinagar but his prayer
meetings were attended by thousands. The State of Jammu
and Kashmir would be legally independent after 15 August,
but would have to join either India or Pakistan. He summed
up his estimate of the situation in the following words:

The State had a predominantly Muslim population. But
he saw that Sheikh Saheb had fired Kashmiris with
local patriotism.... They had one language, culture and,
so far as he could see, they were one people. He could
not distinguish readily between a Kashmiri Hindu and
a Kashmiri Mussalman.... Common sense dictated that
the will of the Kashmiris should decide the future of
Kashmir and Jammu. The sooner it was done the better.
How the will of the people would be decided was a fair
question. He hoped the question would be decided
between the two Dominions, the Maharaja Saheb and
the Kashmiris. If all the four could come to a joint
decision, much trouble would be avoided.[36]

Chapter IX

On the Brink

On 8 July 1947, a British jurist who had never been to India before, or taken interest in it, arrived in New Delhi to conduct the most complex and potentially explosive act of socio-political surgery in history. As Chairman of the Boundary Commission, Sir Cyril Radcliffe was given just five weeks to draw a line on the map through Punjab and Bengal which would separate the new Dominions of India and Pakistan. Political leaders had decided to allow Muslim-majority areas in these provinces to secede from India without anticipating the problems involved or the mass savagery and suffering that would ensue. The process of partition went down to district level and further; it could involve cutting through villages, even homes.

As far as Punjab was concerned, Sir Cyril's brief was "the Boundary Commission is instructed to demarcate the boundaries of the two parts of Punjab on the basis of ascertaining the contiguous majority areas of Muslims and non-Muslims." This would be difficult enough, but the instructions continued: "In doing so it will take into account other factors." The other factors were not defined. To make matters worse, his Hindu and Muslim fellow-judges on the commission seldom agreed. So a man who had never seen the heavily populated territory or the people he was partitioning proceeded to do so on the basis of maps and census reports. In view of the highly explosive nature of his undertaking, he had to work in complete secrecy as far as possible.

That few would be satisfied with the outcome was inevitable in these circumstances, as was the likelihood of charges of bias. Sir Cyril finished his job and returned to Britain on 15 August, the day the subcontinent was partitioned. He was so upset by criticism of his award that he returned the fee of two thousand pounds that he had received.[1] Later, he remarked:

> Amazing people. They had absolutely no conception. They asked me to come in and do this sticky job for them, and when I had done it they hated it. But what could they expect in the circumstances? Surely, they must have realised what was coming to them once they had decided on partition. But they had made absolutely no plans for coping with the situation. Strange chaps. Just didn't do their homework.[2]

One of the decisions taken on the basis of maps that was controversial proved to be crucial in determining the future of Jammu and Kashmir, which was outside Sir Cyril's scope of operations. This concerned Gurdaspur district, which adjoined Jammu. He divided the Muslim-majority district and awarded the three eastern *tehsils* to India, thus providing road access to Jammu which would not have been available otherwise. The "other factors" of which he took account to justify this decision are a matter of speculation. They probably related to his intention of minimising the impact of partition on Punjab's canal irrigation networks. In his report, he referred to "factors such as the disruption of railway communications and water systems that ought in this instance to displace the primary claims of contiguous majorities."

However, the strategic advantage that this decision gave India prompted the Pakistani leadership to assume that it was the outcome of a conspiracy between Nehru and Mountbatten, who had influenced Radcliffe. Rumours had

reached them before the award was anounced. On
11 August, Liaquat Ali Khan, who would soon be Pakistan's
first Prime Minister, sent a verbal complaint to the Viceroy's
Chief of Staff, Lord Ismay, that Gurdaspur, or part of it, was
being awarded to India and he regarded this as a breach of
faith. Ismay indignantly denied that Mountbatten had
anything to do with the Boundary Commission,[3] which the
Viceroy had also been telling anone who had sought his
intervention.

Nevertheless, the conspiracy thesis survived.
Mountbatten's friendship with Nehru and coolness towards
Jinnah, particularly after Jinnah countered Mountbatten's
desire to become Governor-General of both new Dominions
after partition by opting to be Pakistan's first Governor-
General himself, were evident during the last phase of
British rule. The thesis was bolstered by a note about
Punjab's canal irrigation system by A.N. Khosla, Chairman
of the Central Waterways, Irrigation and Navigation
Commission, which mentioned Gurdaspur but without
making as strong a case for retaining it in India as some
other areas. This was sent by Nehru to Mountbatten on
9 August,[4] who refused to send it on to Radcliffe. "I hope you
will agree," he wrote, "that I should not do anything to
prejudice the independence of the Boundary Commission,
and that, therefore, it would be wrong of me even to forward
any memorandum, especially at this stage."[5]

In view of variations between earlier maps delineating
Radcliffe's award and the final one relating to Punjab being
advantageous to India (in contrast to his award on the
Bengal-Assam border which gave the non-Muslim
Chittagong Hill Tracts to Pakistan on grounds of accessi-
bility), the impression of intervention by Mountbatten
gained ground. The release of his last personal report as
Viceroy dated 16 August furthered this impression. He
reported that Hari Singh was talking of holding a
referendum to decide whether to join Pakistan or India,
provided that the Boundary Commission gave him land
communications between Kashmir and India (which it had

by providing access through Gurdaspur). This enabled
Mountbatten to claim incorrectly, in his usual grandiloquent
style: "It appears, therefore, as if this great problem of the
States has been satisfactorily solved within the last three
weeks of British rule."[6]
     In his book on Kashmir, Indian author-journalist
M.J. Akbar, who had also researched and written a
biography of Nehru, states categorically, though without
supporting documentation, that "during private meetings,
he [Nehru] persuaded Mountbatten to leave this Gurdaspur
link in Indian hands."[7] Pakistan was incensed and later
denied Mountbatten entry.

*T*he strategic importance of the link was demonstrated
some ten weeks later. The rough, unmetalled, fair weather
road through Gurdaspur to Jammu and over the Banihal
Pass to the valley was used by the Indian army to rush
armoured cars and tanks to bolster the infantry units
airlifted to Srinagar on and after 27 October to repel the
tribal raiders investing it. Work on improving the surface
and bridging streams and rivers en route had begun earlier,
together with improving landing facilities at Jammu and
Srinagar airports, again strengthening the impression that
Hari Singh was keeping the option of joining India open,
and New Delhi was responding.
     Although Hari Singh had earlier rejected Mountbatten's
suggestion of military links with either Dominion, on
13 September, his Government approached New Delhi for the
loan of an Indian army officer, appropriately named Lt. Col.
Kashmir Singh Katoch, to replace Major General Scott as
Commander-in-Chief[8] (though it appears that he functioned
only as military adviser). A week later, Patel wrote to Hari
Singh appreciating his decision to appoint Mehr Chand
Mahajan, an Indian judge and protégé of Patel (who later
became Chief Justice of the Supreme Court) as Prime

Minister and promising "our best to help your State in this
critical period".[9]

Patel was more specific in a letter to the Maharaja on
2 October:

> In the meantime, I am expediting as much as possible
> the linking up of the State with the Indian Dominion
> by means of telegraph, telephones, wireless and roads.
> We fully realise the need for despatch and urgency and
> I can assure you that we shall do our best.[10]

Patel's correspondence reveals a letter from Kashmir's
Deputy Prime Minister, B.L. Batra, the next day, that
speaks for itself:

> An indent for military equipment was sent to you on
> 1 October, and another letter connected therewith is
> being sent today. I trust this would receive your earliest
> attention.I am writing to say that Mr Justice Mahajan
> after meeting you at Delhi conveyed the hope that it
> would be possible for the Indian Dominion to
> concentrate some military force at Madhopore [on the
> East Punjab-Jammu border] or at any equally near and
> convenient centre for rendering this State succour in
> case it is needed.[11]

The same day, Communications Minister Rafi Ahmed
Kidwai informed Patel of the arrangements being made by
the railways to carry telephone and telegraph stores to
Pathankot for onward transmission to Jammu.[12] These
preparations could not be kept secret, especially those
pertaining to Jammu and Kashmir. On 27 September, a
Pakistani newspaper reported:

> Orders have been issued by the Kashmir Government
> that a temporary boat bridge should be constructed over
> the Ravi near Pathankot so that vehicular traffic could
> be maintained between Jammu and the Indian Union.
> The metalling of the road from Jammu to Kathua is also
> proceeding at top speed. The idea is to keep up some sort

of communication between the State and the Indian
Union, so that essential supplies and troops could be
rushed to Kashmir without having to transport them
through Pakistan territory.[13]

On 7 October, Sardar Patel urged Defence Minister
Baldev Singh to expedite supply of arms and ammunition
to Kashmir and to send them by air if necessary: "There is
no time to lose if the reports which we hear of similar
preparations for intervention on the part of the Pakistan
Government are correct."[14] Nehru discovered later that the
arms had not been sent; and still later that some had been
diverted to the RSS in the State.

The reasons for this urgency are contained in a
remarkably perspicacious letter from Nehru to Patel on
27 September anticipating events in Kashmir a month later.
He asked Patel to urgently use his influence with Hari Singh
to take the steps he suggested to avert an impending crisis.
Referring to many reports he had received, he wrote:

> The Muslim League in the Punjab and the NWFP are
> making preparations to enter Kashmir in considerable
> numbers. The approach of winter is going to cut off
> Kashmir from the rest of India.... Therefore it is
> important that something should be done before these
> winter conditions set in. This means practically by the
> end of October or, at the latest, the beginning of
> November. Indeed, air traffic will be difficult even before
> that. I understand that the Pakistan strategy is to
> infiltrate into Kashmir now and to take some big action
> as soon as Kashmir is more or less isolated because of
> the coming winter....
> It becomes important, therefore, that the Maharaja
> should make friends with the National Conference so
> that there might be this popular support against
> Pakistan. Indeed, it seems to me that there is no other
> course open to the Maharaja but this: to release Sheikh
> Abdullah and the National Conference leaders, to make
> a friendly approach to them, seek their cooperation and

make them feel that this is really meant, and then to declare adhesion to the Indian Union. Once the State [accedes] to India, it will become very difficult to invade it officially or unofficially without coming into conflict with the Indian Union. If, however, there is delay in this accession, then Pakistan will go ahead without much fear of consequences, specially when the winter isolates Kashmir.

It seems to me urgently necessary, therefore, that the accession to the Indian Union should take place early. It is equally clear to me that this can only take place with some measure of success after there is peace between the Maharaja and the National Conference and they cooperate together to meet the situation. This is not an easy task; but it can be done chiefly because Abdullah is very anxious to keep out of Pakistan and relies upon us a great deal for advice. At the same time he cannot carry his people with him unless he has something definite to place before them....[15]

The Prime Minister's letter dovetailed the political and military strategy being followed in relation to Kashmir. As long as he had to work with Hari Singh, he tried to implement it through Patel, who retained the Maharaja's confidence. Patel implemented the policy faithfully, though not without misgivings. The impact of Indian pressure on Hari Singh gradually became evident, but his reluctance to give up his dream of independence upset the timing of an essential element of the strategy. He did not share the ability to ride the horse of history that enabled his ancestor, Gulab Singh, to found the Dogra empire a century earlier.

Abdullah was freed on 29 September and promptly began a campaign for popular government and communal harmony, which he said must have priority before deciding which Dominion to join. The British Chief of Kashmir's army was replaced; and Kak, sacked on the eve of the transfer of power (after Mountbatten, too, had criticised his obstinacy), was replaced, after an interval, by Mehr Chand

Mahajan, with whom Nehru was uncomfortable because
Mahajan distrusted Abdullah. But instead of acceding to
India to head off an incursion from Pakistan, Hari Singh
did so *after* the event when he had no other option. There
were also delays on the ground. On 12 October, for instance,
Batra complained to Patel that neither Lt. Col. K. S. Katoch,
whose services his Government had requested, nor the
promised arms and ammunition had arrived.[16]

In a letter, Nehru congratulated Abdullah on his release
from prison, but was embarrassed by the communal killings
in India: "the last six weeks have just been a series of
horrors." He interpreted them as more fascist than
communal, but they did not help relations with Muslim-
majority Kashmir. He returned to the theme on 10 October.
While insisting that Pakistan "is in an infinitely worse
position and I doubt very much if it can survive at all,"
Nehru proceeded, as was his wont, to place Kashmir in the
context of world politics to sustain the argument that it
should keep clear of Pakistan:

> On no account do I want Kashmir to become a kind of
> colony of foreign interests. I fear Pakistan is likely to
> become that if it survives at all. It may well be that the
> Pakistan people look upon Kashmir as a country which
> can yield them profit.[17]

*U*ntil mid-October, a week before the fateful tribal
incursion, Hari Singh was still hopeful of independence,
thouh, at the same time, preparing contingency plans for
support from India. On 12 October Batra told the press in
New Delhi:

> Despite constant rumours, we have no intention of
> joining either India or Pakistan, and the Maharaja and
> his government have decided that no decision of any
> kind will be made until there is peace on the plains.

[And significantly] the only thing that will change this
decision is if one side or other decides to use force
against us.... The Maharaja had told me that his
ambition is to make Kashmir the Switzerland of the
East – a State that is completely neutral.[18]

Mahajan followed up three days later by visualising
Kashmir as the home of "learned people in the sciences, arts
and literature from India, Pakistan, Asia and other
countries of the West and America and the USSR".[19]
Abdullah had also been keen to make Kashmir an Asian
Switzerland, but without a Maharaja. After his release from
prison, he seemed to realise that independence was not
feasible and focussed on the need to form a people's
government before deciding on accession. His emphasis on
such a government representing all religious communities
was interpreted as disfavouring Pakistan.[20]

At the verbal level, the conflict between India and
Pakistan, and the Maharaja's delaying tactics, began, as we
have seen in the previous chapter, before 15 August 1947.
His first diplomatic move to gain time, too, was taken on
the eve of the transfer of power. On 12 August his
Government sent telegrams to New Delhi and Karachi
proposing standstill agreements that would assure that
arrangements for trade, travel, communications and other
services would continue as with British India. Pakistan,
which inherited most of the links, agreed. India asked for
time to discuss the details and, in fact, never signed such
an agreement.

Karachi had no reason to hesitate. It lost nothing by
signing a standstill agreement. Pakistan retained control of
Kashmir's post and telegraph and banking services; of the
bulk of its external trade; of the transport bringing in
essential supplies along the main road access to the valley
from Rawalpindi; of the rail link with Jammu from Sialkot;
and of the rivers down which valuable Kashmiri timber, a
major export item, was floated down to the plains. But why
did India delay? The reason given by V.P. Menon (Secretary
to the Ministry of States, who was Mountbatten's
Constitutional Adviser and then helped Sardar Patel

persuade the princely States to join the Indian Union in a matter of weeks) is hardly adequate. In an otherwise convincing account of the background to Kashmir's accession, all he says in explanation is: "... our hands were already full and, if truth be told, I for one had simply no time to think of Kashmir."[21]

The Indian Government could hardly be as unconcerned with evolving a post-independence relationship with Kashmir as these words suggest, given the interest it had already shown. Since Kashmir did not depend on India for communications and supplies, no suffering was involved by not signing a standstill agreement. Observers suspicious of India, however, see it as evidence that New Delhi felt certain that the State was already in the bag.[22] It could equally be interpreted as a signal to Hari Singh that India would not accept the status quo indefinitely.

As for Menon, he may have been literally honest. On stepping into office on 15 August, the new Indian Government was faced with a delicate problem with grave implications for the future. Sir Mahabatkhan Rasulkhanji, the Nawab of Junagadh, a small princely State embedded in Kathiawar – with a population of 670,719, of whom 80 per cent were Hindus – had announced his accession to Pakistan. Junagadh was surrounded by Indian territory but could boast of a sea link with Pakistan, over 300 miles of water, from its port of Veraval. Repeated telegrams were sent to Karachi and messages were sent through emissaries asking whether the Pakistan Government was accepting the Nawab's accession. Finally, on 13 September, Karachi replied that the accession had been accepted.

Lord Ismay, Chief of Staff to Mountbatten who was now India's Governor-General, visited Karachi and reported that Junagadh's accession had the appearance of a trap. Pakistan was posing as a small country threatened by a bigger neighbour. The trap confronted New Delhi with an acute dilemma, as brought out by H.V. Hodson, Constitutional Adviser to a previous Viceroy, Lord Linlithgow, who had access to State papers and British officials in both Dominions. Hodson was later Editor of the *Sunday Times* of London. He wrote:

> If the Indian Government acquiesced [in Junagadh's accession to Pakistan], admitting the undoubted legal right of the Ruler to decide which way to go, the precedent of a Muslim Prince taking a Hindu-majority State into Pakistan, notwithstanding geographical and communal arguments to the contrary, could be applied to the far greater prize of Hyderabad. If the Indian Government intervened with force, besides the harm it would do itself with outside opinion, it would set up a contrary precedent, to be applied by Pakistan to Kashmir, were the latter's Maharajah to accede to India. If India demanded, as the alternative to force, a plebiscite in Junagadh, this could be adopted as a general principle which when applied to Kashmir and Jammu would, in Karachi's estimation, take the State to Pakistan.[23]

Serious as the situation was, it did not lack a comic aspect. Nawab Mahabatkhan seemed miscast as the originator of this masterly strategy: Jinnah was clearly pulling the strings. Te Nawab's ruling passion was for dogs; he had little time for anything or anyone else. Leonard Mosley describes the palace scene:

> Around his palace he had built a series of elaborate kennels (rooms would be a better description) in which he kept his favourite pets -- about a hundred and fifty of them -- each with his own bath, serving table, bed, attendant and telephone. There was a palace vet, an Englishman, to look after them. When dogs were brought in, they were placed on palanquins and carried by retainers into the Nawab's presence. When two of his dogs were mated, the Nawab invariably declared a public holiday in the State....

The Nawab [after Indian forces intervened] had already fled to Pakistan in his private plane. He crammed aboard as many of his dogs as he could, plus his four wives. One of them discovered, at the last moment, that she had left her child behind in the palace and asked the Nawab to wait while she fetched her. The moment she left the airfield, the Nawab loaded in two more dogs and took off without his wife.[24]

The Nawab's eccentricities did not reduce the scale of the problem posed. Menon rushed to Junagadh, but was unable to see Sir Mahabatkhan who (like Hari Singh) claimed to be sick, and made do with trying to make his Dewan realise how dependent Junagadh was on surrounding Indian territory. The Dewan, incidentally, was Sir Shah Nawaz Bhutto, father of a future Prime Minister of Pakistan. Over the next weeks, administrative and military pressures were built up, combined with people's demonstrations. The Nawab's administration began to crumble. Pakistani protests multiplied and there was talk of war. In early October, New Delhi proposed a referendum to determine Junagadh's future as a gesture to avert hostilities.

By now it was evident that Jinnah had lost Junagadh, which he never had a chance of getting, but he had won a valuable diplomatic weapon in exchange. Nehru was forced into a corner. He could not deny the right given to rulers of princely States to join whichever Dominion they preferred without establishing that Junagadh's people wanted to join India, which could be demonstrated only by a referendum. But the commitment set a precedent for Kashmir -- Pakistan's real objective. This emerged at a meeting between Nehru and Liaquat Ali set up by Mountbatten to defuse the hostility. As Governor-General, Mountbatten continued to report regularly to his King. About this meeting, he wrote:

... [Nehru] said that India would always be willing to abide by a decision obtained by a general election, a plebiscite or a referendum, provided it was conducted

in a fair and impartial manner. I emphasised the
importance of Pandit Nehru's statement to Mr Liaquat
Ali Khan, and assured him that India would abide by
it, and that Pandit Nehru would agree that this policy
would apply to any other State, since India would never
be a party to trying to force a State to join their
Dominion against the wishes of the majority of the
people. Pandit Nehru nodded his head sadly. Mr Liaquat
Ali Khan's eyes sparkled. There is no doubt that both
of them were thinking of Kashmir.[25]

Even so, Nehru considered a counter-strategy, indicated
by the words "general elections". This actually came into
play when the plebiscite promoted by the UN Security
Council did not fructify and New Delhi decided that the
future of Jammu and Kashmir could not remain undecided
indefinitely. Accordingly, elections in the State were treated
as an adequate test of public opinion, though Pakistan
questioned their fairness.

Patel was unhappy with the offer of a referendum in
Junagadh, where India's control could not be challenged on
the ground. But he is said to have gone along because there
was no reference to UN supervision. As recalled by his
private secretary, he remarked: "Don't you see we have two
UN experts – the Prime Minister and the other Lord
Mountbatten – and I have to steer my way between them."[26]

Nehru publicly announced much of what he said at his
meting with Liaquat in a press communiqué on 6 October,
but left out the "general elections":

Any decision involving the fate of large numbers of
people must necessarily depend on the wishes of the
people. This is the policy that the Government of India
accepts in its entirety and they are of an opinion that a
dispue involving the fate of any territory should be
decided by a referendum or plebiscite of the people
concerned.

There was no response from Pakistan. On 9 November
Indian troops entered Junagadh without resistance.

Pakistan protested. A referendum was actually held on 20 February 1948. Out of the 190,870 persons who voted, only 91 favoured Pakistan. But official Pakistani maps have continued to paint Junagadh green.

Another precedent that would affect Kashmir, set during the Junagadh confrontation, was a formal note from the British Chiefs of Staff of the three armed services to the Government of India stating that they would not be able to participate in a war between the two Dominions.[27] It had serious implications because the higher ranks of the armed services in both Dominions were then manned by British officers, but with Pakistan more dependent on them than India.

Yet another development which would have both positive and negative consequences for India was the decision to ask Mountbatten to chair the Defence Committee of the Cabinet which had been set up at his suggestion. A precedent had been set in early September when he was invited to chair the Emergency Committee to plan operations to stop the spread of post-partition killings. Now the Governor-General, supposed to be a constitutional Head of State, and a foreigner, could play a decisive role in deciding, evolving and executing military policy. His wartime experience as Supreme Commander of Allied Forces in South-East Asia proved to be of great value. But his strategic objectives were constricted by British and international concerns, which explained his insistence on involving the UN and reining in the armed forces when they were on the offensive.

*U*nlike Kashmir, the province of Jammu had no mountain barriers to separate it from the post-partition massacres in divided Punjab. Nor did it have the same eclectic historical and cultural heritage. There was more rivalry between the two communities because neither predominated in terms of population. While in the valley, Muslims formed over 93 per cent of the population, according to the 1941 census, in

Jammu, the figure was 77 per cent. Inevitably, communal
violence flowed over the State border into Jammu, where,
according to Pakistan, there was an organised campaign to
drive out Muslims.[28] Organised or not, many Muslims were
killed; others fled into Pakistan.

The flashpoint was Poonch, adjoining Pakistan and
inhabited by Muslims with close trans-border links. The
men of Poonch had a martial background and a history of
friction with the Maharaja. Many Poonchis had served in
the British-Indian army during the Second World War. They
organised an armed revolt, undoubtedly encouraged by
Pakistan, but provoked by Dogra oppression. The campaign
was led by Sardar Mohammed Ibrahim Khan, who later
founded the 'Azad' Kashmir Government on the Pakistan
side of the cease-fire line. Dogra troops responded with
customary brutality.

A report on the revolt by Richard Symonds, a Quaker
social worker, recalled previous accounts of the manner in
which the Dogra dynasty taxed its subjects: "There was a
tax on every hearth and every window. Every cow, buffalo
and sheep was taxed and even every wife. Finally, the
Zaildari tax was introduced to pay for the cost of taxation,
and Dogra troops were billeted on the Poonchis to enforce
collection."[29]

Pakistan portrayed the uprising in Poonch as a legitimate revolt against the Maharaja's misrule, with the Pathan
tribals entering to help when the situation developed into
a widespread pogrom against Muslims in Jammu. Vengeful
Hindu and Sikh refugees, who had fled Pakistan, had joined
the campaign. The large-scale movement of Muslims from
their homes in Jammu to Pakistan and reports of attacks
on Muslims lent credence to this view, which was endorsed
by several foreign observers and influenced the UN Security
Council when it considered the issue. Among them was Josef
Korbel, a member of the United Nations Commission who
visited Kashmir. He concluded that "there is little doubt that
Kashmir was brewing with revolt against the Maharaja long
before the tribesmen invaded the country."[30]

The trouble in Poonch led to a flurry of telegrams between the Governments of Pakistan and Kashmir. The language clearly hinted at future developments. Pakistan began on 12 October with a veiled warning:

Men of Pakistan army who recently returned from leave at their homes in Poonch report that armed bands, which include troops, are attacking Muslim villages in the State.... One feature of the present situation in Poonch which, however, makes it particularly dangerous to the friendly relations that the Pakistan Government wishes to retain with Kashmir is that Pakistan army obtains a large number of recruits from Poonch. Feeling in the battalions to which these men belong is rapidly rising and the situation is fraught with danger....

The Kashmir Prime Minister's reply on 15 October was less well drafted, but the sting was in the tail:

This Government has ample proof of infiltration. As is the result in every Government, including Pakistan Dominion, military has to take action when disturbances cannot adequately be dealt with by civil administration.... If, unfortunately, this request is not heeded, Government, much against its wishes, will have no option but to ask for assistance to withstand aggressive and unfriendly actions of the Pakistan people along our border.

On 18 October, the newly appointed Prime Minister of Kashmir, Mehr Chand Mahajan, sent a more detailed telegram directly to Jinnah which left no doubt of what was intended if provocations continued. It described the problems that the State was facing due to the virtual blockade imposed by Pakistan in spite of the standstill agreement; attacks on Kashmiri nationals on the Kohala border; armed infiltration into Poonch; and propaganda against the Maharaja's Government in Pakistani media. The last line carried the same warning: "If, unfortunately, this request (to stop all these iniquities) is not heeded the

Government fully hope that you would agree that it would
be justified in asking for friendly assistance and oppose
trespass on its fundamental rights."

At about the same time, an emissary sent by Jinnah to
Srinagar, Major A.S.B. Shah, called on Mahajan. "From his
talk," according to Mahajan, "it was clear that he was
suggesting immediate accession to the State of Pakistan and
that if this was not agreed to, there was bound to be
trouble." Mahajan insisted that the blockade, at the border,
of lorries bringing supplies to Kashmir should be lifted
before the question of accession could be considered. But
the response from Jinnah was in the negative. Instead,
Mahajan was asked to meet Jinnah in Lahore, which he
refused to do. Then, "towards the close of the interview, the
attitude of Major Shah became a bit aggressive and he told
me that my refusal to decide the question of accession
immediately might result in serious consequences. When he
said that, I blurted out that a threat of that kind would
throw the State into the lap of India."[31]

Karachi's official rejoinder contained a counter-threat.
"The Pakistan Government must take a most serious view
of a state of affairs in which Muslims in Kashmir are
suppressed and forcibly driven out," it stated. Then taking
note of the reference to joining India, which it interpreted
as a *coup d'état* against Muslims, it warned: "If this policy
is not changed and the preparations and the measures that
you are now taking in implementing this policy are not
stopped, the gravest consequences will follow for which you
alone will be held responsible."

Jinnah thought he matter serious enough to send a
personal telegram to Hari Singh on 20 October (by when
the tribal raiders were already on the move). It contained
a catalogue of charges against the Kashmir Government,
including its domestic policies. He contrasted the favourable
treatment accorded to Abdullah's National Conference with
the continued detention of Ghulam Abbas and the leaders
of his Muslim Conference; charged Kashmir with
"suppressing Muslims in every way" and driving them out

of the State, and concluded: "...the real aim of your Government's policy is to seek an opportunity to join the Indian Dominion through a *coup d'état* by securing the intervention and assistance of that Dominion."[32]

Unlike the official response from Karachi, Jinnah did not threaten "grave consequences". He must have been aware that such consequences were already on their way: in the shape of the Pathan tribal raiders being helped to invade Kashmir from adjoining Pakistan territory.

*I*n Kashmir itself, the campaign again launched by Abdullah for representative government, after his release from prison, displeased the Maharaja as well as his conservative Prime Minister. Patel, aware that accession would require popular sanction, tried his best to make them realise that times had changed. In a letter to Mahajan, and through him to Hari Singh, written on 21 October, Patel observed:

> I myself feel that the position which Sheikh Abdullah takes up is understandable and reasonable. In the mounting demands for the introduction of responsible government in the States, such as you have recently witnessed in Travancore and Mysore, it is impossible for you to isolate yourself. It is obvious that in your dealings with the external dangers and internal commotion with which you are faced, mere brute force is not enough. We, on our part, have pledged to give you the maximum support and we will do so. But I am afraid, without some measure of popular backing, particularly from amongst the community which represents such an overwhelming majority in Kashmir, it would be difficult to make such support go to the farthest limit that is necessary if we are to crush the disruptive forces which are being raised and organised. Nor do I think [here Patel touched on a continuing grievance of Kashmiri Muslims] it would be

possible for you to maintain for long the exclusive or the predominant monopoly of any particular community in your security services.

Mahajan's reply two days later (the tribal invasion had begun) showed signs of panic but not of accepting Patel's advice:

> I note your views about the constitutional position in the State but the situation in the State at the present moment is such that one cannot get a moment to think of politics. We are practically working on a war basis and every moment of our time is taken up with the border situation which is worsening every day. Practically the whole of our Muslim military and police has either deserted or has not behaved in a proper manner. The help that you kindly promised has not arrived and we are surrounded on all sides....[33] [His tone changed in his next letter to Patel after Indian troops had landed.]

Chapter X

Invasion and Accession

*M*ountbatten was attending a dinner reception for the visiting Foreign Minister of Siam (Thailand) at the Prime Minister's house on 24 October 1947 when Nehru took him aside to tell him that news had been received of a large-scale invasion of Kashmir by Pathan tribesmen.[1] Nehru's worst fears had come true (see letter to Patel on 23 September quoted in the previous chapter). Now it was a question of whether the motorised tribal *lashkars* would take the valley before Indian forces could intervene. And India could not intervene until Hari Singh asked for help and, as Nehru saw it, gained popular support by inducting Abdullah into the administration. Without this support, the limited forces India could send could not function. Popular support was also essential in the event of a plebiscite.

Despite Nehru's anticipating the incursion, and the orders to improve road and communication links with Jammu and Srinagar and to airlift arms and ammunition (which never landed), implementation was tardy. Then, as later, the Indian Cabinet lacked the swift decision-making and enforcing ability essential to meet such emergencies. Mountbatten began to preside over the crucial Defence Committee during the Junagadh episode and did the same when India faced its first major military challenge in Kashmir. The Commanders-in-Chief of the three armed services and the senior operational commanders, too, were British as were their opposite numbers in Pakistan. So was Field Marshal Sir Claude Auchinleck, Supreme Commander of the short-lived Joint (Indo-Pakistan) Defence Council, the most senior and experienced army officer of them all.

It was an unusual situation in which to organise military operations. British officers could not take active part in the fighting and did not visit operational areas; they could only plan and organise from a distance. After expressing initial operational misgivings, those on the Indian side made an unprecedently good job of organising the opening response to the incursion. The desire to save the lives of the couple of hundred British citizens in the valley, some of whom had been killed and raped by the rampaging Pathans, acted as a spur. Later they showed less enthusiasm and, presumably under Mountbatten's guidance, sought to limit the fighting, even when Indian forces were well placed.[2]

The army chiefs in India and Pakistan remained in telephonic touch throughout the Kashmir conflict and there were indications of leakage of operational orders. Within months, General Sir Rob Lockhart had to be replaced as Commander-in-Chief, India, by another British officer, General Roy Boucher. Only when Lt. General K.M. Cariappa (later the first Indian Commander-in-Chief) took over what was then designated the Delhi and East Punjab Command, which extended to Kashmir, were offensive operations conducted during the closing stages of the war. One of them, pushed through though disapproved by General Boucher, resulted in the capture of the Zojila Pass (in a tank attack unprecedented at such a height) and the road beyond to Leh, which was of crucial value in defending Ladakh first against Pakistan and later against China.[3]

Mountbatten's personality and objectives inspired and limited the Kashmir operations. As Chairman of the Cabinet Defence Committee, he was in his element in planning for the airlift that saved Srinagar. It recalled similar operations planned when he was Supreme Commander of the South-

East Asia Command during the Second World War.
Comparing them later, he said that Srinagar beat SEAC
hollow. At the same time, he insisted on Kashmir's accession
which delayed India's response. After Srinagar, and the
British citizens resident there, had been saved, he became
anxious to avoid escalation and to secure a cease-fire,
irrespective of India's strategic objectives, and to leave the
the issue to the United Nations. H.V. Hodson, who knew
Mountbatten well, writes:

> Over Kashmir his leadership was decisive in adoption
> of the policy of accepting accession subject to an
> eventual plebiscite and of immediately sending troops
> into the State: in this, and thereafter, his prime and
> unexceptionable object was to avoid war between the two
> Dominions and, as he repeatedly urged, "stop the
> fighting". The reference to the United Nations as
> peacekeeper was made under his strong pressure.[4]

*B*ritish officers on the other side were initially inhibited
by the fact that Pakistan did not formally enter the war in
Kashmir until May 1948. But it was Major William Brown,
commanding the Maharaja's Gilgit Scouts, who presided
when his men rebelled and raised the Pakistan flag in that
northern outpost of Kashmir on 4 November 1947, soon
after the tribals had invaded the valley. His Scouts went on
to join the raiders in attacking the State forces guarding
Skardu and other places in the north that came under
Pakistan's control.

Lt. General Sir Douglas Gracey, acting Commander-in-
Chief of the Pakistan army (in the absence of General Sir
Frank Messervy), however, played a part in preventing an
immediate outbreak of war with India when New Delhi
accepted Hari Singh's accession and flew troops to Srinagar.
Jinnah was so incensed (the airlift had upset his plans) that
he ordered Gracey to move troops into Kashmir forthwith.

Gracey insisted on consulting Auchinleck who held that Kashmir was legally part of India after the Maharaja's accession and that if the two Dominions went to war, British officers would have to be withdrawn from both, which would hurt Pakistan more than India. Jinnah angrily withdrew his orders.[5]

But this did not mean that British sympathy for Pakistan had waned. It was on Gracey's advice (he had taken over from Messervy as Commander-in-Chief) that Pakistan troops were openly thrown into the fighting when Indian forces began to approach its borders in Kashmir in May 1948. He told the UN Commission later that Pakistan had received reports that the Indian army was preparing for a general offensive to finish the Kashmir campaign. But the reasons he gave to justify introducing Pakistan regulars into the fighting ranged from persuasive to fanciful. They included: an Indian advance would create a refugee problem for Pakistan; it would give India control of rivers flowing into Pakistan; it would threaten the strategic railway linking Peshawar to Lahore and Pakistan's links with the distant northern principalities of Chitral and Swat; it would provide an opportunity for India to join Afghanistan in a pincer movement against Pakistan and provide a corridor to Pakhtunistan.[6]

In Sir Francis Mudie, Governor of West Punjab, which adjoined Jammu and Kashmir, Pakistan had secured the services of an inveterate critic of India who had belonged to the Indian Civil Service. It was he who disclosed a secret letter that gave rise to the suspicion that Sir Cyril Radcliffe had altered his award to favour India on Kashmir. Mudie was most upset when Gracey first opposed Jinnah's order to send his troops into Kashmir.[7] His antipathy to independent India and expectations from Pakistan, not unique among those who had served the Raj, expressed itself in a letter to a Pakistani politician dated 20 October 1948:

The facts of the situation are that Pakistan is situated between a hostile – a very hostile – India and...an

expansionist and unscrupulous Russia. As long as
relations between Pakistan and Britain are good, and
Pakistan remains in the Commonwealth, an attack by
Russia – and also I am inclined to believe, an attack by
India – on Pakistan brings in the UK and the USA on
Pakistan's side. If these conditions do not hold, then
Pakistan stands alone and sooner or later will be
swallowed up by Russia or India or more probably
partitioned as Poland was.... I can assure you that the
feeling in Britain is strongly pro-Pakistan, whatever
Mountbatten and [Sir Stafford] Cripps may do, and that
it is increasingly so. I know this from the letters I
receive from home.[8]

Pakistan was almost entirely dependent on British staff
to man senior civil as well as military posts. It was hardly
possible that they were ignorant of the preparations for the
tribal raid, of which Karachi denied responsibility or
foreknowledge, but no warning was conveyed to New Delhi.
According to Hodson, General Messervy, as Commander-in-
Chief in Pakistan, was aware of the agitation by the
tribesmen to be allowed to invade Kashmir and had strongly
advised Liaquat Ali Khan against such a course. Shortly
before the invasion, Sir George Cunningham (Governor of
the North West Frontier Province) asked him what was the
Pakistan Government's policy, as the Chief Minister of the
NWFP, Khan Abdul Qaiyum Khan, was encouraging
tribesmen to go into Kashmir and collecting Frontier Scouts
and militia transport for a tribal invasion. Within the next
few days a conference was held in Lahore among Jinnah,
Liaquat Ali Khan and Qaiyum Khan. Its outcome was
unknown to General Messervy, then in England, but was
evident from events on the ground.[9]

There was sufficient evidence of Pakistan's complicity
in the tribal invasion. Five thousand or more tribals could
not have passed through its territory without official
knowledge. Provision of lorried transport, petrol, rations,
automatic weapons, mortars and ammunition and all the
requirements for a large-scale invasion meant participation.

There had been earlier evidence of Pakistani army involvement, with tanks deployed against Bhimbar in Jammu on one occasion, and in the uprising in Poonch that preceded the tribal invasion. That was not all. As subsequently admitted, officers and men of the regular army – technically on leave – joined the raiders. The invasion, code-named 'Operation Gulmarg', was masterminded by a regular officer of the Pakistan army, Major General Akbar Khan, functioning under the pseudonym 'General Tariq', after the Moroccan general who crossed the Straits of Gibraltar to invade Spain. He had his headquarters in Rawalpindi.

Even so, New Delhi had no intelligence of these preparations. When the raiders struck on 22 October, they had the advantage of total surprise. They were joined by sections of the Maharaja's army which was spread thinly over the many trouble spots in the State. Muzaffarabad, the last town on the Pakistan border, was protected by a battalion, half of which was comprised of Muslims from Poonch, where a revolt had been in progress against the Maharaja's impositions. Early that morning, they revolted, killed their comrades and commanding officer and opened the road into the valley. The operation bore all the signs of careful advance planning. Travelling in lorries and with just over a hundred miles of good road before them, the threat to Srinagar could be counted in hours.

Lt. Gen. L.P. Sen, who, as Brigadier, commanded the first units flown into the valley, pointed out later:

> One might form the impression from these incidents in Jammu and in Muzaffarabad-Domel area that the Muslims in the State had risen against the Government and wished to join Pakistan. Nothing could be further from the truth. Thousands upon thousands of Muslims in the Government, the State Forces and in the National

Conference, the political party led by Sheikh Abdullah, braved death in stemming the invasion. Many Muslim officers and men of the J&K State Forces were later absorbed into the Indian Army.[10]

With no regular units available, the chief of the Kashmir State forces, Brigadier Rajinder Singh, jumped personally into the battle. Collecting a motley force of some two hundred men, he rushed from Srinagar and deployed them near Uri the next day. There he held up the enemy transport column by blowing up a river bridge. But some of the tribals got across. Rajinder Singh was forced to fight a delaying action against superior odds until he fell mortally wounded. Srinagar realised how near the raiders had come when the lights failed on 24 October: the raiders had reached the power station at Mahura, about fifty miles away. But the Brigadier had gained his capital a respite of at least forty-eight hours at the cost of his life. Only now did New Delhi get the bad news. And only now did Hari Singh's Government appeal for help. "On 24th October," writes Mahajan, "the Deputy Prime Minister [Batra] left Srinagar for Delhi carrying a letter of accession from the Maharaja and a personal letter to Pandit Jawaharlal Nehru and another to Sardar Patel asking of military help in men, arms and ammunition."[11]

*N*ew Delhi did not respond as fast as the situation demanded. The appeal was received the same evening, but three vital days elapsed before help was sent. Mountbatten's insistence on completing the legal formalities of accession and working out the modalities of consulting the people before troops were sent delayed the response. Nehru differed but went along, though he later told Parliament in March 1951 that "irrespective of accession we would have had an obligation to protect the people of Kashmir against aggression." His desire to ensure that the Maharaja associate Abdullah with his Government may have slowed the process. As for Patel, he did not think that accession should be treated as a prerequisite for help.

The Defence Committee of the Cabinet met on 24 October. A report from the Commander-in-Chief, General Lockhart, informed them that his opposite number in Pakistan had sent a belated message that some 5000 tribesmen had entered Kashmir some three days previously and seized and burnt Muzaffarabad on their way to Srinagar. Next day, Nehru contributed the information that they had reached Uri, and complained (Mountbatten was in the chair) that the arms that his Government had ordered to be rushed to Kashmir earlier that month had not been delivered. The orders, presumably, were to be implemented by British army officers.

It was at this point that the committee decided to instruct the Service Chiefs to make plans for an airlift of troops to Srinagar by chartering civil aircraft, but was undecided on the modalities of accession. V.P. Menon was instructed to fly to Srinagar, meet Hari Singh and discuss the different options. One suggestion by Mountbatten – the formula finally accepted – was that the Maharaja offer temporary accession until the will of the people could be ascertained after law and order had been restored. Nehru insisted that Abdullah's cooperation be secured. A biographer of Nehru asserts, without disclosing his source, that Hari Singh "would have been content to join India with Jammu alone, leaving the rest of Kashmir to its fate. But it was the Muslim valley of Kashmir, as Nehru impressed upon the Maharaja and later upon Patel, which was most worth fighting for...".[12]

Menon gives a graphic account of his hurried visit to Srinagar:

> The road leading from the aerodrome to Srinagar was deserted. At some of the street corners I noticed volunteers of the National Conference with *lathis* who challenged passers-by; but the State police were conspicuous by their absence.... The Maharaja was

completely unnerved by his sense of lone helplessness.
There were practically no State forces left and the
raiders had almost reached the outskirts of Baramula.
At this rate they would be in Srinagar in another day
or two.... I advised him to leave immediately for Jammu
and to take with him his family and his valuable
possessions.[13]

That there was an element of bargaining in Menon's
mission, however, emerges from Mahajan's recollections.
Menon told him that nothing could be done about sending
military help without Mahajan's going to New Delhi
personally, although Mahajan pointed out that Batra had
already gone with a letter of accession and he had earlier
been assured military aid if required. The reason became
clearer the next morning.

Mahajan accompanied Menon to New Delhi. He drove
straight from Safdarjang airport to Nehru's residence. There
a dramatic scene was enacted in which Abdullah
participated. Mahajan, clearly overwrought, insisted that
military help be rushed immediately to Kashmir. Nehru,
according to him, seemed in no hurry and talked about the
difficulty of sending troops on the spur of the moment. So,
he played his last card: "Take the accession and give
whatever power you desire to the popular party. The army
must fly to save Srinagar this evening or else I will go to
Lahore and negotiate terms ,with Mr Jinnah." Nehru angrily
asked Mahajan to leave, but Patel, who was present,
intervened. Just then, a slip of paper was passed to Nehru.
It came from Abdullah who was in an adjacent room,
listening in to the conversation. Mahajan then records: "He
[Abdullah] now strengthened my hands by telling the Prime
Minister that military help must be sent immediately.... The
Prime Minister's attitude changed on reading this slip."[14]
Recalling the incident later, Abdullah confirmed that Nehru
was brought round only after he intervened to assure him
that he and the National Conference supported accession.[15]

Yet it is hard to imagine Nehru being quite so casual
about Kashmir. More likely the intention was to secure

Mahajan's cooperation in the decision to bring Abdullah, whom Mahajan disliked and distrusted, into the State administration. This also fits with Menon's care to avoid making any commitment in Srinagar. Evidently, the Prime Minister could be a tough bargainer even on issues on which he sounded sentimental.

Soon after Menon returned to New Delhi he reported to the Defence Committee. Mountbatten now pushed his proposal more strongly, arguing that it would be improper to move troops into what was still an independent country. It would be proper only if Kashmir acceded to India, but in view of the composition of the population, the accession should be made conditional. A plebiscite should be held to ascertain the will of the people after the raiders had been expelled. Nehru and other ministers readily agreed, according to Menon.

Menon then describes his flight the same day (26 October) to Jammu:

> On arrival at the palace, I found it in a state of utter turmoil with valuable articles strewn all over the place. The Maharaja was asleep; he had left Srinagar the previous evening and had been driving all night. I woke him up and told him of what had taken place at the Defence Committee meeting. He was ready to accede at once [a letter was sent two days earlier, according to Mahajan]. He then composed a letter to the Governor-General describing the pitiable plight of the State and reiterating his request for military help. He further informed the Governor-General that it was his intention to set up an Interim Government at once and to ask Sheikh Abdullah to carry the responsibilities in this emergency with Mahajan, his Prime Minister.... He also signed the instrument of accession.
> Just as I was leaving, he told me that before he went to sleep, he had left instructions with his ADC that if I came back from Delhi, he was not to be disturbed as it would mean that the Government of India had decided

to come to his rescue and he should therefore be allowed to sleep in peace; but if I failed to return, it meant everything was lost and, in that case, his ADC was to shoot him in his sleep.

Hari Singh's letter seeking accession indicated that he was still considering the option of independence until the tribal invasion forced him to accede to India. "I wanted to take time to decide to which Dominion I should accede," he wrote, adding, "[also] whether it is not in the best interest of both the Dominions and my State to stand independent, of course with cordial relations with both." But these hopes had been shattered by the tribal raid. "The wild forces thus let loose on the State are marching on with the hope of capturing Srinagar.... With the conditions obtaining at present in my State and the great emergency of the situation as it exists I have no option but to ask for help from the Indian Dominion. Naturally they cannot send the help asked for me without my State acceding to the Dominion of India. I have accordingly decided to do so and I attach the Instrument of Accession for acceptance by your Government."

As required, the Maharaja swallowed an even more bitter pill: "I may also inform Your Excellency's Government that it is my intention at once to set up an Interim Government and ask Sheikh Abdullah to carry the responsibilities in this emergency with my Prime Minister."[16]

The next day, Mountbatten replied by informing Hari Singh that he was accepting the Instrument of Accession (see Appendix for its text) with the condition that after law and order had been restored, the question "should be settled by a reference to the people" (see next chapter). The accession document signed by the Maharaja defined and limited the areas in which New Delhi could extend its legal jurisdiction to Jammu and Kashmir.

Alastair Lamb makes much of what he interprets as a discrepancy between Mahajan's version of his visit to New

Delhi and Menon's account to argue that Indian troops landed in Srinagar before and not after Hari Singh signed the Instrument of Accession, and were thus as much intruders as the tribal raiders.[17] But Mahajan writes specifically that what was left for the following day was to get the Maharaja's signature to "certain supplementary documents". Before leaving on 27 October for Jammu, he got a handwritten note from Nehru setting out the conditions on which military help was being provided. The first was accession in defence, external affairs and transport [communications], which Mahajan notes was "already done". Others related to democratisation of, and involvement of Abdullah in, the administration.

Only after Menon returned with Hari Singh's Instrument of Accession were orders given by the Cabinet to fly an infantry battalion to Srinagar the next morning (i.e., 27 October). For quite some time, the Cabinet Committee debated the modalities of the accession. Eventually, Mountbatten's formula that it be accepted with a proviso for plebiscite was formally approved. But by now the troops could not be sure whether Srinagar airport was in friendly or enemy hands. No reconnaissance flights seem to have been made. If unsure on arrival, they were instructed to land at Jammu.

Orders for the unprecedented airlift to Srinagar were finalised on the evening of 26 October. Major S.K. Sinha (later Lt. General and Vice-Chief of Army Staff) was then serving on the staff of Lt. General Dudley Russell, chief of the New Delhi and East Punjab Command. According to Major Sinha, it was ten at night by the time the staff were rounded up and assembled, and "most of us were dressed in our dinner jackets and to add colour to our costumes, the duty officer was in his pyjama suit". The signal despatched to the First Battalion of the Sikh Regiment, then posted in nearby Gurgaon, brings out the dramatic urgency of the operation, less than six hours away:

YOUR BATTALION LESS TWO COMPANIES WILL CONCENTRATE

PALAM AIRFIELD BY 0400 HOURS 27 OCTOBER(.) ONE BATTERY
13 FIELD REGIMENT IN INFANTRY ROLE BEING PLACED UNDER
YOUR COMMAND(.) BE PREPARED TO FLY ON AN OPERATIONAL
MISSION EX PALAM MORNING 27 OCTOBER(.) REMAINDER
BATTALION WILL BE FLOWN 28 OCTOBER.

The only intelligence accompanying the orders was that
Kashmir had acceded to India, Abdullah had been invited
to form a popular government and an unknown number of
armed tribesmen were approaching Srinagar, where the
situation was deteriorating. In view of this uncertainty, the
orders added that if the Battalion did not receive the signal
to land in Srinagar, it would go to Jammu and from there
requisition local transport and go as far north as possible.[18]

The efficiency of the improvised airlift and the speed
with which the troops went into action – it was the first
combat mission to which free India's forces had been
committed – made up for the Cabinet's delay, but only just
and not without cost. Even Mountbatten was impressed
with the courage and devotion of the Indian Air Force and
civil pilots who flew repeated sorties to airlift three hundred
soldiers and their arms to Srinagar on that first day, with
as many sorties on the following days. It was a hazardous
operation. Landing facilities at the Badgam dirt airstrip
near Srinagar were rudimentary, with no communication
and servicing aids, not even a fire engine. Clouds of dust
obscured the view every time a Dakota landed or took off.

As Menon had reported, only *lathi*-armed National
Conference volunteers were patrolling the streets and the
approaches to Srinagar. Now they also drove buses to the
airfield to ferry Indian troops against the raiders. Without
this popular cooperation, Nehru told the nation in a
broadcast on 2 November, "our troops could have done little".

But the allocation of the Gurdaspur link to India and
the executive role that Mountbatten played after independence as Chairman of the Defence Committee of the Indian
Cabinet convinced Karachi that he was part of a conspiracy
to cheat Pakistan of Kashmir and that India's intervention

was preplanned. To rebut this allegation, the three British
Service Chiefs in New Delhi issued a statement giving a
"true time-table of events, as regards decisions taken, plans
made, orders given, and movements started" beginning on
24 October when the C-in-C, Indian army, received
information that the tribesmen had seized Muzaffarabad.
"Prior to this date," the Chiefs stated, "no plans of any sort
for sending Indian forces into Kashmir had been formulated
or even considered." The first directions from the
Government to prepare such plans were received on
25 October, the same evening orders were issued to an
infantry battalion to prepare to be flown to Srinagar but
only in the event of the Government accepting Kashmir's
accession and deciding to send help. Plans were finalised
the following day and the airlift began at first light on 27
October, "with Kashmir's Instrument of Accession signed."[19]
The emphasis was on legality rather than speed of response.

*H*ow less than a battalion of Indian soldiers saved
Srinagar when the tribal forces had already advanced
beyond Baramula has been written about frequently and
described vividly and in detail by Lt. Gen. L.P. Sen and
Lt. Gen. S.K. Sinha. During the vital three days that the
Cabinet discussed the emergency, the emphasis was on legal
propriety. No effort seems to have been made to secure the
intelligence needed to counter the tribals. The First Sikhs
landed in the valley virtually blind. After securing the
airfield, their commander, Lt. Col. Ranjit Rai, rushed
towards Baramula in an effort to head off the invaders
before they could fan out into the Srinagar plain. But the
tribals far outnumbered his men and were better armed and
led than he had been briefed. He had to pull back to within
sixteen miles of the city and was killed while doing so -- the
second officer to be obliged to lead his men into action with
no idea of the size and intentions of the enemy. (Brigadier
Rajinder Singh of the Maharaja's forces was the first.)

That Srinagar was taken by surprise two days after the tribals attacked was bad enough. For New Delhi to lack all intelligence five days later, while the Indian Cabinet discussed the modalities of accession and Hari Singh bemoaned his fate, was inexcusable. From the start to the cease-fire at midnight of 31 December 1948/1 January 1949, the Kashmir campaign was dogged by lack of operational urgency in New Delhi.

For all the efficiency of the airlift, Srinagar-may not have been saved, and the Indian soldiers may have been forced to land at Jammu, were it not for the sacrifice of Baramula, a small town with a population of 14,000, thirty-five miles from Srinagar on the road from Uri. Baramula was sacked: the tribals did not distinguish among Muslims, Hindus or Sikhs, or the few English citizens there, for that matter. This town was visited by the *New York Times'* correspondent, Robert Trumbull, whose despatch appeared on 10 November 1947:

The city has been stripped of its wealth and young women before the tribesmen fled in terror, at midnight Friday, before the advancing Indian Army. Surviving residents estimate that 3,000 of their fellow townsmen including four Europeans and a retired British Army officer, known only as Colonel Dykes, and his pregnant wife, were slain. When the raiders rushed into town on October 26th, witnesses said: "One party of Masud tribesmen immediately scaled the walls of St Joseph Franciscan Hospital compound, and stormed the convent hospital and the little church. Four nuns and Colonel Dykes were shot immediately...."

Murder, rape, arson, loot and the bestial murder of a local National Conference worker, Maqbool Sherwani, who had rallied local sentiment against the invaders, provided further evidence that they had not come to liberate their fellow-Muslims. He was crucified before being shot,[20] to be remembered as hero.

This proved to be the turning point of the tribal campaign,

though it continued for more than a year. The rapacious halt in Baramula, when the road to Srinagar was open, delayed their advance just long enough to make it possible for the Indian troops to land. After Rai was killed, they put up a defensive screen five miles ahead of the airstrip, which was five miles from Srinagar. That was as far as the raiders got.

The political repercussions of the tribal rampage were anticipated by Mountbatten in a letter to Patel on 27 October, soon after the troops landed. He was uncertain whether they had arrived in time to save the city, but added:

> ...Fortunately the tribesmen are presumably out for loot, and since the Valley has a very small proportion of non-Muslims they are bound to loot and massacre their own co-religionists whilst the forces of India support Sheikh Abdullah against them. This, I feel, will gain us a political advantage, and if Sheikh Abdullah's forces can be rallied in this way the tribesmen can probably be repulsed before they have done too much looting.[21]

The Gurdaspur link proved crucial. Only light infantry weapons could be brought in by air. Heavier equipment, including armoured cars, and later tanks, were rushed up by road. The arrival of the armoured cars, especially, coupled with air strikes against the raiders by the IAF, broke their nerve. On 9 November a devastated Baramula was liberated; four days later Indian troops were in Uri and power was restored to Srinagar from Mahura. But now New Delhi took a decision with fateful consequences.

The British Commander of Delhi and East Punjab Command, Lt. Gen. Sir Dudley Russell, recommended an immediate advance to Muzaffarabad to demolish the two border bridges over the Kishanganga at Domel and Kohala and seal off the valley against further incursions from Pakistan. The Indian commanders on the scene were even keener. It was presumed at that stage that Pakistan's regular forces would not intervene if the Indian army took positions some distance away from the border, which could be patrolled by the Kashmir police.

But New Delhi decided otherwise. L.P. Sen, who was commanding the Brigade, was ordered to divert his column over the Haji Pir pass, to the relief of Poonch, which was under prolonged seige, with 40,000 refugees. Sen writes: "The order took me completely by surprise. I explained to Major General Kulwant Singh (in overall charge in Kashmir) that I had the enemy on the run and unless I kept up the pressure he would recover and come back, and instead of attacking him we would be attacked."[22] S.K. Sinha, then on Russell's staff, was equally unhappy with the decision. In his book, he wrote that the decision was taken at the highest governmental level,[23] and told this writer later that it had come from the Prime Minister.

Indian forces never advanced further, though much later, on 30 May 1948, Nehru wrote to Patel: "I hope within a week we might capture Domel and Muzaffarabad. That will be a major gain and it may be followed by our advance to Kohala." It was then, however, that Pakistan regulars were thrown into the battle. The cease-fire line was drawn just beyond Uri and the opportunity to seal off the valley from incursions by Pakistan, which continued into the future, was lost. It has been argued that apart from the refugees in Poonch that diverted the initial drive on Muzaffarabad, another consideration in Nehru's mind could have been his reluctance to enter territory beyond the influence of the National Conference and closer politically and culturally to Pakistan than the valley. But this is contradicted by his letter to Patel.

Non-military considerations also dictated India's reference of the Kashmir dispute to the UN Security Council when its forces had the upper hand in the valley. Urged by Mountbatten, infructuous talks were held with Pakistani leaders. In one session, Jinnah exposed his hand by offering "to call the whole thing off" if India pulled out of Kashmir.

Again, at Mountbatten's insistence, the untimely decision to approach the UN was taken on 22 December 1947. (The letter was despatched on 1 January 1948.) With New Delhi now committed to seeking an early peace and open to international pressures, military requirements were neglected. Field commanders did not get the reinforcements they wanted and the campaign was reduced virtually to a holding operation.

At that stage, the military situation favoured India. But by May 1948 regular Pakistan formations had entered the battle and the main objective of British officers was to avoid escalation of the fighting. In a letter to Nehru from London on 15 August 1948 pleading that India should not declare war, Mountbatten, no longer Governor-General, argued that "Pakistan is in no position even to declare war, since I happen to know that their military commanders have put it to them in writing that a declaration of war with India can only end in the inevitable and ultimate defeat of Pakistan". Yet, though this meant that India's military objectives were within reach, he insisted that it avoid war and leave the issue to the UN.

UN pressure resulted in a cease-fire exactly a year after the issue was submitted to the world body. Again, strategic concerns were not considered by New Delhi. The date was fixed without consulting its military commanders. The cease-fire prevented, for instance, the recapture of a dangerous bulge on the Uri-Poonch road, including the Haji Pir pass (which figured in another war), that gave Pakistan control of the only road to the Poonch area from Uri and Srinagar. Sinha recalled that his command received warning orders from Army Headquarters in New Delhi as late as the afternoon of 31 December 1948 that a cease-fire was in the offing, followed by executive orders for a cease-fire on all fronts from midnight. They had a sleepless night transmitting these orders together with further instructions.[24]

Sheikh Abdullah, then Prime Minister of Jammu and

Kashmir, complained that the armistice was declared "without consulting us or taking the army into confidence."[25] The direct communication link between the British Commanders-in-Chief of India and Pakistan survived the strain of war. It was used to bring the war to an end. New Delhi took the initiative. On his Government's instructions, General Boucher proposed that he would cease fire with immediate effect if General Gracey responded. He did, and the first round of fighting between India and Pakistan ended on the night of 31 December 1948.

Chapter XI

The Albatross

$\boldsymbol{J}$innah may have lost Junagadh and the best part of Kashmir before he died, but he had hung an albatross around India's neck. Try as New Delhi might, it was unable to get round the commitment to plebiscite made to justify taking over Junagadh when its Nawab preferred Pakistan. The religious composition of the people of Kashmir and its geographical position adjoining both Dominions made the precedent unavoidable. When Hari Singh, escaping from the tribal raiders to his palace in Jammu, reluctantly sought to accede to India, Mountbatten, as Governor-General, introduced a proviso in his letter of acceptance, dated 27 October 1947, destined to haunt India long into the future:

> Consistently [sic] with their policy that when the issue of accession has been the subject of dispute the question of accession should be decided in accordance with the wishes of the people of the State, it is my Government's wish that as soon as law and order have been restored in Kashmir and her soil cleared of the raider; the question of State's accession should be settled by reference to the people. Meanwhile, in response to Your Highness's appeal for military aid, action has been taken today to send troops of the Indian Army to Kashmir to help your own forces to defend your territory and to

protect the lives, property and honour of your people. My Government and I note with satisfaction that Your Highness has decided to invite Sheikh Abdullah to work with your Prime Minister.[1]

There was no mention of any reference to the people in Hari Singh's formal Instrument of Accession; nor in the eloquent appeal he had penned the previous evening. New Delhi later made much use of the unconditionality of his accession to maintain that its international legality was unquestionable. On the issue of reference to the people, the escape route indicated by Nehru in his talks with Liaquat Ali on the Junagadh issue – that general elections could also be a test – was attempted. But Mountbatten made this difficult by proposing a plebiscite under UN auspices to Jinnah at a meeting in Lahore called by the Pakistan Governor-General on 1 November. Nehru had been reluctant to go because he objected to the offensive language of a Pakistan statement on the eve of the meeting and took ill. Possibly he was influenced by Patel's comment: "For the Prime Minister to go crawling to Mr Jinnah when we were the stronger side and in the right would never be forgiven by the people of India." Mountbatten proceeded to Lahore on his own and laid the foundations of a commitment that India would regret.[2]

The next step involving the UN came a month after Indian troops had been ordered to fly to Srinagar. Mountbatten continuing his role as neutral middle-man, managed to get Nehru to confer with Liaquat Ali in the face of Nehru's objections to the Pakistan Prime Minister calling Sheikh Abdullah a quisling and charging New Delhi with trying to eliminate the whole Muslim population of Kashmir. The outcome entailed proposals described as a basis for discussion, initially disfavoured by Nehru, but which eventually became the approach of the UN. The key proposals were:

Pakistan should persuade the 'Azad' Kashmir to cease fighting, the tribal raiders to withdraw and prevent

further incursions; India should withdraw the bulk of
its forces; and the UN should be asked to send a
commission to hold a plebiscite and suggest steps to
ensure that it was fair and unfettered.[3]

Mountbatten's drive to involve the UN in Kashmir was
briefly checked when the Cabinet received reports of fresh
concentrations of would-be raiders on the State borders and
of further atrocities in tribal-held Kashmir. Its reaction was
to suggest enhanced military operations and to propose a
demilitarised belt along the State's border with West Punjab.
Any movement within this belt would be attacked from the
air, after due notice. Mountbatten had the proposal referred
to the three British Commanders-in-Chief and got them to
reject it as unfeasible. He soon returned to his primary
objective. Nehru and Liaquat met again in Lahore on
9 December. Mountbatten's next report to the King reflects
his patronising above-the-squabbling attitude:

> The first two hours or so were spent (at my instance)
> in mutual recriminations -- which, as a method of
> clearing the air, served a good purpose.... So the talk
> went on, round and round, on the whole very friendly,
> but with occasional outbursts, such as when Pandit
> Nehru flared up and declared that the only solution was
> with the sword, and that he would "throw up his Prime
> Ministership, and take a rifle himself, and lead the men
> of India against the invasion...". Eventually, after trying
> every means I knew to find common ground between the
> two parties, I realised that the deadlock was complete
> and the only way out now was to bring in some third
> party in some capacity or other. For this purpose I
> suggested [not for the first time] that the United
> Nations Organisation be called upon.[4]

Considerations of furthering British policy as well,
however, may not have been entirely absent from
Mountbatten's mind. His press secretary, Alan Campbell-
Johnson, had returned from a visit to London where he met
those concerned with the subcontinent and influencing its

affairs. Among them was the Commonwealth Secretary, Philip Noel-Baker, who later strongly criticised India in the Security Council. Reporting to Mountbatten, Campbell-Johnson said that Noel-Baker suggested that it was through international agencies that "British help and influence both in India and elsewhere might be most effectively brought to bear".[5]

Differences between Nehru and Mountbatten were now sharpening. Mountbatten defended his stance on the UN and plebiscite in a long letter to Nehru, of which the kernel was:

> When first I suggested bringing UNO into this dispute, it was in order to achieve the object I have quoted above – to stop the fighting and to stop it as soon as possible.... Surely the main object should be to bring UNO here at the earliest possible moment – to come out and deal with the business and help to stop the fighting, within a matter of days? Can we do nothing to hasten this object?[6]

Nehru was angry but polite. He made it plain that only after the raiders were driven out of the valley and peace and order established would the question of plebiscite arise. Pakistan's involvement in the invasion was evident. Areas adjoining Kashmir had become a military training ground for the invaders:

> The only inference to draw from this [Nehru concluded] is that the invasion of Kashmir is not an accidental affair resulting from the fanaticism or exuberance of the tribesmen, but a well-organised business with the backing of the State.... We have in effect to deal with a State carrying on an informal war, but nevertheless a war. The present objective is Kashmir. The next objective is Patiala, East Punjab and Delhi. "On to Delhi" is the cry all over West Punjab.

In the circumstances, he proposed two parallel lines of action. One was to approach the UN, which must have pleased the Governor-General. The phrasing of the other disturbed him considerably:

> Complete military preparations [should be made] to meet any possible contingency that might arise. If grave danger threatens us in Kashmir or elsewhere on the West Punjab frontier then we must not hesitate to march through Pakistan territory towards the bases[7] [a strategy that Prime Minister Lal Bahadur Shastri implemented in 1965].

With his influence over Nehru waning, Mountbatten lost his composure. He telegraphed Prime Minister Clement Attlee to fly out to prevent what he saw as an immediate threat of war between the two Dominions, which Attlee declined to do because he saw no specific role to play. In reply to a letter from Nehru (who had earlier informed him when rushing troops to Kashmir) Attlee urged caution. It was then that New Delhi forwarded its complaint to the UN,[8] in an effort to combine firmness with respect for international opinion. But the move was made without thinking through its consequences and the great power interests that would come into play.

Far from being dubbed aggressor, Pakistan was given equal status with India and benefited from the prolonged debate in the Security Council. The urgency India placed on stopping Pakistan from aiding the tribal invaders was overlooked; instead the Council focussed on how to arrange for a plebiscite, with it even being suggested that India pull out and a "neutral" administration be installed in Kashmir. India's representatives relied on moral rather than political arguments and were at sea at the UN, in contrast to Pakistan's Sir Mohammed Zafrullah Khan. Against the background of partition and its massacres, widely reported abroad, it was not difficult for Zafrullah to paint the subcontinent into a green Muslim Pakistan and a saffron Hindu India, in which the eclectic iridescence of Kashmir was obscured but its Muslim majority could be projected. Global Anglo-American strategies designed to construct

their own version of an iron curtain around the Soviet
Union and Communist China, into which Pakistan was
drawn, influenced the Security Council.

The Indian complaint to the Security Council under
Article 35 of the UN Charter detailed the assistance given
by Pakistan to the raiders and warned:

> ... The Government of India request the Security Council
> to call upon Pakistan to put an end immediately to the
> giving of such assistance, which is an act of aggression
> against India. If Pakistan does not do so, the
> Government of India may be compelled, in self-defence,
> to enter Pakistan territory, in order to take military
> action against the invaders. The matter is therefore of
> extreme urgency and calls for immediate action by the
> Security Council for avoiding a breach of international
> peace.

Nehru's threat to enter Pakistan territory had little
effect. Pakistan was not deterred. After first denying
complicity in the invasion, it later admitted sending in
regular troops. The Security Council took its time. A
commission landed in Kashmir six months later. No
condemnation of Pakistan followed. The focus shifted to
arrangements for a plebiscite regulated by the UN, the start
of a long, tortuous debate. Whether Nehru's threat was
serious or not, the reference to the UN had ensured that it
could not be implemented while the UN was seized of the
issue, as Pakistan as well as the members of the Security
Council must have realised. For India, the unnecessary
internationalisation of the dispute was a serious setback and
an obstacle to political reconciliation in Kashmir.

Exchanges between Nehru and Attlee became
progressively less cordial after Nehru's first telegram on
25 October informing the British Prime Minister of the
serious threat posed by the tribal invasion. He emphasised
the havoc created by the raiders in the valley and the
danger posed to Srinagar if they were not stopped. But
Attlee continued to advise against Indian armed intervention

and expressed concern over the possibility of it leading to "an open military conflict" between the two Dominions.[9]

Nehru was livid when the views Noel-Baker had expressed at the UN, particularly in a conversation with Abdullah, who was one of India's delegates, were reported to him. On 8 February 1948, he virtually ticked off Mountbatten, who cabled Attlee in a tone of unaccustomed mortification: "Any prestige that I may have previously had with my Government has of course been largely lost by my insisting that they should make a reference to the UNO with the assurance that they would get a square deal there."

Nehru then cabled Attlee in chilling tones. Noel-Baker had told Abdullah, he said, that India's charges that Pakistan had given assistance and encouragement to the raiders were untrue and that he was satisfied that the Pakistan Government was blameless. "You will forgive me if I say frankly," Nehru warned, "that [the] attitude revealed by this conversation cannot but prejudice continuance of friendly relations between India and the UK."[10]

Although London was the prime mover in India's discomfiture at the UN, Nehru saw Washington as also keen to support Pakistan for its own strategic objectives. As early as 17 January 1948, he cabled Gopalaswami Ayyangar, who was leading India's delegation to the UN, that diplomatic reports suggested that if Pakistan was willing to cooperate with the US in providing military facilities against the Soviet Union, Washington might support it on Kashmir. This came true when Pakistan became a member of both the CENTO and SEATO Anglo-American military pacts. But Nehru managed to combine awareness of *realpolitik* with continuing naïveté. His letter to his sister, Vijayalakshmi Pandit, on 16 February indicates the process of learning in its simplest terms:

> The USA and the UK have played a dirty role, the UK probably being the main actor behind the scenes. I have expressed myself strongly to Attlee about it and I propose to make it perfectly clear to the UK Government

what we think about it. The time for soft and
meaningless talk has passed.[11]

Indo-British relations never recovered fully. Nehru told
Mountbatten that he bitterly regretted going to the UN. In
one of his last reports to the King as Governor-General,
Mountbatten said Nehru was shocked to find that power
politics and not ethics were ruling the UN; that it was being
run by the Americans; that Noel Baker had been nearly as
hostile as them. The belief in India was that the United
Kingdom wished to appease the cause of Muslim solidarity
in the Middle East and the US wanted to rehabilitate their
position with the Arabs after advocating the partition of
Palestine.[12] Mountbatten left India on 21 June 1948.

*T*he uncertainty aroused by the commitment to plebiscite
had serious consequences within the State, especially in
Jammu. In 1947, Muslims comprised 60 per cent of the
population of Jammu (as against over 90 per cent in the
valley). The communal rioting in Punjab had spilled over
into bordering areas of Jammu, with non-Muslims fleeing
into Jammu and Muslims into West Punjab. The uprising
in Poonch, which the State troops tried to put down
ruthlessly, was a continuing sore. Muslims became suspect
in much of Jammu; many were forced to flee across the
border. The Governments of Pakistan and Kashmir had
exchanged angry notes, virtually accusing each other of
complicity in these outrages.

The situation did not improve after accession. On 5 and
6 November two convoys carrying 5000 Muslims from
Jammu city to the Pakistan border were ambushed by
Hindu and Sikh refugees from Pakistan, with heavy
casualties. The Indian troops guarding the second convoy
beat off the main attack. On 7 November, Nehru expressed
his frustration to his secretary, Dwarkanath Kachru, who
was liaising for him in Kashmir:

We are all agreed here that the Maharaja's attitude has been bad and is bound to lead to trouble. The attempt to evacuate Muslims from Jammu was an amazingly stupid thing to do.... I am quite clear that the Maharaja is played out and has no understanding of the situation. Nevertheless in the present legal context he can create difficulties. These should be avoided.[13]

On 9 November, Kanwar Dalip Singh, who was appointed to the newly created office of Agent to the Government of India in Jammu and Kashmir, reported on the tragedy:

The refugees from West Punjab and of the local villages are extremely bitter. It is impossible to control their lust for vengeance.... The troops, the [Indian] Brigadier assures me, are unable to give protection to Muslim citizens in Jammu city. The Muslims were concentrated in two *mohallas* (localities).... Shots used to be exchanged between them and the Hindus round about and much alarm and panic caused. It was in these circumstances that it was decided to evacuate them to Pakistan. I went to their camp today and one man came up to me and said that he, a member of the National Conference and a loyal subject of His Highness was being treated the same as a [Muslim] Leaguer. I believe he was telling the truth. But I can think of no method of keeping back selected persons and giving them protection from Hindus and Sikhs in the city....[14]

Abdullah had no doubt that the Jammu killings "were organised by the Maharaja, his bigoted wife and Mahajan. In this hate intrigue, [Maharani] Tara Devi played an important role. She was under the influence of a mysterious guru, Sant Dev [also mentioned by Karan Singh], described by some people as the Rasputin of Kashmir."[15]

To Gandhi, as to Nehru, Kashmir represented a model of

intercommunal amity to be held up to the rest of India. After the horrors of partition and its aftermath, he saw hope, as we have seen, that the valley "would become a beacon light in this benighted subcontinent". And Sheikh Abdullah became the epitome of a secular leader. Gandhi became involved with the Kashmir campaign even before the troops took off for Srinagar (Nehru had informed him in advance) and, despite his commitment to non-violence, did not object to armed force being deployed to counter tribal savagery. He kept in close touch with the developments. Brigadier L.P. Sen, for instance, was asked to give him a personal briefing before taking off from Delhi to command the forces protecting Srinagar.[16] Thus he was able to project the vital issues involved at his public and prayer meetings far more effectively than the official media. Though he spoke in Hindustani, Gandhi invariably issued an authorised English translation to the press to ensure that his message got through. It was broadcast over All India Radio.

Soon after the leading contingents of the troops were despatched on 27 October 1947, he explained the circumstances in which Kashmir had acceded to India and the commitment to a plebiscite. He repeatedly stressed the great role of "Sheikh Sahib, who was affectionately called Sher-e-Kashmir, the Lion of Kashmir". Gandhi described the havoc caused by the tribal raiders, who must have been encouraged by Pakistan. It was right, in the circumstances, for India to send troops. He depicted a sacrificial outcome that seemed possible then to convey the urgency as well as the lessons to be drawn from the situation:

> He would not shed a tear if the Union force was wiped out like the Spartans, bravely defending Kashmir, nor would he mind the Sheikh Saheb and his Muslim, Hindu and Sikh comrades, men and women, dying at their post in defence of Kashmir. That would be a glorious example to the rest of India. Such heroic defence would infect the whole of India and we would forget that Hindus, Muslims and Sikhs were ever enemies.[17]

Gandhi was quick to protest against the campaign against Muslims in Jammu. He realised the political problems it would create for Abdullah, who was now entitled Head of the Emergency Administration, but shared powers with State Prime Minister Mahajan. Abdullah had visited Jammu to assuage Muslim sentiment. On 27 November, Gandhi told his prayer audience that though there were just a handful of Hindus and Sikhs in the valley, Abdullah took pains to carry them along. What had happened in Jammu was shameful for Hindus and Sikhs. Yet Abdullah did not lose his balance and his visit to Jammu had borne good fruit. He pointed out that Kashmir's link with India lay through a strip of territory (the Gurdaspur link) running through East Punjab in which Muslims felt unsafe. It was the duty of the East Punjab Government and the Centre to see that the land route was safe for transit and trade.

The next day, Gandhi took Abdullah to a meeting to celebrate Guru Nanak's birth anniversary in Delhi, where Sikhs had earlier taken the lead in attacking Muslims. It was a tense occasion. Gandhi's words, gentle as ever, capture the event:

> You see Sheikh Abdullah Saheb with me. I was disinclined to bring him with me, for I know that there is a great gulf between the Hindus and the Sikhs on one side, and the Muslims on the other. But the Sheikh Saheb, known as the Lion of Kashmir, although a pucca Muslim, has won the hearts of both, by making them forget that there is any difference between the three. He has not been embittered. Even though in Jammu recently, the Muslims were killed by the Hindus and Sikhs, he went to Jammu and invited the evil-doers to forget the past and repent over the evil they had done. The Hindus and Sikhs of Jammu listened to him. I am glad, therefore, that you are receiving the two of us with cordiality.[18]

Friction between Abdullah and Mahajan, who was backed by the Maharaja, continued in Kashmir, always threatening to take on a communal form. On 25 December, Gandhi intervened and touched off a furore: he publicly supported Abdullah and held the Maharaja responsible for the killing of Muslims in Jammu. The authorised version of his speech was in the third person:

> He had heard of the murders of numberless Muslims and of the abduction of Muslim girls in Jammu. The Maharaja of Kashmir must own the responsibility. The Dogra troops were under his direct control. He had not yet become the mere constitutional head and, therefore, must be held responsible for all the acts, good or bad, of the people under his rule.... The speaker would advise the Maharaja to step aside along with his minister, in view of what had happened in Jammu and give the fullest opportunity to Sheikh Abdullah Saheb and the people of Kashmir to deal with the situation.

Four days later, Gandhi replied to the criticism that his speech had evoked, in a written address read out at his prayer meeting. There was a touch of sarcasm in what he wrote; yet the address went to the root of what was at stake in Kashmir:

> I have been lately taken to task for daring to say what I have stated about Kashmir and the Maharaja.... I have simply tendered advice which, I suppose, the lowliest can do.... He is a Hindu prince, having under his sway a very large majority of Muslims. The invaders have called their invasion a holy war for the defence of the Muslims reported to be ground down under Hindu misrule. Sheikh Abdullah Saheb was called by the ruler to his task at a critical period.... It must be evident to the outsider, as it is to me, that Kashmir must be lost to the invaders, otherwise called the raiders, if Sheikh Abdullah Saheb's efforts to hold together the Muslims and the minority fail....

Then came the heart of the message, encapsulating the ultimate test of success or failure:

It is on Kashmir soil that Islam and Hinduism are being weighed now. If they pull their weight correctly, and in the same direction, the chief actors will cover themselves with glory and nothing can move them from their joint credit. My sole hope and prayer is that Kashmir would become a beacon light in this benighted subcontinent.[19]

Gandhi's near-despair at continuing threats to Muslims in and around Delhi led him to undertake his last fast on 13 January 1948, which ended with prominent leaders of all religions pledging to allow Muslims to live in peace. But he paid the price with his own life on 30 January. His assassination by a Hindu fanatic for protecting Muslims aroused doubts in Kashmir about the wisdom of being tied to India. According to Abdullah, "the Maharaja openly sided with the RSS and dispersed the condolence rally organised by the National Conference. RSS volunteers distributed sweets in Jammu. According to eye-witnesses, trays full of sweets arrived at the Palace gate."[20]

As Minister of States and Home Affairs, and Deputy Prime Minister, Sardar Patel had some responsibility for Kashmir, though major decisions were taken by Nehru, a situation that sometimes caused friction and once provoked a decision to resign. The issue was sensitive from the start. As early as 8 October 1947, when contingency preparations had begun for a possible conflict in Kashmir, Patel reacted sharply in a letter to Nehru to a remark from Kachru (Nehru's secretary) which he saw as a reflection on himself: "I do not think that anything which could have been done in Kashmir has been left undone by me; nor am I aware of any difference between you and me on matters of policy relating to Kashmir. Still it is most unfortunate that persons down below should think there is a gulf between us. It is also distressing to me."[21] But Nehru depended on Patel's excellent management skills to get decisions implemented.

He found him particularly useful in dealing with Hari Singh who found Patel more sympathetic than Nehru.

It was Patel who persuaded Hari Singh to release Abdullah from prison. On 21 October, Patel argued with Mahajan, his own protégé, but as inflexible as Kak, that it was essential to secure Abdullah's cooperation. When, as a condition of accession, the Sheikh was inducted into the State administration, Patel tried to pacify Mahajan who was describing him as a dictator. When it finally became clear that Abdullah and Mahajan could not work together, he suggested on 10 December that Mahajan resign. But Mahajan launched into an attack on Abdullah's "Hitlerian methods" and "gangster rule", the first shots in a long campaign.[22] And Hari Singh insisted that his Prime Minister retained his confidence and he was "not going to appease anyone" by letting him go. Not till March 1948 did Mahajan actually go, after considerable pressure from Nehru and Gopalaswami Ayyangar, who, as Minister without Portfolio, had been asked by Nehru to liaise with Kashmir (much to Patel's displeasure).

A tiff between Patel and Gopalaswami snowballed into a Cabinet crisis towards the end of December 1947, indicating differences below the surface which had inevitable repercussions on Kashmir. Patel objected to Gopalaswami not going through his Ministry in making arrangements for Kashmir's request for motor vehicles. Gopalaswami replied that if all he was to do was to act as a post office, he would "disconnect myself and my Ministry from all matters relating to Kashmir, including the negotiations now in progress connected with the setting up of an Interim Government there". He sent a copy to the Prime Minister.

Patel tried to make up the next day by explaining that his objection concerned ordinary transactions between "the Kashmir authorities and the Government of India. There was no question of its affecting in any way the conduct of negotiations over which you are engaged; that the Prime Minister is already managing with your collaboration and in consultation with me wherever necessary in supersession of the normal ministerial responsibility." But it was already too late: the copy of Gopalaswami's letter had been seen by Nehru.

On 23 December, Nehru wrote angrily to Patel:

> I do not appreciate the principle which presumably the States Ministry has in view in regard to its work. That Ministry, or any other Ministry, is not an *imperium in imperio*, jealous of its sovereignty in certain domains and working in isolation from the rest.... The present issue relates to Kashmir. This raises all manner of connected issues – international, military and others – which are beyond the competence of the States Ministry as such. That is why it has to be considered by the Cabinet as a whole frequently and by various Ministers separately or together. And that is why I have to take personal interest in this matter as P.M. to bring about co-ordination in our various activities... I do not understand why the States Ministry should intervene and come in the way of arrangements being made [for sending vehicles to Kashmir]. All this was done at my instance and I do not propose to abdicate my functions in regard to matters for which I consider myself responsible.

Patel drafted a reply the same evening expressing the "considerable pain" Nehru's letter had caused. He added:

> In any case, your letter makes it clear to me that I must not or at least cannot continue as Member of Government and hence I am hereby tendering my resignation. I am grateful to you for the courtesy and consideration shown to me during the period of office which was a period of considerable strain.[23]

The letter technically remained a draft. According to V. Shankar, Patel's secretary, the resignation went no further due to personal discussions between Nehru and Patel.[24] But that was to avert an immediate crisis, for neither side climbed down. Later that evening, Nehru responded expressing regret at having caused Patel pain, but insisting that "it seems that our approaches are different, however much we may respect each other. If I am to continue as Prime Minister, I cannot have my freedom restricted...". Patel concluded the dignified exchange next day by rejecting any thought of Nehru's resignation, assuring him of his continued help but making the point that he could not continue "as an ineffective colleague."[25] It was a polite standoff, serious enough to be referred to Gandhi, who played for time. A month later, the crisis was dissolved in the tears they shed as they embraced each other over Gandhi's body.

Even so, Patel again felt it necessary to consider resigning when the Home Ministry was blamed for not giving enough protection to Gandhi. Rejecting any such suggestion, Nehru wrote in a letter full of emotion, "... I have been greatly distressed by the persistence of whispers and rumours about you and me, magnifying out of all proportion any differences we may have.... Anyway, in the crisis that we have to face now after Bapu's death, I think it is my duty, and if I may venture to say yours also, for us to face it together as friends and colleagues."[26]

Nevertheless, it was a meeting of hearts rather than minds. Differences remained on many issues, including the role of Sheikh Abdullah.

Chapter XII

Rival Loyalties

*T*he only person who can deliver the goods in Kashmir is Abdullah.... I have a high opinion of his integrity and his general balance of mind. He has striven hard and succeeded very largely in keeping communal peace. He may make any number of mistakes in minor matters, but I think he is likely to be right in regard to major decisions. But the real point is that no satisfactory way can be found in Kashmir except through Sheikh Abdullah.

This was the central thrust of a letter from Nehru to Hari Singh two weeks after Kashmir had acceded to India. The Maharaja was unhappy about transferring powers to Abdullah, to which he was committed by the terms of accession. Nehru had to remind him that the "great changes" that had occurred in Kashmir could not be ignored "and the path of wisdom is to recognise them and adapt oneself to them."[1] Hari Singh was not persuaded. He countered Nehru's support for Abdullah by promoting Hindu communal reaction against the special status given to Kashmir which threatened the privileges that Hindus had enjoyed. This made Abdullah and the Muslims of the valley question the value of the link with India; which, in turn, embarrassed Nehru and paved the way for the breach in their long friendship.

Nehru has been criticised for hinging his Kashmir policy on Abdullah. But it was Abdullah who had come to symbolise the secular principle that buttressed India's claim to Kashmir and whose example Nehru, and Gandhi, projected to the rest of the country. Nehru had fostered their friendship with an eye to drawing Kashmir towards India. In the context of the stated Congress policy that popular opinion was an essential element in determining accession of princely States, and especially after Junagadh, Abdullah's support for accession was crucial. Kashmir had not thrown up any secular leader of equivalent stature. Nehru had no option but to back him; until he had to do without him.

Abdullah's primary loyalty was to the valley. He reflected his people's deep-rooted resentment of exploitation by outsiders, including the Dogra dynasty based in Jammu. His first preference was independence. When forced by the tribal invasion, he opted for India. He knew that Kashmir would be given more autonomy, and his socialist views would receive more sympathy, in Nehru's India than in Jinnah's Pakistan. In spite of the communal killings accompanying and following partition, he hoped that Gandhi's influence would help inoculate New Delhi against Hindu communalism. In any case, his campaign against the two-nation theory and criticism of Jinnah ruled out joining Pakistan.

When Gandhi was assassinated, Abdullah felt he had only Nehru to rely on. Though they were close friends, he was aware of Nehru's tendency to compromise. He himself was committed to social revolution and was determined to implement the Naya Kashmir programme, unlike the manifestos adopted by the Congress. He wanted to cut the links with the past, represented by Maharaja Hari Singh, and was not satisfied with the gradualism of a transfer of power on the model of the transfer from British to Indian hands in New Delhi. When, for instance, he wanted to end *jagirdari* without payment of compensation, Nehru urged caution in view of the situation in other States. But this was precisely Abdullah's justification for restricting to a

minimum the areas in which Kashmir was subject to New
Delhi's supervision and control. For him Kashmir's interests
were paramount; for Nehru the national interest came first.
When they clashed, a breach became inevitable.
Thus, their friendship was subject to severe stresses, but
endured within the parameters of their political compulsions. When in February 1948, Pakistan's representative at
the UN, Zafrullah Khan, suggested that it was his
friendship with Nehru that influenced his decision to join
India, Abdullah replied: "I feel honoured that such a great
man claims me as his friend. And he happens to belong to
my country; he is also a Kashmiri, and blood is thicker than
water.... But that does not mean that because of his
friendship I am going to betray the millions of my people
who have suffered with me...."[2] Abdullah was critical of
Nehru when he was dismissed and jailed but stayed at the
Prime Minister's house when freed and was sent on a
mission to Pakistan during Nehru's last days. He rushed
back to be present at Nehru's cremation on 27 May 1964. A
diplomatic observer noted: "Before the fire had died down
Sheikh Abdullah leapt on the platform and, weeping un-
restrainedly, threw flowers onto the flames."[3]

When Abdullah was appointed Head of the Emergency
Administration in Kashmir, he stepped into an improvised
office which would have taxed the expertise of a skilled
administrator and the finesse of a diplomat. He was neither.
And the cards were stacked against him. His designation
was devised to fulfil Nehru's demand that he and the
National Conference be involved in the Government of the
State. It was also important in preparation for a plebiscite,
which was expected to be held early. He was impatient to
demonstrate the change in administration by giving
Muslims the jobs and the land that they had been denied.
But Maharaja Hari Singh was still Head of State, with his
own Prime Minister (Mehr Chand Mahajan) and other

ministers. He had been forced to appoint Abdullah by Nehru
as a prerequisite for military help when the tribal raiders
were menacing Srinagar, and resented and distrusted him
from the start. And Abdullah continued to see Hari Singh
as a Hindu communalist, carrying on the Dogra tradition
of oppressing the Muslims. Yet, the dyarchic arrangement
assumed that they would function in harmony.

While Abdullah was conversant with the problems and
aspirations of the valley, he knew little of those of the other
provinces still under the Maharaja's dominion: Jammu and
Ladakh. The Muslims of Jammu did not share the valley's
eclecticism and had mostly supported the rival Muslim
Conference that favoured Pakistan, and Abdullah had a
limited following among Hindus and Sikhs. In Buddhist
Ladakh, he had no following at all. Nor did he show much
concern for these areas, except when they affected his
position in the valley; as when the eviction of Muslims from
Jammu created doubts in Kashmir. Residents of Jammu and
Ladakh responded by questioning Srinagar's right to
dominate the State.

After fleeing Srinagar, Hari Singh established himself
in Jammu town, the seat of the Dogra dynasty. And when
Abdullah was in town, Jammu became the site of their
clashes. Kanwar Dalip Singh, who had reported to New
Delhi on the Jammu killings, provided a telling account of
the confusion and tension in Jammu on 7 November 1947:

> His Highness is extremely bitter.... The Prime Minister
> [Mahajan] is a man of ability and straightforwardness.
> He is however an Arya Samajist with all the mentality
> and fanaticism of that body.... H.H. personally dislikes
> Sheikh Sahib [Abdullah] and Sheikh Sahib's endeavours
> to maintain authority in Jammu without reference to
> H.H. are merely causing friction and tension.... I should
> also like clear instructions as to what is meant by the
> Kashmir Government. I would suggest that where
> Sheikh Sahib is concerned, he should be mentioned by
> name; where H.H. is concerned, he should be mentioned
> by name; and where the concurrence of both is desired,

the phrase "Kashmir Government" might be used.... It
is not always possible to contact Sheikh Sahib on the
phone and everyone here says the phone is tapped.[4]

On 1 December, Nehru again wrote to Hari Singh,
spelling out the basic facets of India's Kashmir policy (and
several times thereafter for the Maharaja had his own
ideas). The letter raised issues that continued to be relevant
far into the future:

Even if military forces held Kashmir for a while, a later
consequence might be a strong reaction against this.
Essentially, therefore, this is a problem of psychological
approach to the mass of the people and of making them
feel that they will be benefited by being within the
Indian Union. If the average Muslim feels that he has
no safe or secure place in the Union then obviously he
will look elsewhere. Our basic policy must keep this in
view, or else we fail....[5]

But the deep-rooted conflict could not be resolved by
words of advice, however wise. Abdullah and Hari Singh
fought over distribution of Government departments,
especially the State forces and the creation of an armed
home guard (which would mean arming valley Muslims for
the first time). Appointment of Muslims to senior posts, for
which they were not always formally qualified, became
another issue. Abdullah continued to dub the Maharaja
communal. The response came from Mahajan, who
contrasted Abdullah's present stand with a letter he had
written from jail on 26 September 1947 pledging loyalty to
the Maharaja (after which he was released). Mahajan
complained to Patel from Jammu on 24 December:

He [Abdullah] is actively canvassing support of Muslim
Conference leader [Ghulam] Abbas who is in jail and
with whom he is having interviews. Practically in all
matters he is ignoring and bypassing H.H. and is daily
showing communal tendencies.... On hearing from you

I will send you some instances of complete misrule and maladministration on fascist lines.[6]

According to others, Abdullah was trying to win over Abbas in an attempt to gain support from Jammu Muslims, but this was interpreted as communal by Mahajan.[7] Abbas was subsequently released from jail and sent to Pakistan, where he became leader of the 'Azad' Kashmir Government. Mahajan himself was soon a focus of controversy. Nehru had heard that the arms (which had belatedly landed) meant for Bakshi Ghulam Mohammad's (Abdullah's deputy and party manager) home guards had been distributed to the RSS. On 30 December, Nehru wrote to Patel: "I am inclined to think that Mahajan sympathises with these activities and perhaps helps them." Patel could not have been too pleased with this allegation against his protégé, but confined his reply to saying that Mahajan was anxious to quit Kashmir but Hari Singh would not let him go. As for the arms, neither Bakshi nor anyone else in Jammu had informed him of RSS activities and there seemed no evidence of them.[8]

The foundations of future tragedy were now laid. Hari Singh dug his heels in, but eventually had to let Mahajan go; and later left the State himself, handing over office to his son, Karan Singh. However, the damage had been done. The forces of Hindu nationalism, financed by the Maharaja and spearheaded by the RSS, found deep roots in Jammu, while leaders of Hindu parties elsewhere in India began to take interest in Kashmir. Muslims in the valley became uneasy with the ties with New Delhi, where Nehru seemed increasingly isolated in his commitment to secularism. Their fears were voiced by Abdullah who responded by laying greater stress on Kashmir's autonomy, which provided fresh ammunition to his critics, thus initiating a vicious circle. He also began to secretly consult Western diplomats, primarily American, about the possibility of independence.

Nehru did all that he could to sustain Abdullah against Hari Singh, sharing as they did the same commitment to secularism and social justice. The Prime Minister worked through Gopalaswami Ayyangar rather than Patel. It was Gopalaswami who made it clear to the Maharaja that Mahajan was no longer acceptable to New Delhi. Hari Singh's response was as brief as the note to him had been prolix. It was conveyed in a telegram: "Sorry cannot agree." This was too much even for the mild-mannered, diplomatic Gopalaswami, who had once worked for Hari Singh as Prime Minister. "I cannot proceed further with this foolish man," he wrote to Patel enclosing a copy of the telegram, "not having any powers to put pressure on him. I thought I could persuade him, but I have not succeeded."[9]

*N*ehru's concern over the distribution of arms had been conveyed to the Maharaja. Hari Singh's reply to Patel on New Year's Day revealed the depths of his fears and frustration. He was not taken into confidence, he complained, but "according to rumours I hear the supply of modern arms to the Home Guards is dangerous. I also hear the raiders snatch them away and they [presumably Home Guards] are wholly unfit to handle arms". Then came his real objection, "obviously a great effort to create a rival army in the State is being made". And, further, "this seems to me to be only deep propaganda in disguise to drive me to desperation by being bullied right and left. Already there is no rule of law here and if the present policy continues it will be worse". Patel replied to Nehru a week later, stating that according to inquiries by Mahajan (on whom he still depended), the arms had been given to Bakshi and not to the RSS.[10]

Towards the end of January 1948, Hari Singh's frustration spilled over into reconsidering his accession to India. On 25 January, he wrote to Patel complaining that he was being ignored in India's reference to the UN Security Council even though Kashmir's accession could not have been legalised without him. He was also the final authority to decide on the modalities of plebiscite. No commitment should be made to the Council without consulting him.

An even more disturbing letter was delivered on the last day of the month. It began with strong criticism of the Indian troops for failing to retake more territory than they had, especially in Jammu province: "the name of the Indian Army is getting into the mud". He then referred to the possibility "that the State will eventually have to accede to Pakistan as a result of what the Security Council will decide," whereas he had hoped "the State would remain acceded to the Union and my position and that of my dynasty would remain secure." Then came the punchline:

> Sometimes I feel that I should withdraw the accession that I have made to the Indian Union. The Union only provisionally accepted the accession and if the Union cannot recover back [sic] our territory and is going eventually to agree to the decision of the Security Council which may result in handing us over to Pakistan then there is no point in sticking to the accession of the State to the Indian Union.... There is an alternative possible for me and that is to withdraw the accession and that may kill the reference to the UNO because the Indian Union will have no right to continue the proceedings before the Council if the accession is withdrawn. The result may be a return to the position the State held before accession.

Whether Hari Singh meant this seriously or not, his letter indicated a reawakened desire for independence and also his intention to put counterpressure on New Delhi. Yet when he pictured himself leading his army into battle, it was evident he was living in a lost world. Recalling his honorific service as member of Britain's War Cabinet during the Second World War (he liked appearing in the uniform of Lt. General, a rank conferred on him by the British Government in return for his monetary contributions to the war), the Maharaja said he was prepared to take over command of his forces and those of the Indian army (as

volunteers since the State would no longer be part of India)
to evict the raiders. He was confident that his leadership
"would certainly hearten my people and the troops. I know
my country much better than any of your generals will know
it even during the next several months or years and I am
prepared to take the venture boldly rather then merely keep
sitting here doing nothing". But if forced to do nothing, he
might "leave the State (short of abdication) and reside
outside so that people do not think I can do anything for
them". In another paragraph, however, he insisted on
retaining his reserve powers as Maharaja because he was
not satisfied with National Conference Ministers.

Patel sent a copy of the letter to Nehru who played it
down. He welcomed the idea of Hari Singh leaving Kashmir
but felt he should stay on for the present.[11] Then the shock
of Gandhi's assassination put Kashmir, like many other
matters, on hold for some time.

*E*arly in March 1948, Mahajan's tenure as Prime Minister
of Kashmir finally ended. Hari Singh's position was further
weakened when Patel suffered a heart attack on 5 March.
He had always regarded Patel as sympathetic. On 2 October
1947, even before accession, Patel had assured him "of my
abiding sympathy with you in your difficulties; nor need I
disguise the instinctive responsibility I feel for the safety
and integrity of your State".[12]

How shaken Hari Singh was came through in a letter
by Maharani Tara Devi to Maniben (Patel's daughter): "You
are already aware how worried we must be during these
days. And since we learnt of Sardar Sahib's illness, our
anxiety has grown." On 11 April Patel wrote personally to
Hari Singh inviting him to come to Delhi before he left for
Mussoorie for a rest. From Mussoorie, his secretary, V.
Shankar took up Hari Singh's complaint that *jagirs*, large
estates gifted to supporters of the Dogra dynasty, were being
resumed without payment of compensation. He argued that

apart from this being contrary to the practice in the rest of India, "it is also to be borne in mind that probably the jagirdars would be mostly non-Muslims and this measure would probably create a certain amount of discontent and ill-feeling against the Government among the minority community".[13]

Patel was opposed to the revolutionary aspects of the Naya Kashmir manifesto of the National Conference which demanded distribution of such lands to the tiller without payment of compensation, whereas the Indian Constitution prescribed otherwise. He also interpreted Abdullah's desire for autonomy as evidence of disloyalty to India. Abdullah saw communal overtones in New Delhi's stand. This was the start of a confrontation between Abdullah and Patel on the extension of constitutional provisions to Kashmir. Nehru was less concerned with the rights of the Maharaja and his *jagirdars*, though he urged caution, but sided with Patel when he felt that the Centre's authority was threatened.

Dissension between Hari Singh and Abdullah, now Prime Minister, nearly reached breaking point. On 3 April 1948, Nehru wrote to both pointing to the disastrous consequences of an open break between them, at home and abroad, but generally siding with Abdullah.[14] Patel wrote to Nehru on 4 June from Dehra Dun, however, that Hari Singh's rights were not being respected: "I have impressed upon Sheikh Sahib as well as Bakshi the necessity of maintaining the prestige, the rights, and privileges of the Maharaja, but the manner in which the questions of his privy purse, jagirdars and commandeering of office accommodation of his Private Department have been dealt with has left on my mind a most painful impression."[15]

With Patel convalescing, his secretary did his bit to raise the Maharaja's morale: "I hope Your Highness and Her Highness would believe me when I say that both of you are constantly in our thoughts and that we shall do our best to lighten your burden. There are certain compulsions out of which we cannot extricate ourselves.... For the time being, we may have to suffer much. Whatever firmness or definiteness is required is being adopted by us; it is possible matters may prolong [sic] a bit, but I have no doubt that sooner or later we shall find a satisfactory solution."[16] Nehru, however, was still firm. While Abdullah was not always tactful, he conceded to Patel, the Maharaja was oblivious to the need to gain popular goodwill and "behaves in a manner which is completely inexplicable to me and which irritates the people." That was on 5 June 1948. The next day, he followed up with: "My study of the Kashmir situation has led me to believe that the Maharaja cannot play. He just does not know how to."[17]

In fact, the Maharaja and his Prime Minister were barely on speaking terms, as evident from the account the Maharaja gave to Patel of their meeting, arranged by Bakshi after considerable difficulty, on 5 August. Abdullah charged the State forces with atrocities, accused the Maharaja of complicity in the killing of Muslims and suggested that Bakshi be made State Army Minister. Hari Singh countered that such decisions could be taken only by the States Ministry in New Delhi. Abdullah was most excited and burst out: "I have got to turn the minds of Muslims of the State from Pakistan to the Indian Dominion. If the Muslims feel their lives are not safe and things are not done in the way I want them to be done, then there is no use my carrying on and I had better resign." And then: "If the States Ministry wants me to drown myself in the Dal [lake], I for one am not going to do so. I will resign and tell the people that I have done so because I have been hampered both here and in Delhi...."

There was silence. Then, according to Hari Singh: "Sheikh Sahib and Bakshi left the room saying *Khuda Hafiz* [equivalent to goodbye] in a curt manner without even looking towards Her Highness or me. As they neared the door Sheikh Sahib said to Bakshi, 'it is no use. We will have to deal with Delhi and force their hands'."[18]

For his part, even as his actual powers were slipping away, Hari Singh became more insistent than ever on retaining the inherited symbols of his princely authority. On

9 September, he reminded Patel that gun salutes were fired in the State on several Hindu festivals as well as on his and his son's birthdays and "departures and arrivals of myself and Her Highness". His birthday was on 27 September and instructions should be given to the Indian army, which now controlled his army, to fire the salutes (even though fighting was in progress). V. Shankar dutifully replied that the appropriate instructions had been issued.[19]

Patel's support for the Maharaja and animus against Abdullah were now overt. The strain was telling on Abdullah, too. On 29 September, he held a press conference in which he criticised Hari Singh and "his strong friends" in New Delhi, who were holding up reforms in Kashmir. This provoked an angry protest from Patel. "I myself feel bitterly that, after all that we have done for him and the sympathy and the understanding we have extended to him," he wrote to Gopalaswami, "he [Abdullah] should have indulged in such direct and unbecoming attacks on the Maharaja." Patel also drew Nehru's attention to the press conference, objecting, among other things, to Abdullah's mention of Hindu fanaticism in East Punjab. He protested to Abdullah that his charges against Hari Singh were unfair because: "No one knows better than you that today the Maharaja is powerless to resist your wishes."

Abdullah was far from apologetic, contesting Patel's assertion that the reforms proposed by the Abdullah Government had not been obstructed. One was the festering issue of reorganisation of the State forces. It had been agreed, according to Abdullah, that "when the present emergency is over and the Indian forces are withdrawn, the State will be left with a properly organised army of its own to fall back upon." But nothing had been done. Since the State forces "had been a close preserve of a very small coterie of the favourites of the ruling family", it had created problems for Kashmir, which is why he had urged transfer of the army administration to a minister of his Cabinet. This was not accepted. He gave several instances of his Government's decisions being held up.

Abdullah repeated his charges that Hari Singh and his Dogra army were responsible for atrocities against Muslims and again proposed (as he had in a note on 1 June) that Hari Singh should resign in favour of his son. Justifying his going to the press, Abdullah said: "I feel intensely on these matters. We are engaged in a life and death struggle. This is not the time to mince matters. You cannot expect me to watch unmistakable attempts to sabotage us and remain quiet."

Patel responded by denying or by explaining the reasons for the delays of which Abdullah had complained, but his reference to considerations and precedents in India to justify delay in considering Kashmir's radical land reforms only reinforced Abdullah's desire for autonomy. The tone of Patel's letter, accusing Abdullah of a "grossly prejudiced view", among other things, and taunting him with his servile letter to Hari Singh from jail, emphasised and brought to the surface their dislike of each other.

But Nehru did not take the press conference too seriously. He admitted to Patel that Abdullah had been "very indiscreet" in criticising Hari Singh publicly, but that was as far as he was willing to go and he reiterated: "Sheikh Abdullah is, I am convinced, a very straight and frank man. He is not a very clear thinker and he goes astray in his speech as many of our politicians do...."[20]

Though Patel differed more and more with Nehru's handling of Kashmir (he complained to Gopalaswami that Jammu and Kashmir "seems to be an independent State and the Government of India appear to have abdicated their functions..."[21]), he did not risk resignation again and executed the Prime Minister's decisions when asked to. On 17 April 1949, Nehru wrote to Patel that Lt. General Cariappa had reported that the tussle between Hari Singh and Abdullah was having a bad effect even on the army. Referring scornfully to Hari Singh's reported willingness to give up the valley, he added: "If we want Jammu province by itself and are prepared to make a present of the rest of the State to Pakistan, I have no doubt that we could clinch the issue in a few days. The prize we are fighting for is the valley of Kashmir."

A far more serious charge in Nehru's eyes was an intelligence report that the Praja Parishad (the communal Hindu organisation in Jammu) was being financed by Hari Singh. All this made it "highly desirable that the Maharaja should take some kind of leave and not remain in Kashmir."[22]

Despite his reservations, Patel did the needful. After evading several messages, the Maharaja was summoned to Delhi. As recalled by Karan Singh, they were invited to dinner by Patel on 29 April: "After dinner my parents and the Sardar went into another room, and it was there that the blow fell. The Sardar told my father gently but firmly that although Sheikh Abdullah was pressing for his abdication, the Government of India felt that it would be sufficient if he and my mother absented themselves from the State for a few months.... I should be appointed Regent by my father to carry out his duties and responsibilities in his absence. My father...emerged from the meeting ashen-faced.... My mother went to her room where she flung herself on to her bed and burst into tears."[23]

Hari Singh settled in Bombay, where he became a horse-racing aficionado, never to return to Kashmir. Tara Devi preferred Kasauli, near Shimla. Only Karan Singh returned, to take his own revenge on Abdullah for ending the Dogra dynasty, which was abolished before he could inherit the title of Maharaja.

*T*he only point on which Abdullah and Hari Singh had ever agreed, albeit for different reasons, was that they would have preferred Kashmir to be independent. Mahajan recalls a meeting between them a month after accession during which Abdullah "suggested that it would be a very good thing if India and Pakistan were made to recognise the State as an independent unit like Switzerland" and "the

Maharaja nodded assent". Mahajan told them that he could not subscribe to this view.[24] The Maharaja's motive was to preserve his dynasty; Abdullah's to protect his people. Nobody charged Hari Singh with being anti-national, though in his letter of accession he had precisely restricted New Delhi's role to the minimum three subjects of external affairs, defence and communications and later even considered withdrawing accession. But that was the charge that helped topple Abdullah who insisted on maximum autonomy. He trusted Gandhi and Nehru, but not New Delhi.

Though he outwardly rejected the independence option as unfeasible after supporting accession to India, Abdullah continued to consider the possibility. Early in 1948, he went to New York as one of India's representatives at the UN. In his address to the Security Council on 5 February, unlike some of his colleagues, he was able to avoid falling into the pitfalls dexterously laid by Zafrullah Khan. He countered the impression created by Zafrullah that the fighting in Kashmir was a Muslim revolt against the tyranny of a Hindu ruler, pointing out that he himself had led a campaign against the Maharaja for democratic rights but did not accept the two-nation theory. In fact, the valley had been an island of peace when much of the subcontinent was engulfed by communal flames.

Abdullah further asserted that the present situation had been created by the tribal invasion which Pakistan had promoted. It was under these circumstances that "both the Maharaja and the people of Kashmir requested the Government of India to accept our accession". He praised Nehru for making accession subject to ratification by the people, after Kashmir had been freed from the marauders, although he did not have to. More than once he brought up the point that he and his colleagues were still deciding whether Kashmir should accede to India, to Pakistan or be independent, when Pakistan tried to force the issue by sending in the tribal raiders.[25]

What was not known at the time was that while
Abdullah was in New York, he met Warren Austin, the US
representative at the UN. The subject of their conversation
is conveyed by Austin's telegram to US Secretary of State
George Marshall dated 28 January 1948:

It is possible that principal purpose of Abdullah's visit
was to make it clear to US that there is a third
alternative, namely, independence. He seems overly
anxious to get this point across.... He did not want his
people torn by dissensions between Pakistan and India.
It would be much better if Kashmir were independent
and could seek American and British aid for
development of country. I, of course, gave Abdullah no
encouragement on this line and am confident when he
left he understood very well where we stand on this
matter.[26]

American diplomatic messages, now open to public
scrutiny, and also some diplomatic memoirs, confirm that
Abdullah continued to probe Western missions on the
feasibility of independence. But, contrary to the impression
created at the time, he does not seem to have been
encouraged by the US Government (though possibly by
individual Americans). The official US line was laid down
by Marshall in a telegram to his embassy in New Delhi on
4 March 1948:

Re various proposals for Kashmir independence, we
have in the past, as you know, followed line that princely
states should be incorporated in either India or Pakistan
on assumption that Balkanisation of Indian
subcontinent would jeopardise and complicate political
and economic transition and create conditions of
instability ultimately adverse to broad US interests that
area. Our current thinking re Kashmir is influenced by
these considerations subject to proviso that should
concept of independence appear to be basis for GOI-GOP
[India-Pakistan] peaceful settlement of Kashmir issue,

we would probably not oppose such a solution, but would certainly take no initiative in supporting it.

This was confirmed in a State Department memo two years later (when Dean Acheson was the Secretary of State) opposing proposals for an independent Kashmir on the ground that it "(a) would not be economically viable; (b) would quite possibly be taken over by the communists; (c) might otherwise weaken the security of the subcontinent."[27]

There were to be more contacts between Abdullah and visiting Americans and diplomats in the future, leading to strained relations between New Delhi and Washington as well as between New Delhi and Srinagar.

Chapter XIII

The Lion Caged

*H*ari Singh's exile removed the only rival centre of power to Sheikh Abdullah within Jammu and Kashmir, but it increased the latter's differences with New Delhi. For Abdullah, it was no longer the Maharaja who symbolised the reactionary forces curbing his revolutionary programmes, but the conservatism of the Centre. It was no longer the Maharaja who represented Hindu reaction, but the Union Ministry of States and Home Affairs, under Sardar Patel. In fact, the policy of the entire Congress Government was to integrate Kashmir into the Union as closely as any other State; with Jawaharlal Nehru insisting on gradualism so as to honour commitments made to Abdullah. But Patel's attitude made Muslims suspicious.

Abdullah reacted to what he felt were pressures from New Delhi by raising the decibel levels of his campaign for permanent autonomy and using every political and diplomatic weapon to sustain it, including contacts with foreign diplomats. The gap between Srinagar and New Delhi was exposed in the crucial discussions on the provisions being drafted in the Constituent Assembly to specify Kashmir's special status within the Indian Union, with Abdullah once even threatening to resign from the Assembly.

Abdullah's stand was that the Centre had no right to extend its powers in Kashmir beyond those covered by the

three subjects to which Hari Singh had confined accession,
and as endorsed by him. These subjects, as already noted,
were foreign affairs, defence and communications. He
resisted the application of even the provisions for
fundamental rights, citizenship and directive principles in
the Constitution of India to Kashmir. On fundamental
rights, his main objection was to the right to property (later
deleted from the Union Constitution) because it would come
in the way of implementing the land reforms promised in
the Naya Kashmir manifesto. His objection to the clauses
on citizenship was that it might enable outsiders to acquire
property and swamp the locals – a fear rooted in history.
Overall, he opposed any provision going beyond what had
been conceded in the Instrument of Accession.

In the Indian Constituent Assembly, the focus of
dissension then, as later, was Article 370 (then numbered
306-A). In essence, this restricted Parliament's power to
make laws for Jammu and Kashmir State to foreign affairs,
defence and communications. Otherwise, it could do so only
with the consent of the State Government, thus giving the
State a degree of autonomy not enjoyed by any other. This
was broadly in accord with Abdullah's stand, though Patel
was scandalised. On 16 October 1949, he wrote to
Gopalaswami Ayyangar, who had drafted the Article: "I find
there are some substantial changes over the original draft,
particularly in regard to the applicability of fundamental
rights and directive principles of State policy. You can
yourself realise the anomaly of the State becoming part of
India and at the same time not recognising any of these
provisions...any question of my approval does not arise. If
you feel it is the right thing to do, you can go ahead with
it."[1]

On the other hand, Abdullah had wanted iron-clad
guarantees of autonony and was upset that certain phrases
were not in accord with the compromise he had accepted.
He was also unhappy with the Article being described as a
"temporary provision". He felt that the draft had been
pushed through without giving him and his three colleagues

representing Kashmir a chance to speak. So, he wrote to Gopalaswami: "As I am genuinely anxious that no unpleasant situation should arise, I would request you to see if even now something could be done to rectify the position. In case I fail to hear from you within a reasonable time, I regret that no course is left open for us but to tender our resignation from the Constituent Assembly." Gopalaswami did not budge and Abdullah climbed down.[2] In his autobiography, Abdullah insisted that the Centre wanted complete merger of the State with India, which was countered by the Kashmir representatives. In any event, he argued: "India was formally committed to holding a plebiscite in Kashmir, a complete merger was therefore out of the question."[3]

Abdullah used India's commitment to plebiscite, with the implication that Kashmir's accession was provisional, to shore up his campaign. Developments in his own backyard, in Jammu, the seat of Dogra power, which remained loyal to the absentee Maharaja, accentuated his desire for guaranteed autonomy or independence. Jammu now had a Hindu majority which was conscious of the threat that the valley-dominated State Government posed to the privileges that it enjoyed. The Hindu ethos of the Jammu movement against his administration, supported by Hindu communal groups elsewhere in India, made Abdullah concerned about the future of the valley, which he had led into India's embrace, once the secular influence of Gandhi and Nehru disappeared. At the same time, he needed to justify his endorsement of accession to India to his people. The resultant anxiety, sometimes verging on neurosis, underlay his contrary statements and behaviour.

From the start, Jammu threatened to mar the model of communal amity that Kashmir had set up. It began when the communal frenzy of the partitioned Punjab crossed Jammu's border, resulting in the exodus and eviction of Muslims from the province. Gandhi, to whom Kashmir represented a secular beacon, was particularly worried, lest events in Jammu create a reaction in the valley, and

repeatedly condemned atrocities against Muslims there. So
was Nehru, who drew attention to the negative fallout of
the Jammu incidents, at home and abroad, and accused Hari
Singh of financing and inciting these incidents.

The campaign against Abdullah and his National
Conference Government was organised by the Praja
Parishad, founded in 1947 by an RSS activist, Balraj
Madhok, who later became President of the Jana Sangh.
Among the Parishad's concerns was the defence of the
entrenched interests of the Dogra community, to which the
Maharaja belonged, and it came under the leadership of a
veteran political worker of Jammu, Prem Nath Dogra. The
Parishad first clashed with the authorities in early 1949,
when Prem Nath and many others were arrested. This set
the pattern for the next four years. Analysing the motivation
for the unrest, Professor R.N. Kaul, a political worker at the
time, writes: "The Maharaja wanted monarchy to be
restored; the Hindu and Muslim jagirdars wanted the feudal
pattern of society to last forever; the Hindu extremists, who
had acquired wealth in the name of religion, believed that
a status quo could be perpetuated by fanning communal
flames." At the same time, Abdullah's efforts to 'Muslimise'
the administration alienated Jammu Hindus and Ladakh
Buddhists.[4] Also, perhaps fuelled by a sense of insecurity,
Abdullah became increasingly autocratic and put many of
his opponents into jail. In this he was helped by his deputy,
Bakshi Ghulam Mohammed, who was an effective executive
with little concern for democratic and legal procedures.

For New Delhi, the issue of autonomy became a source
of increasing tension. In July 1950, Yuvraj Karan Singh,
who as Regent exercised his father's powers as Head of
State, though still under twenty, had a brush with Abdullah
when he sought New Delhi's approval for Abdullah's
proposals for abolishing *jagirdari* without payment of
compensation. Abdullah insisted that the Yuvraj had
exceeded his functions as constitutional Head of State. His
basic objection was that the measures did not relate to
matters in which the State had acceded to India; therefore,

New Delhi had no jurisdiction. Next day, Abdullah announced the measures in a public speech, though called to Delhi to discuss them. They were finally implemented after some 'grudging' amendments on New Delhi's advice.[5]

The convoking of Jammu and Kashmir's own Constituent Assembly in May 1951 represented the apogee of Abdullah's political career. But it also provided a target on which his opponents could concentrate their volleys. The way had been cleared by Article 370 of the Indian Constitution which came into force on 26 January 1950. Abdullah's was the only State which could have its own constitution. The process did not begin auspiciously. The authoritarian ways of the National Conference Government were reflected in the elections to the Assembly, the first since the State acceded to India. Seventy-two members were elected unopposed on the National Conference ticket. The Jammu Praja Parishad boycotted the elections. But the inauguration of the Assembly on 5 November 1950 gave Abdullah an opportunity to justify his commitment to secular India without reducing his stress on autonomy. He did so in an outstanding address that recalled Kashmir's eclectic culture:

> After centuries, we have reached the harbour of our freedom...once again in the history of this State, our people have reached a peak of achievement through what I might call the classical Kashmiri genius for synthesis, born of toleration and mutual respect. Throughout the long tale of our history, the highest pinnacles of our achievement have been scaled when religious bigotry and intolerance ceased to cramp us, and we have breathed the wider air of brotherhood and mutual understanding.

Referring to the land reforms, that to him were part of the content of freedom, but which had created problems with New Delhi, he took credit for abolishing ownership rights to lands in excess of twelve-and-a-half acres and transferring it to the tillers: "The abolition of landlordism

is thus an accomplished fact and there is no going back on
the decisions already taken."

Next, he emphasised the special autonomous
relationship of the State with India:

> We are proud to have our bonds with India, the goodwill
> of whose people and Government is available to us in
> unstinted measure.... The Constitution of India
> has...treated us differently from other constituent units.
> With the exception of the items grouped under Defence,
> Foreign Affairs and Communications in the Instrument
> of Accession, we have complete freedom to frame our
> Constitution in the manner we like...while safeguarding
> our autonomy to the fullest extent so as to enable us to
> have the liberty to build our country according to the
> best traditions and genius of our people, we may also
> by suitable constitutional arrangements with the Union
> establish our right to seek and compel Federal
> cooperation.

Then he justified his preference for India and dealt with
the gut issue of the future of Muslims in a Hindu-majority
nation:

> The Indian Constitution has set before the country the
> goal of secular democracy based upon justice, freedom
> and equality for all without distinction. This is the
> bedrock of modern democracy. This should meet the
> argument that the Muslims of Kashmir cannot have
> security in India, where the large majority of the
> population are Hindus.... The Indian Constitution has
> amply and finally repudiated the concept of a religious
> State, which is a throwback to medievalism.... The
> national movement in our State naturally gravitates
> towards these principles of secular democracy. The
> people here will never accept a principle which seeks to
> favour the interests of one religion or social group
> against another.

Abdullah did not duck the threat of Hindu communalism, but emphasised the role that Kashmir could play in countering it:

> Certain tendencies have been asserting themselves in India which may in the future convert it into a religious State wherein the interests of Muslims will be jeopardised.... The continued accession of Kashmir to India should, however, help in defeating this tendency.

Criticism of Pakistan was implicit in the early portions of the address. But Abdullah underlined his reasons for opposing any thought of joining it:

> This claim of being a Muslim State is of course only a camouflage. It is a screen to dupe the common man, so that he may not see clearly that Pakistan is a feudal State in which a clique is trying... to maintain itself in power. In addition to this, the appeal to religion constitutes a sentimental and a wrong approach to the question.

He did not leave out the third option, independence, which he had been known to favour, in his review of the choices before Kashmir, but described it as impracticable:

> We have to consider the alternative of making ourselves an Eastern Switzerland, of keeping aloof from both States [India and Pakistan], but having friendly relations with them. This may seem attractive in that it would appear to pave the way out of the present deadlock. To us as a tourist country, it could also have certain obvious advantages. But in considering independence we must not ignore practical considerations. Firstly, it is not easy to protect sovereignty and independence in a small country which has not sufficient strength to defend itself on our long and difficult frontiers bordering so many countries. Secondly, we do not find powerful guarantors among them to pull together always in assuring us freedom from aggression.

Recalling the tribal invasion abetted by Pakistan, he said there was no guarantee against recurrence of similar aggression. But the careful phrasing of the third option suggested that he was still considering it, if international guarantors could be found.

Abdullah was soon able to achieve something that Kashmiris had long desired: the end of the Dogra dynasty, indeed, of princely rule. But he had to accept a compromise, engineered by Nehru, to make it acceptable to New Delhi. The Kashmir Constitution envisaged an elected Head of State titled Sadar-i-Riyasat (unlike the Governors appointed by the Centre to head other States of the Union). The compromise was that Karan Singh be the first Sadar-i-Riyasat to maintain the link with the past and as a gesture to Jammu. Though Abdullah could not have liked it, he made the most of the compromise:

> There is no doubt that Yuvraj Karan Singh, in his capacity as a citizen of the State, will prove a fitting symbol of the transition to a democratic system in which the ruler of yesterday becomes the first servant of the people, functioning under their authority, and on their behalf.

There was more to the compromise formula than Abdullah realised. Hari Singh was furious that his son should be party to the extinction of his dynasty. But he was urged to accept by Nehru in a letter saying he would "thereby put yourself right with your people and do them much service in many ways which may not be so obvious and yet which are important." Karan Singh flew to Delhi to meet Nehru. "For the first time I noticed a slight hint of displeasure in Jawaharlal's remarks about Sheikh Abdullah", he recalled later. "Although he did not say so in so many words, I gathered the distinct impression that he wanted me to be on the scene so that I could be of help if some difficulty arose in the future."[6] Nehru was more outspoken when Karan Singh called on him again in November 1952 and "spoke of the perplexity he was beginning to feel in dealing with Sheikh Abdullah and said that this made it all the more important that I should be on the scene."[7]

Karan Singh complied and was elected Sadar-i-Riyasat for a five-year term on 15 November 1952. It was in this capacity that he dismissed Abdullah from the office of Prime Minister eight months later.

*T*he political estrangement of Nehru and Abdullah, who had depended so much on each other, reflected the tragedy slowly overcoming Kashmir and the mutual suspicion eating into the values that its accession represented. Nehru was large-minded enough not to interpret the desire for autonomy as anti-national but was less liberal in practice. He was irritated when Abdullah continued to oppose his plans for the gradual integration of Jammu and Kashmir into the Indian Union. At the same time, the seeds of distrust of Abdullah planted by Sardar Patel before he died (on 15 December 1950), grew in the Central Government and took on a communal tinge. The process has been described in the memoirs of B.N. Mullik, India's influential Director of Intelligence from 1950 to 1965. In August 1949, he was asked to report on rumours concerning Abdullah's hostility to India and allegations by "large numbers of Kashmiri Pandits and Jammu Dogras, who had access both to the Prime Minister and the Home Minister,...which were generally hostile to Sheikh Abdullah".

The report that Mullik submitted after visiting the valley was that Abdullah's support to India was genuine and that the number of Kashmiris not reconciled to the accession to India was small. Nehru was pleased and had copies of the report distributed to Indian embassies. Patel was upset. In this context, Mullik wrote:

> The Sardar then gave me his own views about Sheikh Abdullah. He apprehended that Sheikh Abdullah would ultimately let down India and Jawaharlal Nehru and

would come in [sic] his real colours; his antipathy to the
Maharaja was not really an antipathy to the ruler as
such, but to the Dogras in general and with the Dogras
he identified the rest of the majority community in
India.

Future events, Mullik went on to note, "proved that the
Sardar was right and I was not. Within three years we found
ourselves fighting against Sheikh Abdullah."[8] As indicated
by his language, Mullik treated Abdullah as an enemy and
built up a case questioning his loyalty as well as his
secularity.

Abdullah was beginning to feel trapped. On 10 July
1950, he wrote to Nehru to express his predicament:

It is clear that there are powerful influences at work in
India who do not see eye to eye with you regarding your
ideal of making the Union a truly secular state and your
Kashmir policy.... While I feel I can willingly go down
and sacrifice myself for you, I am afraid as custodian of
the destinies of 40 lacs of Kashmiris, I cannot barter
away their cherished rights and privileges. I have
several times stated that we acceded to India because
we saw there two bright stars of hope and aspiration,
namely, Gandhiji and yourself, and despite our having
so many affinities with Pakistan we did not join it,
because we thought our programme will not fit their
policy. If, however, we are driven to the conclusion that
we cannot build our State on our own lines, suited to
our genius, what answer can I give to our people and
how am I to face them?[9]

Nehru's defeat with regard to the choice of the first
President of the Indian Republic, when Patel managed to
secure the election of the conservative Rajendra Prasad in
preference to C. Rajagopalachari, possibly occasioned
Abdullah's fears. They must have been reinforced by the
election of the overtly pro-Hindu Purushottamdas Tandon
as Congress President in 1951. The founding of the
Bharatiya Jana Sangh on 21 October that year gave new

life to the Hindutva forces in North India, with widespread criticism of the special status given to Kashmir. These trends were followed with deepening concern in the valley. The pressures began to tell on Abdullah. He made several speeches criticising the Hindu lobby in New Delhi, climaxed by the one at Ranbirsinghpura, on 11 April 1952, which was widely reported by the press. In this speech, he expressed fears about what would happen to Kashmir after Nehru's departure and suggested that Kashmiris think about their future, thereby questioning the finality of accession. Nehru expressed his unhappiness in a letter to Abdullah on 23 April:

> I have felt deeply about Kashmir, because it represented to me many things and many principles. It always has been an axiom with me, quite apart from constitutional position and the like, that the people of Kashmir must decide their own fate. For me the people of Kashmir were basically represented by you. If you feel as you do, then the link that has bound us together necessarily weakens and I have little heart left to discuss such matters.[10]

Abdullah was hurt and said that the press had misinterpreted parts of his speech. He was hurt even more by a letter from Nehru the following month, because he felt it questioned his secular credentials, which was "an article of faith" for him. Nehru had written:

> My government is committed to secular democracy. You, too, have been working for this sacred cause. I am at a loss to understand your present attitude. I am afraid Kashmir is heading in an adverse direction. Unfortunately, it is going to affect the Indian situation in the same manner as the Indian situation affects Kashmir.[11]

Nehru and Abdullah made another attempt to patch up their differences in June 1952. The outcome was the Delhi Agreement which reiterated the provisions of Article 370. Controversial issues such as the extension of fundamental rights and the jurisdiction of the Supreme Court were left for further examination. The Kashmir flag, which had been the standard of the National Conference during the struggle against the Maharaja's rule, was retained, though Abdullah explained: "The Union flag to which we continue our allegiance as a part of the Union will occupy the supremely distinctive place in the State." Kashmir continued to be outside the purview of provisions authorising Central intervention embodied particularly in Article 356, enabling the President to take over the administration of other States. Kashmir also continued to have the right to elect its own Head of State, but the Delhi Agreement laid down specifically that such a person would hold office "during the pleasure of the President".

But the Delhi Agreement soon came under attack. Joined by the Jana Sangh elsewhere in the country, the Praja Parishad launched a massive campaign in Jammu, where the police found themselves opposing demonstrators carrying the national flag and President Rajendra Prasad's portrait before them. The National Conference Government was portrayed as the enemy of nationalism, a sentiment conveyed by a rhythmic chant that soon spread widely:

Ek desh mein do vidhan; ek desh mein do nishan:
Ek desh mein do pradhan; nahin chalenge, nahin chalenge.

(Two constitutions, two flags, two Heads of State in one country will not be tolerated.)

Nehru was greatly concerned, for it was evident that the target of the Praja Parishad demonstrators went beyond Abdullah to his own policies. The campaign was part of a wave of communal passion being aroused throughout the country. He was worried enough to repeatedly write to State Chief Ministers about the threat. On 4 December 1952, for instance, he wrote: "There are two aspects of these disorders in Jammu which have to be kept in mind. The far-reaching land reforms in the State have naturally not pleased some of the old landlord elements and they have joined this agitation against the Government there. In this they are being helped directly by some communal elements in other parts of India.... In the name of closer association with India, they are acting in a manner which might well imperil that very association."

Two weeks later, Nehru wrote a special letter to the Chief Ministers drawing their attention to various linked agitations in the country. One was the Jammu campaign; the second to respond to the influx of refugees from East Bengal by evicting Muslims; and the third to ban cow slaughter. "The people at the back of these agitations," he stated, "belong to communal organisations like the Hindu Mahasabha, the Jana Sangh, the RSS and the Ram Rajya Parishad. Appropriately, Master Tara Singh and his Akali Dal have lined up with them...". Again, on 27 January 1953, he observed: "The Jammu agitation, about which I have written to you previously, is again a remarkable instance of folly or of mischief. [It] plays into the hands of Pakistan. It is clear that the objective of these [communal] organisations is not confined to Jammu and that they are aiming at bigger quarry. Their dislike of the Government of India and the secular policy that it pursues is so great that, in order to injure it, they are prepared even to harm our relationship with Jammu and Kashmir State."[12]

The President of the Jana Sangh, Shyama Prasad Mookerjee, played on the threat of Muslim separatism that had led to the creation of Pakistan, overlooking the fact that it was the autonomy promised to Kashmir that persuaded its Muslim majority to prefer India to Pakistan. But by equating the demand for autonomy with anti-nationalism, he was able to arouse national opinion against Kashmir's special status. Mookerjee unintentionally helped accelerate Abdullah's fall. He entered the State illegally on 8 May 1953 and on 23 June died of heart failure while in detention at Srinagar. His death touched off a wave of indignation in the country, provoked by rumours that he had been murdered. Abdullah was sacked six weeks later.

Abdullah's strategy was two-pronged. The first entailed
the campaign for perpetuating Kashmir's special status. But
he was unsure whether the special status would survive,
since the national leadership, including Nehru, regarded it
as a temporary feature, as noted in Article 370. The second
prong involved securing international, primarily US,
backing for an independent Kashmir. On 29 September
1950, he met the US Ambassador to India, Loy Henderson.
Henderson's cable to the State Department on the secret
talks summarised his thinking:

> In discussion [of the] future of Kashmir, Abdullah was
> vigorous in restating that in his opinion it should be
> independent; that overwhelming majority of the
> population desired their independence; that he had
> reason to believe that some Azad Kashmir leaders
> desired independence and would be willing to cooperate
> with leaders of National Conference if there was
> reasonable chance such cooperation would result in
> independence. Kashmir people could not understand
> why UN consistently ignored independence as possible
> solution for Kashmir. Kashmir people had language and
> cultural background of their own. The Hindus by custom
> and tradition widely different from Hindus in India, and
> the background of Muslims quite different from Muslims
> in Pakistan. Fact was that population of Kashmir
> homogeneous in spite of presence of Hindu minority.

Asked by the US Ambassador if an independent
Kashmir could remain stable without the support of India
or Pakistan, Abdullah replied that it would need US
assistance, directly or through UN. He then went on:

> Adherence of Kashmir to India would not lead in
> foreseeable future to improving miserable lot of
> population. There were so many areas of India in urgent
> need of economic development, he was convinced that
> Kashmir would get relatively little attention.
> Nevertheless, it would be preferable to Kashmir to go

to India than to Pakistan. It would be disastrous for Kashmir to be brought under control of government with medieval outlook.[13]

This is the fullest account of Abdullah's outlook available from diplomatic sources. Though, as Abdullah told Henderson, only the US could prop up an independent Kashmir, he also discussed the possibility with other diplomats. Walter Crocker, High Commissioner for Australia at the time, recalls Abdullah suggesting independence when he met him in Kashmir in 1952.[14] While preferring independence, Abdullah consistently favoured India to Pakistan if obliged to choose between them.

In the first week of May 1953, Abdullah's prolonged meetings with Adlai Stevenson, a US presidential candidate, aroused widespread speculation concerning US interference in Kashmir. Ambassador George Allen cabled Washington on 13 July 1953 for authority to contradict such speculation, explaining that:

> Indian leaders certain to show concern over reports that individual Americans have encouraged Abdullah to favour independence for Kashmir and have held out hope of US economic assistance, possibly in return for US air bases. Ref to increased intransigence of Abdullah following Adlai Stevenson's talks with him in May. There has been veiled implication that Stevenson was charged with special mission by present US administration. Nehru appears convinced of this and may have originated reports.

Washington cabled Allen to assure Nehru that "US government made no suggestion, officially or unofficially, encourage Kashmir government seek satisfaction any set demands. You may assure Nehru Stevenson given no mission to discuss Kashmir with Abdullah or anyone else." Washington also asked American embassy staff to refrain from visiting Kashmir.[15] Stevenson denied that he had encouraged Abdullah's "casual suggestion that independent status might be an alternative solution" Nehru believed him.[16]

In the new political equation set by Abdullah's search for supporters for independence or near-independence as a solution for Kashmir, he became less condemnatory of Pakistan (Nehru had earlier suggested he use less harsh language.) The gap between India and Pakistan was narrowing in his eyes. Pakistan had survived, contrary to the predictions of many, including Nehru, and its economy was prospering. Jinnah, his arch-enemy, was dead. And, in India, the medieval communal forces, which he had condemned in Pakistan, appeared to be on the rise. And, so, as he wrote to Nehru, what was he to tell his people? He also complained of discrimination against Muslims in recruitment to the army and the postal and other services.

For Nehru, however, independence was the worst possible solution for Kashmir. He was highly suspicious of moves by Washington to secure bases against the Soviet Union (and later China) at strategic places near the Soviet border. At the same time, he was worried about penetration of Soviet ideology and funds. "India does think that international communism is aggressive," he wrote in a note on foreign policy in February 1950, "partly because of communist philosophy and partly because communism today is very much Slavism."[17]

We do not know if Nehru was aware of Abdullah's talks with US diplomats, but Abdullah's preference was obvious from his public pronouncements. This led to the parting of the ways. Nehru wrote to Maulana Azad in March 1953:

I fear that Sheikh Sahib's mind is so utterly confused that he does not know what to do. All kinds of pressures are being brought to bear upon him and he is getting more and more into a tangle. There is nobody with him who can really help him much, because he does not trust anyone fully, and yet everyone influences him.... My fear is that Sheikh Sahib, in his present state of mind, is likely to do something or take some step, which might make things worse.[18]

When Nehru went to Srinagar the following month, he
ruled out any possibility of an independent Kashmir, while
agreeing that the quantum of autonomy could be discussed.
Abdullah continued to seek "full autonomy". Nehru
interpreted this as independence and told him that he would
rather give Kashmir to Pakistan on a platter than allow
international intrigue to dangle Kashmir over the heads of
India and Pakistan like a sword of Damocles.[19] Another issue
was Abdullah's reluctance to honour commitments made in
the Delhi Agreement. This was embarrassing Nehru. They
were now set on opposing courses. On returning to Delhi,
Nehru invited Abdullah for further talks, but Abdullah
declined to attend. On 28 June, Nehru wrote a letter in
terms that, for him, were harsh:

> To me it has been a major surprise that a settlement
> arrived at between us should be by-passed or repudiated,
> regardless of the merits. That strikes at the root of all
> confidence, personal or international.... My honour is
> bound up with my word.... It is always painful to part
> company after long years of comradeship, but if our
> conscience so tells us, or in our view an overriding
> national interest requires, then there is no help for it....[20]

A visit by Azad to Srinagar did not help in bridging the
gulf.

Abdullah's fate was now sealed. A split in the National
Conference leadership between those favouring close ties
with India and those, headed by him, wanting independence
or permanent autonomy, helped. Though the pro-integration
group, led by Bakshi Ghulam Mohammad, claimed a
majority, they did not follow the democratic procedure of
bringing about a fall of the Government by resigning and
then forming a new one. Neither Bakshi nor New Delhi was
willing to take any risks. Though Abdullah's prestige had
suffered over the years due to his arbitrary ways, his

popularity in the valley was still unrivalled. A shabby undercover operation resulted. The ground was laid by a convenient report from Mullik that "the more the Sheikh was getting isolated, the more desperate he was becoming and there was every apprehension that he would assume the role of dictator or do some other desperate act".

Karan Singh contributed his bit, functioning more as Delhi's representative in the State than as Sadar-i-Riyasat. Describing Abdullah's opponents as "the pro-Indian faction", he reported to Nehru that this faction was strong, adding that Abdullah "seems to have decided to go back upon his solemn agreements...with India and upon his clear commitments. This cannot be allowed, as it will make our position absolutely impossible and be a grave blow to our National interests...."[21]

Perhaps getting wind of the plot, Maulana Mohammed Syed Masoodi, General Secretary of the National Conference and one of its most respected leaders, tried to head it off. He was representing Kashmir in Parliament and on 6 August 1953, three days before what Mullik described as D-day, he issued a statement to the press in New Delhi drawing attention to the attitudes underlying the crisis:

> There is a deliberate attempt on the part of those who do not view Kashmir's present position with favour to cloud the real issue so as to escape responsibility for the harm that has been caused to the Indo-Kashmir relationship by the support given to the recent agitations for Kashmir's merger with India..... If Kashmiris rose as one man against Pakistan it was because they saw that that country wanted to force them into a position which they were not prepared to accept. If today demands are made in India which endanger the present autonomous position of the State and, realising this danger, the people of Kashmir feel inclined towards a third alternative [independence], it is not they who should be blamed for it but those who are at the root cause of it.

Masoodi appealed to "all those people in India who are honestly interested in seeing Kashmir and India thrive together on the basis of a willing, not forced, association" to organise public opinion against the movement for merger and strengthen Abdullah. But it was too late.

*I*t has been widely believed that Nehru did not order the overthrow of Sheikh Abdullah. But if we are to go by Mullik's memoirs, he was personally involved in the planning of the operation. According to the Director of Intelligence, Nehru asked him to strengthen his organisation in Kashmir and personally approved the choice of an intelligence official, D.W. Mehra, to oversee the operation. Then, after a two-hour discussion on 31 July

> finally he [Nehru] came to the point that there was no other alternative but to remove Sheikh Abdullah and install Bakshi Ghulam Mohd. in his place. He hoped that the change would be effected peacefully, but he warned that we must be prepared for the worst, because the Sheikh undoubtedly had a large following in the valley and over this matter the pro-Sheikh group would be supported by the pro-Pakistani elements also.

Nehru, we are told, even gave instructions that Mehra assume control of the State police force and, if necessary, take over as chief executive under Sadar-i-Riyasat Karan Singh. At this point, Mullik adds, the Prime Minister was nearly overwhelmed by emotion. He had never seen him so disturbed before.[22] But the operation had been set in motion and the army alerted. Rafi Ahmed Kidwai and Ajit Prasad Jain, Nehru's Cabinet colleagues, who had been reporting to him on Abdullah's conduct, were to supervise the operation.

A split in the National Conference leadership had dented Abdullah's supremacy while favouritism and corruption in the administration had lessened his popularity, though it was still unrivalled. Suspicious of his colleagues, Abdullah provoked a ministerial crisis by asking his Health Minister, Sham Lal Saraf, to resign on grounds of corruption. This gave three dissident Ministers – Bakshi, Girdhari Lal Dogra and Saraf – an opportunity to formally accuse Abdullah in a letter of precipitating a rupture with New Delhi and asserting that he had lost the confidence of the Cabinet and the people.

A copy of the letter was quickly sent to the Sadar-i-Riyasat, who decided it was sufficient grounds to dismiss Abdullah, though democratic propriety required that the issue be decided by the State Assembly. But as Bakshi was to discover himself, and Farooq Abdullah later, such niceties were not taken too seriously by New Delhi. That much planning had gone into this denouement was, in fact, admitted by Karan Singh when he praised Durga Prasad Dhar, the State Deputy Home Minister who had been keeping in close touch with New Delhi, for tying up all the 'loose ends' of the operation over the previous three days.[23]

On the appointed day, 9 August 1953, since Bakshi was unwilling to take over Abdullah's office while he was still at large and able to organise popular protests, it was decided not only to dismiss but also to arrest him. Karan Singh had expressed his concern to Abdullah over the dissensions in the Cabinet, but without indicating that he was to be dismissed. That evening Abdullah went to Gulmarg for the week-end, ignorant of what was about to happen. The operational plans laid by Dhar and Mullik were implemented by the Sadar-i-Riyasat on grounds that could have been dictated by New Delhi:

> If we gave him [Abdullah] an opportunity to take his case to the streets he would easily arouse acute communal and chauvinistic sentiments among the Kashmiri masses, which in turn would result in serious and violent disturbances. Anti-national elements and agents were active in the valley and, if given the chance, would not hesitate to plunge the State into utter turmoil.[24]

So, near midnight, in pouring rain, a police party rushed
to Gulmarg. Sheikh and Begum Abdullah were asleep. He
was woken up and handed the letter of his dismissal and
the warrant for his arrest. "Who is the Sadar-i-Riyasat to
dismiss me? I made that chit of a boy Sadar-i-Riyasat," he
protested angrily, possibly regretting the compromise in
which Karan Singh was elected to the office. He was taken
to Udhampur, near Jammu, in the early hours and detained
there. According to Mullik, Nehru was kept informed of the
night's operation and his book gives an hour-by-hour
account of how this was done.[25] But according to S. Gopal,
Nehru's biographer who had access to his papers, Nehru
"certainly does not seem to have anticipated the way in
which Abdullah was dismissed, by stealth of night in his
absence [from the State capital], and his prompt arrest
thereafter".[26]

Mullik put an extra stiletto into Abdullah by mentioning
that an emissary from Pakistan was to meet him at
Tangmarg, near Gulmarg. "Suspicions deepened," he wrote,
"when the Sheikh suddenly left for Tangmarg on the
morning of July [presumably August] 8. So the D-day was
automatically determined by the Sheikh's own action, as any
further delay might be attended with unforeseen results".[27]
But Karan Singh had known of his visit to Gulmarg in
advance and, in fact, he left late in the afternoon. Karan
Singh makes no mention of the assignation, though Mullik
suggests that he ordered Abdullah's arrest "as his meeting
the Pakistani emissary would constitute a grave danger to
the State". There was no report of any such meeting having
taken place; nor was it indicated by the circumstances in
which Abdullah was arrested. Having been given the job,
the chief of intelligence was displaying his expertise.

Nehru summed up the historic dimensions of the
tragedy in his letter to State Chief Ministers on 22 August
1953:

There can be no doubt that one of the most powerful
elements at the back was the Praja Parishad-Jana

Sangh agitation which created a great effect not only
in Sheikh Abdullah's mind but in the minds of the people
of the valley. The agitation embittered them and it
appeared to them that the Jana Sangh and its
supporters represented the prevailing sentiment in
India and that frightened them. The people began
looking in other directions. Sheikh Abdullah became
particularly bitter and rather lost his moorings. We can
criticise Sheikh Abdullah for going astray and forgetting
the principles on which he had long stood, but that does
not help much in understanding a situation which at
first gradually and then rather suddenly confronted us.
This situation was primarily the result of this communal
agitation which went on in Delhi, in the Punjab and
some other places of India for many months. Thousands
of Kashmiri labourers, who come down to India in the
summer, went back with bitterness in their hearts....
The situation developed as some inevitable tragedy
which could not be stopped. It has left a bad taste in the
mouth and I have felt unhappy, for much that has
happened has not been good and a long trail of
consequences will flow from it. If we believe as we have
and must do, that the people of Kashmir must decide
their own fate, then obviously things have happened
which have weighted the scales against us.[28]

Chapter XIV

The Bakshi Brothers

*B*akshi Ghulam Mohammad could not compete with Sheikh Abdullah as ideologue or orator, but he had other talents. He carried a baton to enhance his authority, which was not merely symbolic; he used it to enforce his orders. He was an outstanding political manager and fixer. People followed or obeyed him not because they were enthused by what he said, but because they wanted something from him or were frightened of him. For many years, he was a useful second man to Abdullah, who could whip up mass fervour with his vision of Kashmir's past and future greatness but had little political skill. Bakshi was accessible, whereas Abdullah was aloof. Above all, Bakshi had considerable organising abilities. As with so many second men, a time came when he saw no reason why he should not be first.

Principally an organisation man, Bakshi was highly pragmatic. He cultivated those who mattered by convincing them that he was dependable and could get things done one way or the other. He had no hangups about autonomy and saw the relationship with India as an arrangement to get maximum financial assistance for the State, with a percentage for family and friends. (The name given locally to his regime was BBC or Bakshi Brothers Corporation.) He was the type of State leader whom New Delhi appreciates and fosters, but who are not always loved at home. When the respect such leaders start with begins to fade, they rely increasingly on intimidation and money power to remain in office.

For New Delhi, Bakshi was an ideal State chief, especially for the bureaucrats in the Home Ministry for whom those opposing Central intervention are anti-national and those who go along pro-India. B.N. Mullik, the Director of the Intelligence Bureau, was a typical prototype. Abdullah was 'anti', and Bakshi very much 'pro'. To what extent they represented the sentiments of their people was less important. And so, Bakshi was described as "a liberal-minded and large-hearted person with his feet planted strongly among the masses.... He was completely loyal to Pandit Jawaharlal Nehru and considered himself an Indian out and out". Mullik was particularly pleased that Bakshi allowed his operatives to function freely in the State (Abdullah wondered whether their role was to spy on him or to counter Pakistan) and allowed police contingents from other States to be stationed in Kashmir. Mullik was most unhappy when Nehru accepted Bakshi's resignation in October 1963 as part of the Kamaraj plan (in which several inconvenient ministers were dropped).[1] A commission of inquiry later confirmed charges of corruption against Bakshi, but this did not lower him in Mullik's estimate.

Bakshi began to correspond with Nehru when the Quit Kashmir campaign against the Maharaja was in progress. He had gone underground, whereas Abdullah was in jail. The information he sent Nehru was not always factual, and Nehru had to modify some of the allegations made about the Maharaja's excesses when he described Srinagar as "almost a city of the dead" (see Chapter 6). As Abdullah's deputy, Bakshi continued to be Nehru's source of inform-ation concerning developments in Kashmir and the Prime Minister trusted him enough to indicate his concern over the direction that they were taking. Bakshi had everything going for him when New Delhi decided against Abdullah, except popular support, as evident from his refusal to take over until Abdullah was safely detained outside the valley.

Bakshi was a competent administrator and made full use of the flow of financial assistance from the Centre. Hydroelectric projects, housing colonies, roads spreading through the valley (though some paid for from the State exchequer were later found to exist only on paper), facilities for tourists, a lower-level tunnel at Banihal to improve communications with Jammu and the rest of India, all appeared. Rice was subsidised. The purpose was to demonstrate the benefits of closer ties with India. But the impact on the public was mixed. Mir Qasim, then a Cabinet Minister, recalls: "The people were happy with our work, but would not forgive us for the plight of the Sheikh and therefore would not fully cooperate in our development projects."[2]

Initially, in keeping with the distaste he professed to have felt over the manner of Abdullah's dismissal and arrest, Nehru did not go out of his way to praise Bakshi. But a month later, he was telling other State Chief Ministers that the National Conference was fully behind Bakshi's Government and that he had "met a difficult situation with great ability and energy". And by October, after he had won a unanimous vote of confidence, that "it is really astonishing how Bakshi Ghulam Mohammad and his colleagues in the ministry have, by their policy and hard work, changed the entire picture and outlook in the state within two months".[3]

Judging from the situation in the valley, however, the transition was not quite so smooth. According to Mullik, the disturbances following Abdullah's arrest lasted for nearly three weeks, with nearly sixty people killed in police firing, mostly in Srinagar. The agitation for his release lasted much longer.[4] Ghulam Mohammad Sadiq and Mir Qasim (both Chief Ministers later) barely escaped with their lives from a menacing crowd of 20,000 at Shopian on their way to Srinagar (Sadiq was known to oppose Abdullah) and, according to Mir Qasim: "Srinagar was in total chaos. Bakshi Saheb's own house, despite the police guard, was under attack. He was nervous and wanted to step down." Abdullah's arrest had generated "a bitter sense of betrayal in Kashmir".[5]

With the arrest of Abdullah, other Kashmiri leaders began to emerge. They were well known in the valley, but had been overshadowed by Abdullah's stature and mass appeal. They found it hard to work together after the common struggle against the Maharaja's rule because of differences at two levels. In ideology, they ranged from Marxist through pragmatic to conservative. They also differed on the degree of independence/autonomy they wanted and the extent to which they felt that they could be associated with India or Pakistan. Those standing for social change were more comfortable with India except when events in India aroused fears of Hindu domination. Those favouring Pakistan, like Chaudhri Ghulam Abbas, crossed over; others were detained or kept out of politics. Occasionally, the charge of being pro-Pakistan was used to detain inconvenient rivals.

Among those arrested along with Abdullah was Mirza Afzal Beg, his constitutional and legal adviser, who had briefly functioned as a Minister in the Maharaja's regime. He was charged, by Mullik, among others, with conspiring with Pakistan, though twenty years later, it was he who worked out an agreement in which Abdullah accepted the finality of Kashmir's accession to India before returning to the State as Chief Minister. Beg was in and out of detention. His primary fault was that he organised the Plebiscite Front, thus reviving the issue that the accession of Jammu and Kashmir to India had yet to receive the promised sanction of a plebiscite. For New Delhi, trying hard to escape the albatross that Jinnah had hung over its neck and harried at the UN, this was equivalent to conspiring with the enemy, which is what the Central Intelligence Bureau proceeded to prove. Letters were produced indicating contact with Pakistan, with phrases interpreted as anti-national. From prison near Jammu, Abdullah supported the Front because it helped mobilise Kashmiri opinion against Bakshi. But he did not join the Front, possibly recalling that it was he who had earlier wanted the Kashmir Constituent Assembly to finalise accession to India. Then, it was Nehru

who had insisted that the question remain open since India
was committed to a plebiscite.

Anyone suggesting that Abdullah was more sinned
against than sinning was smeared. Maulana Syed Masoodi,
General Secretary of the National Conference, until evicted
by Bakshi, had not always sided with Abdullah but was
unhappy with his arrest and Bakshi's takeover. He won over
some leaders in New Delhi with the assistance of Mridula
Sarabhai, of the affluent Sarabhai family in Ahmedabad,
who devoted herself to Abdullah's cause. For Mullik, "her
house in Delhi became a haven for the activities of the
Plebiscite Front leaders, some of whom even made contacts
with the Pakistan High Commission from this place. They
took advantage of her munificence and made her part with
a considerable amount of money...."[6] Yet, it was Masoodi who
helped Mullik calm the passions roused by the
disappearance of the *Moe-e-Muqaddas* (Prophet's hair) from
the Hazratbal mosque near Srinagar nearly ten years later.

The primary target was Abdullah; Bakshi could not feel
secure unless he was totally discredited. One charge that
would destroy his image among the liberals in India,
including Jayaprakash Narayan and Asoka Mehta, who
believed he had been treated unjustly, was that his secular
image was fraudulent. To begin with, a case was filed in
October 1957 against Afzal Beg, Begum Abdullah (suspected
of being a conduit for funds from Pakistan) and nine others
on a charge of conspiring to bring about a violent revolution
in the State to overthrow the Government. After an
intensive search for additional evidence, Abdullah was also
charged, although in detention. Many of the charges were
loosely phrased such as inciting communal disharmony and
fostering hostile feelings towards India, and publishing
inflammatory posters. What was designed to hurt them
more in India were charges of contacts with Pakistan
through alleged emissaries and coded letters. Mullik
summarises the allegations as if they had been established:

It was clear that the range of this conspiracy was wide.

Sheikh Abdullah and Afzal Beg were the directing heads and Begum Abdullah formed one of the important links with Pakistan for receiving money and directions.... Their aim was to antagonise the Muslims of Kashmir against the Bakshi Government and against India. In this way an atmosphere was to be created in which it would be easy for Pakistani agents to operate and undertake explosions, sabotages [sic] and killings.... Pakistan went on financing the conspiracy by pumping in large sums of money and also sending large quantities of ammunition. By 1957, on the basis of the information received from the conspirators, Pakistan considered that the ground was ready for a revolution and sent large groups of infiltrators.... There was no doubt that these frustrated Kashmiri leaders, in conjunction with Pakistan, had conspired to bring about a state of utter anarchy and disorder... with a view to overthrowing the lawfully constituted Government of Jammu and Kashmir.

Mullik's weakness for Bakshi emerges more clearly in the reasons he gives for the defeat of the alleged conspiracy. Those involved got no response from the people of Kashmir because "association with India had brought much material benefit to them and the Bakshi government was popular and, by and large, met the aspirations of the people."[7]

A damning indictment against prominent leaders would have been normally expected to be supported by impeccable evidence. But the ensuing conspiracy case against Abdullah and his co-conspirators, filed in a special magistrate's court in May 1958 in Jammu (his Begum was spared though the accusations against her were more specific), was extended from year to year. It was then committed to Sessions in 1962. Mullik would have us believe that Nehru was kept informed and he approved of these proceedings. He also portrays Nehru as saying that "all the trouble in Kashmir was due to the Sheikh's communal outlook...communalism was a disease with him and he could never get rid of it".[8]

Yet, after another two years, at a high-level meeting in
Kashmir, Nehru banged the table and said about the alleged
conspiracy: "If a damned thing can't be proved in four years
and in six years, then there's obviously nothing to be
proved."[9] Abdullah was freed thereafter and invited to stay
at the Prime Minister's house, where he was received with
a regard and affection that Nehru was unlikely to have
extended to an arch communalist.

Y.D. Gundevia was Commonwealth Secretary in the
Ministry of External Affairs when Nehru exploded, and to
him we owe much of the light shed on the working of the
Home Ministry and its Intelligence Bureau, more so on the
dependability of Mullik's memoirs. Gundevia was close
enough to Nehru to contradict Mullik's suggestion that the
Prime Minister was involved in all the measures leading to
the dismissal and post-midnight arrest of Abdullah. He also
questions the accuracy of Mullik's recollection of what
Nehru allegedly said about Abdullah's communal outlook.

Gundevia casts doubts on the basic points made by
Mullik. He insists

> that Jawaharlal Nehru was not party to Sheikh
> Abdullah's arrest and he had certainly not authorised
> it; he had been poisoned and silenced into acquiescence
> -- once the *coup* was a *fait accompli* -- though this is bad
> enough. Secondly, I find it extremely hard to believe --
> no matter who says it now -- that Nehru was ever
> convinced, at any stage, that Sheikh Abdullah was a
> communalist and was conspiring against India in league
> with Pakistan and the pro-Pakistan elements in
> Kashmir.

Gundevia based this judgement on his close association with
Nehru during the last four years of his life as Commonwealth Secretary and then as Foreign Secretary. Abdullah
and his trial had been discussed at least a hundred times
at various meetings, but not once had the Prime Minister
maligned the Sheikh.[10]

In fact, Nehru was consistently apologetic about detaining

Abdullah. A letter he wrote to Abdullah in jail, in April 1955, suggests that his hand was forced:

> We, who are in charge of heavy responsibilities, have to deal with all kinds of forces at work and often they take their own shape. We see in the world today great statesmen, who imagine they are controlling the destinies of nations, being pushed hither and thither by forces beyond their control.[11]

There is no available record of whether Abdullah replied. But in his autobiography, he said that Nehru "was not happy at my continuing detention. He often advised Bakshi Saheb to release me. On one pretext or another, however, Bakshi managed to avoid it. Being basically fair-minded, Jawaharlal started realising that my captivity was due to no fault of mine". Abdullah cites as evidence Nehru's letter to Karan Singh (still Sadar-i-Riyasat) and Bakshi opposing his detention without trial.[12]

Abdullah was briefly freed in January 1958. The reception he got all the way back to Srinagar (on which Mullik comments sourly: "He behaved as if he was a king returning to his country after exile for re-installation") demonstrated that he had not lost his popularity. Then the Intelligence Bureau got into the act again. Abdullah was reported to be provoking riots and "holding secret meetings in his house in which the questions of demanding a plebiscite for merging the state with Pakistan, large-scale enlistment of Razakars, who could be imparted instruction in the handling of bombs and other arms, which were received from Pakistan, and making contacts with Pakistan were planned." Money was also alleged to be flowing in from Pakistan.

And, so, Mullik writes, with his genius for over-statement: "As things were coming to a climax and it was apparent that the Sheikh was doing everything possible to join hands with Pakistan and by creating disorders in the state to give an excuse to Pakistan to intervene directly, he was re-arrested on 30 April 1958."[13] But, according to

Mir Qasim, "we learnt that the riots were engineered by Bakshi Saheb's supporters to provide justification for the re-arrest of Sheikh Saheb". Although Qasim had been a minister he had not been aware of the conspiracy of which Abdullah was charged. He protested to Nehru against the re-arrest, only to be told that the Prime Minister did not approve of all Bakshi's actions and that he was in Hyderabad when Abdullah was put back in jail.[14] This time, he stayed in jail until 8 April 1964 after Nehru, as Gundevia reported, intervened again, much to Mullik's discomfiture.

The show of development in the State did not increase Bakshi's popularity. Mounting corruption and nepotism had the opposite effect. His cousin, Abdul Rashid, made General Secretary of the National Conference in succession to the respected Maulana Masoodi, was the conduit. Kashmiri society was divided into two hostile sections: the few who benefited from development plans and the many who did not. The elections in 1962 were so thoroughly rigged that Bakshi's hand-chosen National Conference candidates won seventy out of seventy-five seats. Nehru was prompted to tell him: "In fact, it would strengthen your position much more if you lost a few seats to bonafide opponents."[15]

Now, Bakshi's days were numbered. After years of closing its eyes to the corruption in his regime and to the terror squads he mobilised, the national press began to write about them. So far, the press had swallowed the line that such reports would hurt the national interest, aided by the generous hospitality Bakshi provided to visiting journalists. But after nearly a decade, the operations of the Bakshi Brothers Corporation became too notorious to be ignored, even though the Central Intelligence Bureau may have preferred to continue to look the other way. Nehru took the opportunity provided in 1963 by the Kamaraj plan (enabling several inconvenient leaders to be persuaded to quit office) to ease out Bakshi too. But, as so often, he did not apply the broom vigorously enough. Bakshi was able to manoeuvre his protégé Shamsuddin, with no following of his own, into

the chair that he had vacated. The consequences were
disastrous.

One of Kashmir's holiest and most treasured relics is the
Moe-e-Muqaddas, widely believed to be the hair of the
Prophet. It was installed in the Hazratbal mosque, overlooking a picturesque stretch of the Dal Lake near Srinagar,
in A.D. 1700. On 27 December 1963, it was found missing.
The rumour went round that the Bakshi family was
responsible for the theft of the holy relic. Though winter was
at its harshest, crowds from all over the valley gathered in
Srinagar and their antipathy to the Bakshi Brothers
surfaced. When asked by cousin Abdul Rashid to disperse,
they turned on him and he had to be rescued by the police.
The crowd set fire to a hotel and a cinema house owned by
Bakshi's brother, Abdul Majid. The police opened fire, killing
three persons.

Prime Minister Shamsuddin returned from Jammu to
Srinagar, but was confined to his house by hostile crowds,
who identified him with Bakshi. And Bakshi was identified
as New Delhi's agent who had begun the process of eroding
Kashmir's autonomy (described later). He was asked by
Nehru to keep away until the situation simmered down. The
crowds demanded Abdullah's release. Radio Pakistan and
the pro-Pakistan lobby in Kashmir got into the act. There
was nobody of stature to oppose them. There were calls for
jehad (holy war) against "the Hindu rulers of India, who had
outraged Islam".[16]

The developments snowballed into a mass protest
against the rule foisted on Kashmir by the Centre. For more
than a week, a total *hartal* crippled Srinagar. Chanting
crowds filled the streets. Unable to control them, the
administration and police withdrew. A citizens' "action
committee" decided which shops should open and when.
Free *langars* were organised to feed the crowds who had
come in from surrounding villages. The Government's writ

did not run beyond its closely guarded offices. Perhaps because Nehru was still in the saddle in New Delhi, the para-military forces did not move in to crush the demonstration.

Mullik was rushed to Srinagar to investigate the disappearance of the Prophet's hair. On 4 January 1964, he announced that the relic had been replaced in what he mysteriously describes as "an intelligence operation never to be disclosed".[17] With sceptics yet to be convinced that the replaced relic was genuine, disturbances continued. Armed police from outside Kashmir were insulted by the crowds and a contingent from Punjab attacked; they opened fire, killing several persons. A demand for the identification of the relic by clerics in whom people had confidence became widespread. But this was opposed by Mullik and Home Ministry officials who were convinced that the campaign was the work of "evil-minded pro-Pakistani agents" and should be crushed.

Though ailing at the time, Nehru was opposed to confrontation. He did not want to continue to leave the problem to the law and order approach of the Home Ministry. Lal Bahadur Shastri (who succeeded Nehru as Prime Minister) was rushed to Srinagar, where he landed in the depth of winter wearing Nehru's overcoat[18] and, as Mullik remarks disapprovingly, "preferred a political settlement of the issue to a settlement by administrative measures".[19] Against Home Ministry advice, Shastri accepted the demand for a special *deedar* (viewing) by a group of fourteen respected clerics on 3 February. Led by Maulana Masoodi, they identified the relic as genuine and peace returned to the valley.

*A*fter the widespread and prolonged agitation due to the disappearance of the holy relic, it was evident that neither Shamsuddin nor any other political leader identified with Bakshi would be acceptable as Prime Minister of Kashmir.

Consequently, the man chosen for the job was Ghulam Mohammad Sadiq, an intellectual and a Marxist. One of the first group of National Conference leaders, he had served with distinction as Chairman of the State Constituent Assembly. One reason for his acceptability was that, in contrast to the Bakshi family, he was not known to be corrupt. These qualifications impressed Nehru, who used his influence to persuade the Kashmir Assembly to elect Sadiq as leader, although his support in the valley was limited. He took over in February 1964.

But democratic procedures were followed only as long as they were permitted by the Home Ministry. Bakshi, who had earlier benefited from its powers, was now at the receiving end. Since he had hand-picked most of the legislators, he was seen as a threat to the new Government. When it became known that he might press a motion of no-confidence, officials panicked and urged his arrest. According to Mir Qasim, Sadiq and he were willing to face the motion, but the officials, headed by Shankar Prasad, Secretary, Kashmir Affairs, in New Delhi, were adamant. Karan Singh, still Sadar-i-Riyasat and more than ever attuned to the Centre's outlook, arranged a midnight conference. Mir Qasim's account is revealing:

> A heated debate on all aspects of Mr Bakshi's plan for a motion of no-confidence ensued. We repeated our stand that since Mr Bakshi enjoyed the majority in the House, we should let him rule. But our stand was rejected in view of what they called the "national interest". It was decided Mr Bakshi be arrested in "national interest".[20]

This event took place in September 1964, after Nehru's death. Sadiq wanted to consult the new Prime Minister, Lal Bahadur Shastri, but went along after being assured that Shankar Prasad's presence indicated that the Centre approved of the arrest. How limited Kashmir's autonomy was in practice was only too evident. Neither Sadiq nor, subsequently, Mir Qasim, was of the calibre to oppose New Delhi, whatever their objections. And unchecked by Nehru's

scruples, New Delhi pushed ahead with integration
regardless of Kashmiri opinion.

The National Conference had been ailing since
Abdullah's arrest. Instead of reviving the NC, Sadiq and Mir
Qasim combined to virtually eliminate it. They tried to
replace it with the Congress. As approved at the Durgapur
Congress session in 1965, Mir Qasim became the founder-
president of the Kashmir branch of the Congress. Now the
people of the valley had no alternative but to join either the
Plebiscite Front, which held that accession to India was
temporary, or the Congress, seen as an agent of the Centre.
The party that had served to represent their interest even
under the Maharaja's regime and fought for autonomy from
the Centre had been deserted by the leaders of the State
Government.

The collapse of the National Conference revealed the
process of erosion of Kashmir's autonomy at the party level.
Far more damaging was the erosion of the constitutional
guarantees which shielded the valley from imposition of
Central authority. In due course this enabled New Delhi to
impose Governors who dismissed elected governments and
ruled, with military assistance, without any evidence of
popular sanction. The process began under Bakshi. The
initial changes were more symbolic than substantial, but
they marked the beginning of a process that was to further
the alienation of Kashmiri opinion which started with
Abdullah's arrest. Less than a year after Bakshi took over,
on 14 May 1954, certain provisions relating to fundamental
rights in the Indian Constitution were extended to Kashmir
and the range of subjects on which Parliament was
empowered to legislate for the State was extended. More
significant was the administrative integration achieved in
1958 by extending the all-India services, including the
Indian Administrative Service and Indian Police Service, to

the State. Their officers were later to rule unfettered by the supervision of elected representatives.

The Jammu and Kashmir Constitution was adopted on 17 November 1956 and took effect on 26 January 1957, exactly seven years after the Constitution of India, which had authorised a separate Constitution of the State under Article 370. In many respects, it was modelled on the parent Constitution and declared unambiguously: "The State of Jammu and Kashmir is and shall be an integral part of the Union of India." At the same time, it contained several provisions giving effect to the special status of Jammu and Kashmir. The most important was the provision for a Head of State, titled Sadar-i-Riyasat, elected by the State Assembly, and *not* appointed by the President of India. This feature and other crucial aspects of Kashmir's special status were eroded in 1965, after Nehru was dead and Abdullah detained again. The office of an elected Sadar-e-Riyasat was abolished to be replaced by a Governor nominated by the Centre, as in other States. And the Governor was empowered to declare President's rule in the event of a "constitutional breakdown", a device used by New Delhi to topple inconvenient State Governments and rule directly. The title of Prime Minister, which Abdullah and Bakshi enjoyed, was abolished, to be replaced by Chief Minister, as in other States.

Certain residual powers were left to Kashmir under Article 370, but they were largely symbolic. One was to prevent non-residents of the State from owning property – in response to a historical fear in the Kashmiri psyche. But this was not unique to Jammu and Kashmir; similar restrictions have been imposed by other States also, especially in remote, hilly areas where the people fear being swamped by aggressive settlers from the plains. Possibly influenced by his ideological belief in centralised power, the crucial extension of the Centre's powers, enabling it to rule the State directly, took place under Sadiq's regime. The historian Prem Nath Bazaz, who had praised Sadiq earlier, expressed his disappointment in a letter to him on 28 June 1965:

> The biggest problem to present-day Kashmir...is the reconciliation of local nationalism with Indian nationalism. That leader alone has the chance to survive opposition onslaughts and lead the state people to the goal of democracy as a part of Indian Nation who can, during the transition period, wisely strike a balance between the demands and emotions of the Indians and the aspirations, urges and sentiments of the Kashmiris. Only thoughtless people can believe that the aims, inclinations, passions and desires of the two peoples are identical in every respect today; such a notion is misleading and harmful. It is unfair to accuse Kashmiri patriots of parochialism or narrow-mindedness when they display communal tendencies as long as Indian nationalism, despite its tall presumptuous claims, itself remains based on religious beliefs and Hindu mythology.... When last autumn Indian nationalism launched upon an aggressive campaign to demolish the autonomy of the State without the consent of the Kashmiris you faltered and acted according to its bidding.[21]

As Congressmen, Ghulam Mohammad Sadiq and Mir Qasim were subject to the controls of the party as well as the Central Government in New Delhi. Mir Qasim was junior, but they had been colleagues and friends ever since participating in the Quit Kashmir movement. Having installed Sadiq as Chief Minister, New Delhi did not want him to become too independent. So, in 1968, Sadiq and Qasim fell victim to a long-established technique. In Mir Qasim's words: "I must inform my readers that whenever New Delhi feels a leader in Kashmir is getting too big for his shoes, it employs Machiavellian methods to cut him to size." And so, too late, he discovered that: "Alas, Mr Sadiq and I, who in Kashmir politics had become the proverbial David and Jonathan in the past about two decades were trapped in this conspiracy to become each other's political rivals and enemies."[22] Both were reduced to travelling to New Delhi to establish their claims to leadership, where Indira Gandhi, an expert in Machiavellian tactics, was Prime Minister. Mir Qasim had earlier noted that "instead of becoming a source of strength for us, the Congress became a conduit for the flow of all the country's political dirt into Kashmir."[23] Even so, he did not break away from the organisation.

It was at this time, when the National Conference had been virtually extinguished and the Kashmir Congress was split, that the first movement for armed insurrection, Al Fateh, emerged in the valley. Mir Qasim traces its origins to resentment against Bakshi's strong-arm methods. At that time, "the valley echoed with harrowing tales of police brutalities and falsifications. A sense of alienation was growing. There were some Pakistani agencies at hand to canalise the Kashmiri youth resentment."[24] Sadiq was further handicapped by persistent sickness. He died in December 1971 and was succeeded by Mir Qasim.

Al Fateh's most spectacular achievement was the hijacking of an Indian Airlines aircraft on 30 January 1971. It took off from Srinagar and was diverted to Lahore, where the plane was burnt but the passengers rescued. When some of the young men charged with the conspiracy in Srinagar were brought to trial a year later, Mir Qasim, now Chief Minister, took credit for bringing them round by releasing some and helping those jailed to prepare for their examinations. He kept in touch with Abdullah and prepared the ground for his reconciliation with the Centre.

Chapter XV

End of an Era

---

*T*he death of Jawaharlal Nehru on 27 May 1964 marked a watershed in relations between the Centre and Kashmir. He valued the valley for sentimental reasons and its scenic beauty but not primarily as real estate. For him, it was a living demonstration of his faith that Muslims could have confidence in a secular India and could reject the two-nation theory. This made winning the people more important than holding the territory. He shared the Marxist/rationalist belief that economic advance would overcome religious sentiment (he had earlier predicted that Pakistan, as a nation, would fizzle out) and hoped that this would promote Kashmir's gradual integration with the rest of India. He occasionally looked the other way when repressive steps were taken, but this was in the hope that they were temporary and would accelerate economic development, as indicated by his early support for Bakshi. But he would not go along with prolonged injustice, exemplified by the extended detention of Abdullah, mostly on concocted charges.

Nehru's central objective remained to win and secure the confidence of the valley, not to hold it by force. He was willing to part with the valley, if unsuccessful, as promised in his statement to the Lok Sabha on 7 August 1952. This also imbued his commitment to a plebiscite, which was muffled when he feared that Pakistan's alliance with the West would draw Kashmir into Anglo-American geopolitical axis against the Soviet Union. Ultranationalist domestic pressures were also a factor. He favoured a settlement on the basis of territory held rather than religious affiliation. When needing Western assistance during and after the border war with China in 1962, he was subjected to considerable pressure to win over Pakistan by making concessions in Kashmir. He offered to hand over a strip bordering Pakistan in the valley and in Jammu without conceding acceptance of the two-nation theory. But Pakistan wanted the entire State, except for a bit of Jammu, on the basis of the two-nation theory. The negotiations collapsed.

Towards the end of his life, Nehru seemed to realise that the Home Ministry, backed by hardliners in his party, had taken over direction of policy towards Kashmir and other disaffected areas, such as Nagaland. He began to initiate remedial steps. The maximum rethinking was on Kashmir. The crisis caused by the disappearance of the Prophet's hair from Srinagar had demonstrated the degree of Kashmiri disaffection and how near the situation was to open rebellion, until assuaged by Shastri. So, as Gundevia reported, he insisted that Abdullah be freed and the case against him be withdrawn.

Abdullah was embittered by his imprisonment, yet willing to talk to Nehru. He did not question his friend's principles, but was unsure of his capacity to resist pressures. As he recalled later: "Panditji expressed his deep anguish and sorrow at the past incidents. I also became very emotional and told him that I was glad to have convinced him that I was not disloyal to him personally or to India." He then convinced Nehru of the need to resolve the Kashmir problem while he was still alive. Accordingly, Nehru agreed to Abdullah visiting Pakistan and inviting President Ayub Khan to visit Delhi since Nehru's health did not permit him to go to Pakistan.[1]

Opinion in India was sharply divided. A strong lobby, especially in Parliament, took the line that Kashmir's accession must be treated as final. Any hesitation or show of willingness to consider a popular verdict would not only endanger its link with the Union but it would also promote "fissiparous tendencies" elsewhere too. But there were also growing numbers who were disturbed by what they saw as a fascist tendency in the Centre. Among them was Nehru's former colleague Jayaprakash Narayan, an outspoken proponent of unpopular causes. He recalled the provision for reference to the people in Mountbatten's acceptance of Maharaja Hari Singh's accession. He also echoed Nehru's assertion that a democratic India should be held together by consent, not by force. The savage reaction to his article in *The Hindustan Times*, on 20 April 1964, in Parliament and elsewhere showed how strong was the opposite sentiment. But it may have strengthened Nehru's doubts about the Home Ministry approach to policy.[2]

Abdullah stayed for several days at the Prime Minister's house meeting Cabinet Ministers and others. He was now convinced that Kashmir would continue to suffer as long as it was the arena of Indo-Pakistan animosity. There could be no solution without an agreement between these two countries. But after nearly nine years in jail, he did not quite realise how deep was the distrust on either side after the war with China, especially after Pakistan had turned down India's offer to part with some territory in Kashmir as the price for a settlement. Instead, Pakistan had signed a border agreement with China.

After his talks in Delhi, Abdullah travelled to Gandhi's old ashram at Wardha to meet Vinoba Bhave and Jayaprakash Narayan and then on to Madras to meet Rajaji (C. Rajagopalachari). He returned with a proposal, probably suggested by Rajaji, for a confederation among India, Pakistan and Kashmir — the nearest thing to his dream of an independent Kashmir. Nehru was not sure it would work but agreed to allow Abdullah to go to Pakistan to sound out President Ayub's reactions. After revisiting the valley, Abdullah left on 24 May, accompanied by Afzal Beg and Maulana Masoodi. After a big initial welcome, enthusiasm for him cooled in Pakistan: he committed the sin of stressing the need to retain India's secular (a word as taboo in Pakistan as two-nation in India) character.[3]

Ayub Khan would have nothing to do with the confederation proposal, as Nehru's official advisers had anticipated. He saw it as a cunning move to extend Indian hegemony, devised by Nehru, which is what he said later in his autobiography. Referring to "the absurd proposal of a confederation between India, Pakistan and Kashmir," he wrote, "I told him [Abdullah] plainly we should have nothing to do with it. It was curious that whereas we were seeking salvation of Kashmiris, they had been forced to mention an idea which, if pursued, would lead to our enslavement. It was clear that this was what Mr Nehru had told them to say to us: I did not blame them because they were obviously acting under the compulsion of circumstances but they left me in no doubt that their future was linked with Pakistan."[4]

When Abdullah saw the book three years after the meeting, he wrote to Ayub on 1 September 1967 to set the record straight and deny that Nehru had forced them to put forward the confederation proposal. But he tried to keep it alive by suggesting that instead of rejecting it, the best course would be to discuss it around a conference table. "I find certain discrepancies in your statement," he wrote. "We had not taken with us any cut and dried proposal concerning the Kashmir dispute, and to be fair to the late Jawaharlal Nehru, he never forced us to put before you any particular proposal. We are not made that way."[5]

However, Abdullah was successful in persuading Ayub to visit India. From Rawalpindi, he went on to visit "Azad" (Pakistan-held) Kashmir, where, in Muzaffarabad, he was informed of Nehru's death on 27 May. He rushed back to Delhi to be present at his cremation, where he wept publicly. "With his death a glorious chapter of Indian history came to an end," he wrote later.[6] Their friendship had survived severe political strains for a quarter century; the only Indian leader who understood him, even when forced to

differ from him, had gone. Abdullah carried some of Nehru's
ashes for immersion in Kashmir's rivers.

*T*he shift in New Delhi's attitude was perceptible after
Nehru's death. Abdullah described his successor, Lal
Bahadur Shastri (who had played a crucial role in assuaging
the outbursts after the disappearance of the holy relic) as
gentle and moderate, and keen to improve relations with
Pakistan. But Home Minister Gulzari Lal Nanda led those
who took the opposite line and accelerated the erosion of
Kashmir's autonomy. After some months, Abdullah returned
to Delhi for talks with the new Prime Minister and his
colleagues. "Shastri was very cordial and it seemed he was
keen to complete the work-initiated by Jawaharlal Nehru,"
he recalled. "But he lacked Nehru's popular appeal and did
not have the strength to muster his colleagues around to
his viewpoint."[7]

In February 1965, Sheikh Abdullah and his wife went
abroad, initially to Mecca to perform the Haj, then to other
Islamic countries and finally to England. He had always
been a devout Muslim, but his visits to Islamic countries
disturbed many in India. In Mecca, he attended a session
of the Islamic International Conference, where he was
invited as a freedom-fighter. But, as in Pakistan, he stressed
the need to promote Indian secularism and, at his
suggestion, no reference was made to Indian Muslims. What
upset New Delhi, however, was his amicable meeting in
Algeria with the Chinese Premier, Chou En-lai, who invited
him to China. Chou supported self-determination for
Kashmir. With China still regarded as a near-enemy, this
was akin to treason. There was an uproar in Parliament and
he was instructed to return immediately to India on pain
of forfeiture of his passport.

This was an empty threat because many countries,
especially Pakistan, would have been happy to give Abdullah
a passport. But he dutifully flew back to New Delhi, a

gesture that was ignored. He was detained at the airport
and taken to Kodaikanal, a hill resort in Tamil Nadu, far
away from Kashmir. Gulzari Lal Nanda had even less
regard for Abdullah than Patel. This time, his incarceration
lasted three years, though life was made as pleasant as
possible, with his wife permitted to join him.

W hile Abdullah was in Kodaikanal, India and Pakistan
again went to war over Kashmir. "Luckily I was away," he
commented, "otherwise Gulzari Lal Nanda would have
accused me of fomenting trouble."[8] This time the invaders
were not tribals, but trained saboteurs, fewer in numbers
than in 1947, but better disciplined and motivated.
Technically, once again, it was a non-official operation, but
there was even less doubt about the Pakistan Government's
complicity. This has been documented not only by the
Indians involved in resisting these saboteurs but also by the
Pakistanis responsible for infiltrating them. It was a major
operation involving about 7000 armed men, from "Azad"
Kashmir formations, and irregulars, led by regular Pakistan
army officers. Supplies were dropped by the Pakistan air
force. They harried the Indian army and para-military
forces for two months and infiltrated up to Srinagar, where
they set off explosions to announce their presence. But they
failed in their primary objectives: to provoke a general
uprising against India and to set up a revolutionary council
which would appeal for foreign recognition and aid.

The reason they failed was that the Kashmiris did not
cooperate with them. This is admitted by General
Mohammad Musa, Commander-in-Chief of the Pakistan
army at the time. According to him, "the Muslim population
there [in the valley], although by and large willing to help
were unable to cooperate with us fully". Though carefully
worded, the background he provides to the decision to
launch Operation Gibraltar, as it was code-named, makes

it clear that his army was opposed to the operation because
they were uncertain of local support and feared to provoke
an all-out Indian response (which eventually occurred).
They were pushed into it by the Pakistan Foreign Office,
then headed by Zulfiqar Ali Bhutto. Musa discloses that
President Ayub was involved in the planning. The objectives
were:

> Sabotage of military targets, disruption of
> communications, etc., and as a long-term measure,
> distribution of arms to the people of occupied Kashmir
> and initiation of a guerilla movement there with a view
> to starting an uprising in the valley eventually.[9]

Political factors were not ignored in planning Operation
Gibraltar. The re-arrest of Sheikh Abdullah after his Haj
pilgrimage had evoked resentment in the valley. To
capitalise on this factor, the infiltration time-table was
drawn up so as to hit Srinagar on 9 August, the anniversary
of his first arrest, when protest meetings were usually held.
Pakistan's earlier efforts to denigrate Abdullah had failed;
now he was projected as a popular hero. But the infiltrators
got no support. They were killed, captured or withdrawn.
Pakistan's regular forces were thrown into the battle in an
armoured attack on Chhamb (in Jammu district), which
headed for Akhnur, where it threatened to sever India's land
communications with Kashmir. On 6 September Indian
troops crossed directly into Pakistan in response. Kashmir
was no longer the main theatre of war.

Lt. General Harbaksh Singh, then Commander-in-Chief,
Western Command, provides an admirably detailed account
of the entire campaign in the form of daily despatches, with
data on opposing forces, plans and strategies and the
outcome. He admits that the Indian army had no prior
intelligence of the massive infiltration campaign. If the
planners of Operation Gibraltar had not misjudged
Kashmiri sentiment, the infiltrators may have slipped
through the cease-fire line undetected. On 5 August,
however, two of them approached Mohammad Din, a young

man herding cattle near Gulmarg and offered him four
hundred rupees for information. But he informed the police
and an army patrol was despatched, which dispersed the
group. Near Mendhar, Wazir Mohammed was similarly
approached. He reported to the nearby brigade
headquarters. A patrol was sent out and clashed with the
intruders. The captain leading them and three others were
killed before the intruders fled back across the cease-fire
line.

Now the army realised what they were up against. More
troops were despatched and there were encounters
throughout the State, with casualties on both sides. The
infiltrators did not get to Srinagar according to schedule,
but were able to keep its citizens awake on the night of
10 August with sporadic firing. Not until 18 August did the
pressure ease; the last infiltrators were not pushed out until
October.[10] The army took the opportunity to capture Haji
Pir, dominating the route from Uri to Poonch, lost in 1948
by an early cease-fire. Haji Pir was lost again under the
Tashkent Declaration signed by Lal Bahadur Shastri and
Ayub Khan on 10 January 1966 under the eye of Soviet
Premier Alexei Kosygin. The pressures on Shastri to
withdraw Indian troops from areas they had occupied at
great cost, including Haji Pir, for the sake of a settlement
from which India gained little, undoubtedly contributed to
his death in Tashkent. It was not the first, nor the last, time
that gains in battle would be lost at the conference table.

Shastri's death brought in Indira Gandhi as Prime
Minister, the most skilful political operator to occupy the
office, but more concerned with retaining and extending
personal power than its use for the national benefit. She had
an instinct for sizing up an individual's weakness and how
to utilise it. Abdullah, taken ill at Kodaikanal, had been
brought to Delhi for treatment and interned in a bungalow
in July 1967. Those who called on him there (including this

writer) found him unusually pensive and somewhat confused. He had aged. Despite his infructuous meeting with Ayub, he continued to feel that an Indo-Pakistan agreement was essential for the welfare of Kashmir. He did not seem bitter over his long imprisonment, nor in a mood for revenge, but was still convinced that the commitments India had made to Kashmir were yet to be fulfilled.

Abdullah was released from his last detention on 2 January 1968. At a press conference two days later, he was very much the elder statesman, refusing to be provoked, stressing the need for accommodation. The earlier fire and zeal were missing. The only pronouncement to which New Delhi could take objection was his insistence on the right of self-determination for Kashmir, but he phrased it generally; it was "an inherent right of all peoples". At the same time, he said "free elections" were not enough to satisfy him – a hint that plebiscite was still on the cards. The same day, he met Indira Gandhi and seemed impressed: "She had an independent temperament, excellent administrative ability and political sagacity."[11]

The extended authorised interview, published as his *Testament*, provides a glimpse of Abdullah's views after his release. He said that Kashmiri opinion had changed since partition and gave reasons for the change:

There are still those Muslims who shouted the slogans "Long live Gandhi and Nehru" and who wanted to live in peace and friendship with India but the dishonesty of [later] Indian statesmen has weakened their faith in India. They have witnessed riots, corruption, the plight of the poor people in India and the luxury of the wealthy and they are greatly influenced by these things. As a result a significant change has taken place in their outlook.

Abdullah was evasive on the subject of citizenship: "From the constitutional point of view I have accepted the citizenship of India temporarily but the final decision will be taken later." This fitted in with his stress on the need for self-determination, to be implemented through plebiscite. He admitted that he had said that the Kashmir Constituent Assembly was competent to confirm the State's accession to India without a plebiscite, but pointed out that Nehru had held back because of the UN. "Thus," he now argued, "the promise of the plebiscite was reaffirmed and the right of the people of Kashmir to decide their own future was restated."

At the same time, he insisted that he was loyal to India, as shown by his resistance to Pakistani aggression and later by his return to India to face arrest in 1965. "Give me more freedom – I shall not jeopardise the grandeur of India."[12]

Initially, there were no restrictions. He returned to the valley, where he was given the mass welcome he had always received as Sher-i-Kashmir (Lion of Kashmir). But his open support for the Plebiscite Front, emerging as the most popular party in the valley, led to second thoughts in New Delhi. He presided over a people's convention, organised, among others, by his old friend and sympathiser, Jayaprakash Narayan. Politicians of all hues were present, as were some academics and journalists (including this writer). It was a confusing conference; no clear line or viewpoint emerged. In fact, it led to a difference of opinion between Jayaprakash and Abdullah. The former was all in favour of autonomy, but insisted that after the 1965 war, the question of self-determination was theoretical and Pakistan had no role to play. This was unacceptable to Abdullah.

Indira Gandhi dissolved Parliament in December 1970 and called for elections in March 1971. Abdullah decided to stand and advised the Plebiscite Front to contest the elections. When he was about to leave New Delhi for Srinagar on 8 January 1971, a bomb was allegedly discovered on his plane and the flight was cancelled. The next day, he and Afzal Beg were served orders prohibiting them from entering Jammu and Kashmir. Then the Plebiscite Front was declared unlawful, many of its members arrested and offices closed. To make doubly sure, the State Assembly passed a law declaring that members of the Front could not stand for elections. With no opposition in the field, the Congress did well in Kashmir, helping Indira Gandhi to gain a two-thirds majority in Parliament.

Back in New Delhi, Abdullah complained to Gundevia: "What do you want me to do? You have always told me that I must come in and take over responsibilities. This time I decided to fight a democratic election. If I had been elected, I would have had to swear by the Indian Constitution. But you see, they won't even let me come in constitutionally."[13] The ban on his entering Kashmir was lifted in June, well after the elections were over.

A nother Indo-Pak war was looming round the corner. East Pakistan, long treated as a bothersome colony by the ruling West, had risen in revolt, which was being encouraged by New Delhi. The West Pakistan army reacted savagely against the entire population and millions, mostly Muslim, sought refuge in India. Finally, war broke out in December 1971. In two weeks, the Indian army reached Dacca and captured more than 90,000 Pakistani soldiers. Bangladesh came into being. In the West, the fighting was inconclusive. This time, Kashmir was not an issue. But it was affected by the peace negotiations.

Another Indo-Pakistan summit meet took place in Shimla on 28 June 1972. And even more outrageously than at Tashkent, the advantage gained by the Indian army was lost by its civilian masters. Zulfiqar Ali Bhutto, accompanied by his daughter Benazir, pleaded that the terms of settlement should not embarrass his position as Prime Minister. He held that the Indian demand that the cease-fire line in Jammu and Kashmir be converted into an agreed international border would do this. It would be seen at home as equivalent to surrender and make his position impossible. "Bhutto told her [Indira Gandhi] that Pakistan was now convinced that it could never win a war with India, that

Kashmir was lost. *Bharosa keejiye* (trust me) Bhutto pleaded."[14]

And so Mrs Gandhi and her principal advisers (all Kashmiri Pandits, as it happened) were won over. For some reason, Bhutto's political survival was seen as important to India, though they could not have been ignorant of his past record on Kashmir. He was the one who turned down India's efforts for settlement after the war with China in 1962, demanding the entire State because "India was a defeated nation". He instigated Operation Gibraltar in 1965 and excelled previous Pakistani speakers at the UN in spewing vitriol ("Indian dogs" was the epithet he hurled in the Security Council). He had done nothing since to suggest that his antipathy to India, or commitment to gain Kashmir, had waned.

Yet with more than 90,000 prisoners and 50,000 square miles of West Pakistan territory in her grasp, India's iron lady and her advisers let the opportunity slip. Converting the cease-fire line into an international border between India and Pakistan remained unachieved though it was a long-established policy objective. Such an agreement would have ended the dispute between India and Pakistan, with each side keeping what it held, and also would have ended uncertainty in Kashmir about its future.

Verbal changes helped satisfy Indian officials. Much was made of converting the cease-fire line (CFL) into the line of control (LOC), but the agreement had no teeth. The relevant paragraph read:

> In Jammu and Kashmir, the line of control resulting from the ceasefire of 17 December 1971 shall be respected by both sides without prejudice to the recognised position of either side. Neither side shall alter it unilaterally, irrespective of mutual differences and legal interpretations. Both sides further undertake to refrain from the threat or the use of force in violation of this line.

Bhutto was even able to insert a reference to the UN

into the text as well one to further discussions on, among other matters, "a final settlement of Jammu and Kashmir". The future of the State was thus left wide open. The prisoners and the territory were returned. An official spokesman fended off criticism by asserting that it would not be correct to doubt Bhutto's bonafides. India would have to pay heavily for yielding to flattery.

*I*n Kashmir, however, the impact of Pakistan's defeat, and the separation of Bangladesh, was far-reaching. Those who wanted to join Pakistan realised that it did not have the strength to force the issue. Those wanting independence found that Pakistan was not an effective counterpoise to India and the scope for playing one against the other was exhausted. Besides, the emergence of Bangladesh demonstrated that ethnic pulls could be stronger than religious ties. Mir Qasim, who had become Chief Minister, told his people over the radio that Bangladesh had shown the hollowness of the two-nation theory.

On becoming Chief Minister, Mir Qasim promised elections in the State within six months, in the best democratic traditions. But the need for keeping the Congress in office and for pleasing New Delhi took priority. So the Plebiscite Front had to be kept out. In his own words: "If the elections were free and fair, the victory of the Front was a foregone conclusion. And, as a victorious party, the Front would certainly talk from a position of strength. This would irritate Mrs Gandhi, who might give up her wish to negotiate with Sheikh Abdullah. That in turn would lead to a state of confrontation between the Centre and the Jammu and Kashmir Government."[15] The front was debarred from contesting the elections and even Maulana Masoodi arrested.

Even so the opposition did better than ever before, winning seventeen seats out of seventy-four, some of them known Front sympathisers. The Jamaat-i-Islami made an entry into the State Assembly by securing five seats, after its members had taken the oath of loyalty to the Indian and Kashmir Constitutions. Bakshi Ghulam Mohammad emerged from obscurity to contest the elections, and was badly defeated by a journalist.

The loaded elections in the State did not stop Abdullah and his chief political and constitutional adviser, Afzal Beg, from rethinking their strategy after Bangladesh. The emphasis on plebiscite was first to go. The appeal of Pakistan had diminished and independence was more remote than ever. The best that seemed available was to secure as much autonomy as possible. Both men were getting on in age, with years of imprisonment behind them. The temptation to return to positions of power and prestige in Kashmir must have been pressing.

Appropriately enough, it was Beg, President of the Plebiscite Front, who made it known that plebiscite was no longer an issue. The dispute with New Delhi was over the quantum of autonomy. This was in February 1972. Abdullah followed up with an interview to the London *Times* on 8 March which was more specific:

> There is no quarrel with the Government of India over accession; it is over the structure of internal autonomy. One must not forget that it was we who brought Kashmir into India; otherwise Kashmir could never have become part of India.

In his autobiography, Abdullah slurs over the shift in objectives after Bangladesh: "I assured my Indian friends that we had no differences with them over accession. We only wanted Article 370 to be maintained in its original form." Yet later: "Our readiness to come to the negotiating table did not imply a change in our objectives but a change in our strategy."[16]

Now the way was clear. Mrs Gandhi, who had held out against talks with Abdullah on the future of Kashmir so far, told Parliament on 24 March that she "welcomed the change in the thinking of the Plebiscite leaders because they have expressed their willingness to accept the finality of the Kashmir accession". Formal talks began in June. The principals were Indira Gandhi and Abdullah but the detailed negotiations were conducted by Afzal Beg and G. Parthasarathy, a veteran Indian diplomat.

If Abdullah believed that abandoning plebiscite would mean gaining what he wanted in terms of autonomy, he was soon disillusioned. Mrs Gandhi was tougher with him than with Bhutto. He insisted on returning to the relationship between the Centre and Kashmir before he was arrested in 1953. She insisted that the clock could not be turned back, her favourite phrase. He had burnt his boats and was in no position to resist. After more than two years, an agreement was signed by Beg and Parthasarathy on 13 November 1974. It was wordy and full of assurances, but in effect the clock stayed where it was. Abdullah did not even get the commitment he sought: fresh elections so that his sympathisers, who had been debarred from the previous one, could contest.

Article 370 was retained; so were the changes made after 1953 to reduce Kashmir's autonomy. The key provisions enabling the Centre to appoint Governors and take over the governance of the State under Article 356 were unaffected, with drastic consequences a decade later. To make matters crystal clear, the agreement stated:

> Parliament will continue to have power to make laws relating to the prevention of activities directed towards disclaiming, questioning or disrupting the sovereignty and territorial integrity of India or bringing about cession of a part of the territory of India or secession of part of the territory of India from the Union or causing insult to the Indian National Flag, the Indian Anthem and the Constitution.

All that Abdullah got in return were assurances that proposals to repeal changes in the Indian Constitution affecting Kashmir would be "considered on merits". Similarly, if the State Government wished to repeal social legislation enacted by Parliament and extended to the State, it would be "sympathetically considered". Otherwise, the agreement bristled with phrases reiterating the Centre's powers.

What Abdullah did get was technically outside the purview of the agreement, but very much part of it. He was invited to return as Chief Minister of Kashmir. Mir Qasim volunteered to resign and Abdullah was elected in his place by the Congress legislature party, attended by the then Congress President, Dev Kant Barooah (of "Indira is India" fame). The Sheikh could hardly have done more to identify himself with the Congress.

Mrs Gandhi rubbed in his plight with a statement that relations between Kashmir and the Indian Union would continue as before, which was reported by All India Radio. Demonstrations followed in Srinagar condemning the Kashmir accord. This was just before Abdullah was to be sworn in as Chief Minister, but he did not appear for the ceremony. He was livid with rage, according to Mir Qasim. " 'You have made a statement as if I have sold out Kashmir for the chair of chief minister,' he roared. I pleaded that he should not be influenced by the radio version of the statement [by Mrs Gandhi]."[17]

Abdullah was persuaded to accept office and was sworn in as Chief Minister on 25 February 1975, returning to the post after nearly twenty-two years. As usual, he received an enthusiastic welcome, but his popularity had suffered. There was continuing criticism in the valley of his deal with Mrs Gandhi. And he had never been popular in Jammu and Ladakh, where his return was resented. Why did he do it? Admirers of the earlier Abdullah found his compromise hard to understand. But there were traces of tiredness with martyrdom in his behaviour for some time. And the struggle for full autonomy seemed futile. He liked family life and his family liked the good things of life. But he soon regretted his association with the Congress and came to doubt Indira Gandhi's assurances. As he recalled later: "Forgetting my past experiences, I agreed to cooperate with Congress, but soon had to regret my decision."[18] As for Mrs Gandhi, she was exploiting and demonstrating Abdullah's weakness in order to erode his image in Kashmir, but not to use the opportunity to revive secular forces committed to India, as her father might have.

But Abdullah did not give up entirely. The rest of his term in office, and of his life, was a tug-of-war with Congress and with rising Islamic forces. He revived the National Conference — to replace the Plebiscite Front — as a counterweight. He demonstrated his independence by ending the Central subsidy on rice even at the cost of sending up prices and giving Congress an issue to attack him with. He then attempted to come to terms with Congress by offering them an equal number of seats in his Cabinet, but was turned down. When Indira Gandhi, imposed her emergency in June 1975, he refused to go along and condemn his old friend, Jayaprakash Narayan. On a visit to Delhi, he was shocked by demolitions in the Turkman Gate area (predominantly inhabited by Muslims) and the unhappy fate of those evicted. The then Chairman of the Delhi Development Authority, Jagmohan, was unable to "give me any plausible explanation for these deplorable conditions. In Khichripur [rehabilitation colony] some people told me about the atrocities they suffered at Turkman Gate."[19] Jagmohan was to later become Governor of Jammu and Kashmir.

When the Congress was virtually wiped out in the 1977 elections to Parliament, Abdullah persuaded the new Prime Minister, Morarji Desai, to hold fresh elections. In March 1977, the State Assembly was dissolved and Governor's rule imposed (an unfortunate precedent). Though less popular than before, there was still no rival to Abdullah in the valley, although the Janata Party, now ruling in New Delhi, also entered the fray. The main plank of Abdullah's programme was the restoration of Kashmir's autonomy, an objective he had failed to secure in the Kashmir accord. Unable to campaign due to illness, he recorded a cassette with the message that the election was a referendum on Kashmir's self-respect; that they could now show the world they were masters of their destiny and that Delhi could not dictate their future.[20] The cassette was played throughout the valley.

The election results demonstrated how Kashmiris felt. In the first really free and fair elections in Kashmir, the National Conference won forty-six of the seventy-five seats in the Assembly (forty-two in the valley). Congress was cut to size (ten in all; none in the valley). Janata did slightly better (thirteen; with only two in the valley). Candidates sympathetic to Pakistan did not do well. Jamaat's representation came down from five to one. Abdullah returned to office on 9 July strengthened politically but in failing health.

His last years were unhappy. He was unable to persuade New Delhi to make any meaningful gestures towards restoring Kashmir's autonomy. Congressmen who had got used to enjoying the fruits of power, though with minimal support in the valley, kept trying to dislodge him. Among them was Mufti Mohammad Sayeed, who switched to Janata when the pickings were better there and was to play a disastrous role as Union Home Minister in V. P. Singh's Government. Abdullah was never a good administrator; in bad health, he was worse. Corruption mounted, with his own party in the lead. Worse, his family got into the act and grabbed some of the best real estate in the valley.

Islamic groups, always latent, began to gain support. The transformation of Iran by Ayatollah Khomeini into a disciplined Islamic country, where crime and corruption were said to be effectively punished and religious norms imposed, especially attracted those in the villages who envied the prosperity that development had brought to the towns, Srinagar in particular. They were offended by what they saw as the loose, Westernised culture promoted by films and by the prevalence of liquor, but most of all by the ease with which those known to have committed crimes – who in Islamic countries would have merited dismemberment – evaded any punishment at all. Khomeini's name was familiar to the valley; his ancestors had once lived there.

The sudden access to oil-generated wealth in the most conservative Arab countries, especially Saudi Arabia, in the late seventies, made plenty of money available for fundamentalist causes from abroad. Among the beneficiaries was the Jamaat-i-Islami of Kashmir, which had planted its green flag in the valley as early as 1942 and campaigned for it to become an Islamic state. It did not do too well on the surface as long as the National Conference and the Congress did not fight each other and communal rioting did not appear endemic in India. The Jamaat was successful in creating a network of schools where pupils got a grounding in its narrow, fundamentalist version of Islam, as opposed to the tolerant, eclectic tradition the valley had inherited from the Sufis, Rishis and the wandering mystics. The indoctrination continued in the youth organisation set up by the Jamaat, the Jamaat-i-Tulba.

Sheikh Abdullah was sufficiently disturbed by these activities to order the closure of Jamaat schools in 1975. He described them as "centres for spreading communal poison" and went on to ban a massive convention planned by the Jamaat-i-Tulba in Srinagar in 1981.

In June 1982, Abdullah suffered a heart attack, his second. He did not recover fully. Now he behaved as a conventional potentate; he took steps to ensure that the succession remained in the family. On 21 August, he pinned the badge of President of the ruling National Conference on the chest of his son, Farooq. He also made him a Cabinet Minister. Except for his height and bearing Farooq had little in common with his father. Much of his adult life had been spent abroad and he loved a luxurious life. He knew little of politics, from which he had distanced himself. He was handsome, well-meaning and had a foreign wife. The similarity with Rajiv Gandhi was striking. He tried his best when given the job, but his political ineptitude cost Kashmir dear.

On 8 September 1982, Sheikh Mohammad Abdullah finally succumbed to a prolonged heart ailment. With him died something of Kashmir. The tradition of *Kashmiriyat*, the unique, common, eclectic, secular culture of the valley, suffered a severe setback. He had withstood Pakistani attempts to infuse religion into Kashmiri politics; he had resisted Indian efforts to swamp its distinct personality. It was fifty years since he had taught his people to resist oppression. No leader of stature played the same role after him. They swung either to one side or the other; the middle ground was eroded. With a rising generation who knew little of the past, the stage was set for a less civilised mode of confrontation. And there was no Jawaharlal Nehru at the Centre to modify New Delhi's responses.

For all his preoccupation with Kashmir's autonomy, Sheikh Abdullah contributed much to India. As he recalled before his death:

> One can say without fear of contradiction that the two-nation theory suffered its first severe defeat in Kashmir. Kashmir played a vital part in keeping the torch of secularism lit in India.[21]

Chapter XVI

Violence Erupts

*I*n happier times, Farooq Abdullah could have proved an ideal leader for Kashmir. Tall, handsome, engaging, and forthright, he attracted crowds easily, making them believe that he would lead them out of the uncertainty, intrigue and corruption that darkened the last days of his father. But he was also impulsive, gullible, easy-going, and a novice in administration and politics. He may have learnt in time, if he had someone to rely on. In his enthusiasm to clean the dirt of the past, however, he antagonised those who had benefited from it, among them the two most influential ministers in the Sheikh's Cabinent, Ghulam Mohammad (Gul) Shah and Devi Das Thakur. They had been antagonists, but were now united in their desire for revenge. The intrigue disrupted the family: Shah was Farooq's brother-in-law as well as his main rival. Only Farooq's mother stood by him. Then, before he had time to achieve political maturity, he antagonised the most powerful and unscrupulous politician in the country, Indira Gandhi, with predictable consequences. (She had returned to power after the January 1980 general elections.)

Farooq's political naïveté provided ammunition to his foes. When living in London in 1974, he visited Pakistan-held Kashmir to attend a convention organised by the Plebiscite Front there. This was before his father gave up

the demand for self-determination and reconverted the
Plebiscite Front on the Indian side into the National
Conference. Farooq held the status of 'observer' at the
convention, where he listened to speeches stressing
Kashmir's demand for independence. This was to become
the slogan of the Jammu and Kashmir Liberation Front
(JKLF). The JKLF leader, Amanullah Khan, was present,
as were Mohammed Maqbool Butt and Hashim Qureshi,
who would hit the headlines as terrorists. His own
intentions were transparent; he went on to New Delhi to
brief Mrs Gandhi about the convention.[1] Then and later,
however much he criticised the Centre, Farooq never
qualified his commitment to the permanence and finality
of Kashmir's accession to India. But he failed to realise that
his visit across the cease-fire line could be used against him,
as it was.

Farooq never quite got rid of the playboy in him.
Although forty-seven, he dashed around the valley on a
motorcycle, teenager fashion. One exotic passenger on his
pillion was the film star Shabana Azmi, whom he took all
the way up from Srinagar to the mountain resort of
Gulmarg. He spent much of his time playing golf, for which
he laid out an extra course beside the Dal Lake. He looked
impressive and spoke with passion, but his commitment and
his capability began to be doubted. Yet, he was the only
symbol the valley had of the struggle for autonomy.

Within days of becoming Chief Minister, Farooq Abdullah
inherited an explosive political issue, which occasioned his
first brush with the Centre. The Resettlement Bill – a
measure giving anyone who was a citizen of Kashmir before
May 1954, or his descendant, the right to return provided
the person swore allegiance to the Constitutions of both
India and Kashmir – had been passed during his father's
regime. The Bill was awaiting the assent of the Governor,
who had returned it to the Assembly for reconsideration. It

was a gesture to the thousands of Muslim citizens who had fled Hari Singh's persecution to Pakistan-held Kashmir but aroused fears in New Delhi of Pakistani agents and sympathisers being able to freely cross the border and settle down in Kashmir.

The reaction in Jammu was hostile. Hindu and Sikh refugees from Pakistan who had been resettled on property left behind by the departing Muslims felt threatened. There were fears that Jammu may regain its Muslim majority. Communal sentiment, aroused by the Praja Parishad agitation in the early fifties, was still strong. In any case, New Delhi felt that legislation concerning citizenship was a Central prerogative. Farooq would have been happier if the issue had not arisen, but felt he would lose face in the valley if he backed down on a measure introduced by his father. He got the Bill reconsidered and passed again by the Assembly. But a confrontation with the Centre was avoided by agreeing to refer it to the Supreme Court.

Farooq was keen on early elections to enlarge his following in his party. But Indira Gandhi was anxious to re-establish her party in the valley and insisted on a Congress-National Conference poll alliance, which he and his party advisers knew would be suicidal. All he was willing to offer her was to field weak candidates in three or four constituencies, where the Congress would be allowed to win. She was affronted and angrily turned down the offer.

Polling was fixed for 5 June 1983 and the election campaign proved disastrous for relations between Kashmir and the Centre. Mrs Gandhi devoted ten days to her campaign. With little prospect of winning in the valley, she concentrated on gaining seats in Jammu, where her speeches were distinctly communal in tone and focussed on the Resettlement Bill. But in the valley, she was provoked by placards describing Congress as Muslim-killers (after the Assam riots); in Srinagar, a few boys in the crowd stripped to demonstrate their alienation. She insisted that Farooq had arranged the spectacle though he denied it. Their relations could not have been worse.

The results were a morale booster for Farooq. The National Conference won only one seat less than in 1977, when it was led by his father, despite Mrs Gandhi's bitter campaign. The valley's voters still supported the NC's stand on autonomy. However, Farooq was not successful in eliminating dissidents. Shah had managed to infiltrate a handful. As for Mrs Gandhi, she got Congress a block of twenty-four seats in Jammu, which was also to prove crucial. Though the pro-Hindu Bharatiya Janata Party had fielded as many as twenty-seven candidates there, none was elected; they were upstaged by the Prime Minister.

Electorally, Congress had been virtually eliminated in the valley, but its local leaders still had influence in New Delhi. Indira Gandhi's anger with Farooq for turning down her proposal for an electoral alliance was intensified by the humiliating Congress defeat in the valley. According to Mir Qasim, "she was like an injured tigress seeking an opportunity to pounce on Dr Farooq and his government".[2]

Unlike other Kashmiri leaders, Farooq's vision was not limited to the valley. Flushed with the National Conference victory, he felt big enough to join the challenge to the Congress at the national level on the issue of regional autonomy. And Congress seemed vulnerable. N.T. Rama Rao, the Chief Minister of Andhra Pradesh and Ramakrishna Hegde, the Chief Minister of Karnataka, had scored over Congress by stressing regional sentiment, as had Jyoti Basu of West Bengal and M.G. Ramachandran of Tamil Nadu before. Except for Ramachandran, who had worked out his own equation with New Delhi, the others decided to evolve a common front on Centre-State relations.

Farooq promptly joined the conclave of opposition parties. This could have been welcomed as bringing Kashmir into mainstream politics. But that was not the kind of integration Indira Gandhi wanted; it had to be a relationship of subservience, with her party in command. (In contrast, Jawaharlal Nehru had not permitted Congress to function in Kashmir; he worked through the National Conference.) Farooq took part in the first session in

Vijayawada on 31 May 1983, which was attended by fourteen parties. As a result, Kashmiris took interest in developments outside the valley for the first time.[3]

Farooq volunteered to hold the next session in Srinagar, in October (when the valley is at its scenic best). This turned out to be an even bigger show than Vijayawada, with five opposition Chief Ministers present, including himself. Among the party leaders who attended were Chandrashekhar (Janata) and Prakash Singh Badal (Akali Dal). The citizens of Srinagar turned out in force for the occasion, especially for ex-film star Rama Rao in his saffron robes. They had never seen so many party leaders expressing problems similar to theirs. Opposition politics was creating a feeling of shared concerns with the rest of the country in Kashmir; years of Central pressure to integrate had had the opposite effect.

But all this was anathema to Indira Gandhi. Always insecure, she now felt gravely threatened. Large-scale violence was erupting in Punjab and Assam. And her remedy was far from providing the enhanced autonomy that the opposition demanded; it lay in increased Central power and whatever measures were needed to maintain Central power. Farooq was the most vulnerable target for a counter-offensive, and he had also slighted her personally.

The official media paved the way for the toppling operation. At a one-day cricket match on 13 October 1983, a section of the crowd cheered the West Indian visitors and booed the Indian team. Green Jamaat party flags were waved. Officials, who should have known better, and most visiting journalists described them as Pakistani flags. Farooq was repeatedly portrayed by Doordarshan (Government-controlled TV) and All India Radio as soft on Pakistan (one thing he never was), with Mrs Gandhi chipping in to criticise him.

The fateful year 1984 began with a warning by Indira Gandhi that the Centre would not allow anti-national activities to continue in Kashmir. Congress demonstrations began to be held in the valley coupled with representations to the President in New Delhi accusing Farooq of patronising secessionist forces. In February the kidnapping and killing of Ravindra Mhatre, a junior Indian diplomat posted in Birmingham (UK), by the little-known Kashmir Liberation Army (KLA), which was associated with the JKLF, led to increased pressure against Farooq. Recalling his visit to Pakistan-held Kashmir, he was a accused of having links with the JKLF. Mhatre's killing hastened the trial for murder of Mohammed Maqbool Butt, a colourful double agent used both by India and Pakistan. He was associated with the Plebiscite Front and his execution evoked strong reactions in the valley.

Meanwhile, the Congress went ahead with its plans to unseat Farooq in alliance with the Gul Shah faction of the National Conference. The Congress had twenty-six members; Shah's group claimed thirteen. Together they could claim a majority in the seventy-five-member Assembly. They approached the Governor, Braj Kumar Nehru who happened to be a cousin of the Prime Minister, asking whether he would dismiss Farooq if they proved their majority before him. He insisted that this majority be established on the floor of the Assembly, though they argued that fear of physical attack and bending of the rules could preclude a fair vote.

B.K. Nehru was upset with Farooq because he had called and won a snap vote of confidence in breach of the usual requirement of seven days' notice for such motions. This barred another such motion being moved during the session. Accordingly, he warned Farooq:

> I write to say that in these circumstances, if and when such a delegation were to come to me and I were convinced through counting of heads -- a procedure which I have hitherto stubbornly refused to follow – that you had lost your majority I would have no option but to dismiss your government as all proper constitutional process has now been unfairly pre-empted.[4]

However, Nehru had no intention of paving the way for
Farooq's dismissal; he only wanted to discipline him. In fact,
he believed that Farooq's presence was essential to retain
Kashmiri support. He regarded Farooq as basically decent,
though immature, in contrast to Gul Shah who could not
be trusted. When Indira Gandhi suggested that Farooq be
unseated, he demurred. But she was determined; so cousin
or no, he had to go. On 31 December 1983, Nehru was asked
to resign; later to accept a transfer to Gujarat. He initially
insisted on resigning, but agreed to the transfer when told
by the Prime Minister's secretary that his resignation at
that time would embarrass her personally. He was pressed
to leave Kashmir soon, to expedite the next step, but he
refused to move until April.[5]

Indira Gandhi replaced B.K. Nehru with her tried and
trusted agent, Jagmohan. He had proved himself during the
emergency which she had imposed eight years earlier. As
chief executive of the Delhi Development Authority, he had
faithfully carried out Sanjay Gandhi's clean-up operations,
irrespective of the suffering caused. In the old city itself,
one area from which people were evicted was the
predominantly Muslim locality of Turkman Gate; this did
not promote his reputation for secularity in Kashmir.

As soon as Jagmohan arrived in Srinagar, it became
evident that Farooq's days were numbered, except possibly
to Farooq himself. In May, Shah's faction in the National
Conference formally broke away, with his wife Khalida
(Farooq's sister) as president. Prominent among the
dissidents were the former ministers whom Farooq had
dropped on charges of corruption. He was now accused of
questioning his father's wisdom in appointing them. They,
too, joined in levelling the charge of his being soft on
elements favouring Pakistan.

All was set for the final act. According to Jagmohan's
version, he was informed that the Shah group wished to

meet him at 10.30 p.m. on 1 July 1984 and he sent word
that they could come the next morning. Jagmohan insists
that he was surprised at the hint that they wanted to topple
Farooq (though they had approached his predecessor). Only
after getting the call did he begin to make arrangements
to maintain law and order (though that was still the
responsibility of Farooq's Government). With unaccustomed
speed, a contingent of the Madhya Pradesh armed police
landed in Srinagar early next morning, suggesting that they
had been alerted a day or more earlier. The army, too, was
standing by. Arrangements fell into step like clockwork. Yet
he maintains it was all unplanned.

The sequence of events on 2 July could not have been
staged better. Thirteen members of the Assembly, twelve
belonging to the National Conference (two of them
nominated) and one Independent, met the Governor early
in the morning and pledged their support to G.M. Shah, who
was a member of the Legislative Council. Shah submitted
a letter signed by them authenticating withdrawal of their
support to Farooq. "Simultaneously", according to the
official press release on the occasion, "the leader of the
Congress Legislature Party, Moulvi Iftikhar Hussain Ansari,
presented a letter to the Governor in person informing him
that the twenty-six members of the party had decided to
support Shah."

The Governor promptly summoned Farooq to tell him
that he had lost his job. Both of them, according to
Jagmohan, preferred that he (Jagmohan) should take over
by imposing Governor's rule (possible under the State
Constitution) rather than hand over power to Shah.
Jagmohan also formally wrote to Farooq telling him that
he did not enjoy the support of the majority of the Assembly
and had forfeited his right to continue as Chief Minister.
He should therefore resign. By now Farooq seemed to have
realised what was at stake and wrote back to suggest that
the Assembly be summoned to test his strength, or
alternatively, it should be dissolved so that the issue could
be taken to the people. A disappointed Jagmohan replied

that the question of accepting Farooq's advice did not arise since he had lost the confidence of the Assembly. The exchange ended with with a curt note from the Governor to Farooq:

> I am satisfied that you have lost the confidence of the majority of the MLAs in the Legislative Assembly. I, therefore, regret to inform you that I have dismissed you from the Chief Ministership of the State and dissolved the Council of Ministers headed by you.

More was to be done that same day. Shah was invited to form the Government and submit a list of his Council of Ministers. This he did straightaway. All the thirteen who were with him were rewarded with ministerships. Before the day was out, the Governor administered the oath of office to all of them, as well as to Shah, the new Chief Minister. Jagmohan's plans to rule himself would have to be postponed; New Delhi insisted that the bargain with Shah be kept.[6]

Not everyone was as convinced as Jagmohan was of the legitimacy of his actions. Four non-Congress Chief Ministers (from Andhra Pradesh, Karnataka, Tripura and West Bengal) walked out of a National Development Council meeting to protest Farooq's dismissal. They were joined by leaders of nineteen political parties in describing the dismissal as undemocratic and urging the removal of Jagmohan from Kashmir. Leading national papers were even more critical, insisting that the entire dismissal scenario had been worked out in advance in New Delhi and Jagmohan had set a dangerous precedent.[7]

Some former Governors were also unhappy. The doyen was L.P. Singh, who had also been Home Secretary. He felt it would have been more correct to summon the Assembly to test Farooq's majority.[8] And B.K. Nehru, Jagmohan's predecessor, described the dismissal as a shabby operation and spoke of money being flown in from Delhi to facilitate the change.[9] A later Governor, General Krishna Rao, said Farooq had been removed by "dubious means".[10]

The reaction in Kashmir to the change in government, and the crude way in which it was engineered, was summed up by Mir Qasim:

> Mr Jagmohan's unconstitutional act was another nail in the coffin of the Kashmiri's faith in Indian democracy and law.[11]

More nails were to be driven in. Gul Shah had been given a month in which to prove his majority on the floor of the Assembly. The House met on 31 July 1984. Two non-Congress members, who may have voted against, were prevented from attending the session by the police. Quoting the anti-defection law in the State, the Speaker, Wali Mohammad Itoo, disqualified the twelve National Conference dissidents who brought down the Farooq Government (the High Court ruled they were not defectors). Shah's supporters did not believe in debate; they picked up the Speaker and removed him from the chamber. Farooq and his followers walked out in protest, leaving the others to elect a new Speaker and express a unanimous motion of confidence in Shah.

However, Shah did not last long. He was not as popular as Farooq, and his political opportunism and venality surfaced when in office. In any event, he had been made Chief Minister only as an instrument to oust Farooq. This accomplished, his utility was over. And Jagmohan had been waiting to take the reins of government under his exclusive control. This he could do under the separate Constitution that Kashmir enjoyed under Article 370 of the Indian Constitution, a provision he otherwise condemned and took steps to erode.

Using these powers (originally designed for an elected Sadar-i-Riyasat), Jagmohan dismissed Gul Shah on 7 March 1986 and imposed Governor's rule on Kashmir. Jagmohan had a bureaucratic contempt for popular government and could hardly wait to display his administrative ability. His sense of exaltation at taking power is best expressed in his own words, as recorded in his diary that same day:

...I have an opportunity to show the nobler, the purer, the more radiant face of power. I can now demonstrate how Government can function in a poor and developing country, how a person, inspired by a higher purpose can serve as a model administrator, how domination of the elites can be done away with, how power-brokers can be eliminated, how exploitation by communalists and obscurantists can be prevented, how youth can be weaned away from fundamentalism, how justice can be established as a new religion and the vicious circle of underdevelopment and exploitative democracy can be snipped. I can also show that administration is not merely pen, pencil, paper and red tape; it is much more than this. It is imagination. It is vision. It is creativity. It is commitment. It is compassion. It is catharsis. It is sympathy. It is tact....[12]

Jagmohan initially went ahead with what he knew best: civic improvement. Srinagar, long neglected, appreciated the clean-up campaign. The administration, too, improved. He worked long hours supervising the work; the officials had never known such pressure. He turned his attention to corruption and nepotism, which there was in plenty, but not more than in some other States. It began to be noticed, however, that as a result of his intervention, the appointment of Muslims to jobs and their admission to educational institutions decreased sharply. Hardly any Muslims were left in Raj Bhavan, the Governor's office and residence. Then, in a throwback to the Maharaja era, he reissued an order banning the slaughter of sheep on Janmashtami day in deference to Hindu sentiment, though there was no such ban in the rest of India. This was seen in the valley as conclusive evidence of an underlying communal bent.

Political reactions were not slow in coming. Qazi Nisar, a fiery young preacher of Anantnag, insisted that law should not be used for religious purposes. He collected a large crowd and slaughtered a sheep in full public view. He was

arrested but became an instant celebrity with a considerable
following. He called himself Mirwaiz – a title with religious
and historical overtones – of south Kashmir. The other
established Mirwaiz, resident in Srinagar, was Maulvi
Farooq, who had survived an uneasy relationship with New
Delhi on the one side and the National Conference on the
other.

Another development that would cast its shadow on the
future was the emergence of the Muslim United Front, an
umbrella organisation of communal groups openly
challenging the secular polity that the National Conference
had nurtured. With the NC divided and out of office, its
organisers faced limited opposition and made the most of
the Governor's pro-Hindu image. The MUF called for
hartals in the valley to demonstrate its growing strength.
Among the groups that joined it were the remnants of the
Shah faction of the National Conference. On being ejected
from office, Shah became openly communal and supportive
of Pakistan.

*R*ajiv Gandhi, who had succeeded his mother as Prime
Minister after her assassination on 31 October 1984, was
about the same age as Farooq Abdullah and got on better
with him. But he shared Mrs Gandhi's ambition to impose
the Congress party on the valley. In view of their friendship,
Farooq found it impossible to resist, as he had similar moves
by her. He agreed to a coalition government followed by a
National Conference-Congress electoral alliance. The
outcome was disastrous. The National Conference lost the
image of being committed to Kashmir's autonomy, the most
effective counter to Pakistan and Muslim communalism. It
was seen as an agent of the Centre.

Farooq had been pressing for elections ever since
Governor's rule was imposed. But even after its six-month
limit was over, New Delhi delayed elections and imposed
President's rule instead – the administration was still under

Jagmohan who was in no hurry to hand over power. Thus Kashmir got the worst of both Constitutions. Eventually, on 7 November 1986, Rajiv reappointed Farooq as Chief Minister to preside over an interim National Conference-Congress regime. The coalition evoked protests in the valley, but Farooq was able to announce the Prime Minister's promise of Rs. 1000 crores of special Central assistance to the State, which was never received. (In an interview earlier, he told this writer that he realised that the National Conference would be hurt by an alliance with the Congress, but there was no other way to get the funds needed for Kashmir's development from the Centre.)

Elections followed on 23 March 1987. But they were preceded by arrests of many Muslim United Front leaders and election agents; this paved the way for persistent charges of rigging. The National Conference secured thirty-six seats, a sharp drop from the forty-six it won in 1983. The BJP registered its presence with two seats and the MUF with four. Thus, communal parties now openly gained representation. And the MUF began a widespread campaign, insisting that it would have done much better but for rigging. It had got more than 30 per cent of the vote, and many seats had been won by slender, questionable majorities.

*T*he 1987 elections lost the electoral process the credibility gained in 1977. A new generation of Kashmiris, who knew little or nothing of the freedom movement against the Maharaja's rule or the tribal invasion, had gone to the polls, and were disappointed. They had benefited from the free education -- from primary to university levels -- available since the early fifties, but were frustrated because there were few jobs available for them. Educated unemployed are the most eruptive element in any society; here, they blamed lack of opportunities in the rest of India for their plight. And the new jean-attired generation felt a degree of contempt

for their gentle *phiran*-wearing elders. In the countryside,
they were joined by those indoctrinated in the Jamaat-i-
Islami schools.

Both groups became responsive to the slogan that if the
ballot was ineffectual, then there was no alternative to the
bullet. And, further, that a disciplined Islamic state was
preferable to corrupt, unstable, so-called democratic
governments. The glittering wealthy image projected by the
oil-rich Arab countries, who claimed to be Islamic, disguised
the tyrannical nature of their regimes.

Widespread militancy in neighbouring Punjab after the
tragic military operation against armed militants in the
Golden Temple in Amritsar in June 1984 contained a
message for the discontented youth of the valley. Militancy
there was seen as another movement for freedom from New
Delhi. Indira Gandhi's assassination in October 1984,
together with charges of top-level corruption, did not
increase respect for New Delhi.

More menacing, as seen from the valley, was the steady
rise of Hindu communalism in other parts of the country.
Communal rioting had become endemic, with Muslims being
the main sufferers, and the police often appearing partial.
Ayodhya became symbolic after a magistrate ordered
opening of the gate of the Babri Masjid/Ram Janambhoomi
complex in 1986 after it had been kept locked for thirty-
seven years to avoid communal friction. The manner in
which the issue was handled by the administration
suggested complicity with the Vishwa Hindu Parishad and
associated groups. These fears mounted with the conducting
of the Shilanyas programme in February 1989, followed by
BJP President L.K. Advani's incendiary *rath yatra* in
November the following year. The process culminated in the
destruction of the Babri Masjid on 6 December 1992. It was
no longer hard for those who preached that Muslims had
no future in India to get a hearing. Against this background,
the mounting pressure for closer integration with India was
particularly counterproductive. No attempt was made to
appreciate the sentiments of those who stood for greater

autonomy; to a return to the status Kashmir enjoyed until Sheikh Abdullah was imprisoned in 1953. Nor was much heed paid to those who maintained that the State's accession to India was provisional and its future was yet to be finally determined by its people. They were dubbed subversive and anti-national and clubbed with pro-Pakistani militants, whom some were then tempted to join.

Developments in the international arena, too, had their impact on the valley, especially on the youth. The word *mujahideen* (holy warriors) became international currency in the seventies, when they were depicted as committed guerrillas risking their lives against the godless Soviet-supported regime in Afghanistan. For this reason, they were given the most sophisticated weapons by the United States of America via Pakistan. These weapons made it possible to think in terms of small groups taking on modern armies. It was not too difficult to draw a parallel with the situation in the valley, for those who wished to. Then came signs of eastern Europe freeing itself from Soviet domination and later of the break-up of the mighty Soviet Union itself into independent ethnic nations.

Seen from Pakistan, it was a tempting scenario, another chance to make up for the failures of 1947 and 1965, coupled with the desire to take revenge for the loss of Bangladesh in 1971, in which Indian infiltrators had played a role. New Delhi helped, without realising it, by insisting on the deportation of Amanullah Khan, who had been propagating the cause of the Jammu and Kashmir Liberation Front (JKLF) from the safety of London. The JKLF became an embarrassment to the British Government after the murder of Ravindra Mhatre. Amanullah moved to Pakistan-held Kashmir in 1986, from where he could organise violent disturbances on the Indian side without technically involving the Pakistan Government.

There was a difference this time in contrast to 1947 and 1965. All the *mujahideen* did not come from outside. They were mostly young Kashmiris who sneaked across the line of control (LOC) to acquire training in the use of advanced

weapons and in guerrilla tactics. They then returned to
show their muscle, eliminate selected official targets, take
hostages, provoke police and para-military reaction against
local people and generally try to paralyse the administration. They knew their way around the valley and could
count on sympathisers. Pakistan helped by setting up
training camps and contributing sophisticated arms and also
money. But this time it avoided provoking a military
confrontation with India.

Kashmir had a relatively peaceful 1987. There was an
outburst of demonstrations and *hartals* towards the end of
the year, but this was sparked off by a local problem. Ever
since the Maharaja era, the movement of the State capital
from Jammu to Srinagar in summer, and back in winter,
was seen as an index of the equal importance of the two
regions. When Farooq tried to locate certain departments
permanently in the two places for reasons of economy, he
evoked traditional jealousies and had to climb down.

The valley began to feel the impact of armed militancy
in 1988. In an interview to a Pakistani paper, on 31 July
1988, Amanullah Khan said "uprising had become an armed
struggle". In fact, increased firing across the LOC began
earlier in the year and by the end of April, dusk-to-dawn
curfew had to be imposed in all the border districts. The
explosion of an ammunition dump in Pakistan occasioned
a memorial demonstration in Srinagar. It got out of hand
and the police dispersed it by firing, killing two persons. The
demonstrations continued the next day. Organising
reactions to disasters in Pakistan became a way of
promoting solidarity with it. This was repeated when
President Zia-ul Haq of Pakistan died in a plane crash on
17 August. Curfew was imposed. Police opened fire in
several towns in the valley to quell rioters and five persons
died. Riots between Sunnis and Shias erupted in the tense
atmosphere. Meanwhile, on 15 August, India's Independence

Day, there were widespread clashes between the police and demonstrators. Two weeks passed before peace could be restored.

More serious than increasing unrest, however, were six direct attacks on the security forces and the spate of bomb explosions during the year, indicating availability of arms, explosives and training in how to use them. In September, militants fired at a senior police officer, Ali Mohammad Watali, and a retired Sessions Judge, Neel Kanth Ganjoo, who had sentenced Maqbool Butt to death (the attacks were to be repeated). There were other instances of firing. But the objective seemed to be to frighten rather than kill. Young men caught during these incidents confessed that they had received training across the line of control. Some two to three hundred had returned after training, according to Indian intelligence.

Worse was to follow in 1989, a year in which domestic unrest and foreign-equipped militants confronted the valley with a bigger crisis than it had faced before. The National Conference had lost its appeal as representing Kashmiri aspirations after its forced association with the Congress. There was no alternative secular force with a popular following willing to work with India. Farooq Abdullah, the last symbol of secular *Kashmiriyat*, remained a lightweight, given to helicopter sorties over the stricken valley; to elitist projects to attract tourists, while basic facilities were ignored; and to foreign trips.

The fourth anniversary of Maqbool Butt's execution on 11 February provided an early start for anti-Indian demonstrations in the valley in 1989. News of the publication of Salman Rushdie's *Satanic Verses* soon after provided another occasion for violent demonstrations, although New Delhi had banned the book. They continued for nearly a week. The frequency of demonstrations increased steadily. Heavy-handed police reaction, which often hurt the innocent, provoked further protests. The aged father of Shabir Shah, the popular leader of the People's League (one of the organisations that had sprung up

demanding independence) died in police custody in
Anantnag, provoking widespread disturbances in early
April. The house of Revenue Minister P. L. Handoo, also in
Anantnag, was burnt down. Burning buses and bridges
emerged as part of a plan to paralyse transport and
humiliate the administration. Bomb blasts enforced a *bandh*
on 15 August, India's Independence Day.

After Jagmohan's tenure was over, he was replaced
by General K.V. Krishna Rao (retired), former Chief of
Army Staff and more recently Governor of the troubled
north-eastern States. The expertise gained there in anti-
insurgency operations was seen as a qualification for
Kashmir. But he had no experience of politics and soon
found that the valley posed problems very different to those
in the north-east.

The militants stepped up their campaign from threats
to actual kidnapping and killing. The shooting of
Mohammad Yusuf Halwai, a National Conference leader, on
21 August 1989, began a series of targeted attacks designed
to terrorise those who did not go along with the militants.
The next prominent figure was Tika Lal Taploo, Vice-
President of the State unit of the BJP (14 September). His
murder revived the BJP campaign to dismiss the Farooq
Government and repeal Article 370. Then Neel Kanth
Ganjoo, who had been fired upon earlier, was shot dead in
a Srinagar street on 4 November. Repeated bomb attacks
on Mujahid Manzil, the Srinagar headquarters of the
National Conference, indicated that some militant groups
regarded it as their main enemy. Threats against, and
attacks on, Hindu residents of the valley resulted in a
campaign to push them out.

By now it was hard to distinguish between the various
militant groups that were springing up and their objectives
and targets. Almost all groups, except for criminal ones
exploiting the opportunity for extortion, were financed and
equipped by Pakistan. But these motley groups differed in
their political and social objectives and techniques. The
Jammu and Kashmir Liberation Front, now directed from

across the line of control by Amanullah Khan, was best
known and had the oldest cadres, but tended to split up into
rival groups. Despite getting support from Pakistan, it was
committed to independence and not to joining Pakistan. Its
Pakistani patrons went along because of its widespread
organisational roots and popular appeal. But they favoured
new groups such as the Hizbullah Mujahideen and Allah
Tigers, which were directly under their control and
propagated the advantages of joining Pakistan. After the
militant campaign had assumed the character of full-fledged
insurgency, Amanullah Khan told *Newsline* of Pakistan in
February 1990:

> We basically stand for reunification of our motherland
> which has now been divided into four parts: Indian
> Kashmir; Azad Kashmir and Baltistan – which are
> currently with Pakistan; and Aksai Chin under the
> Chinese. We want these parts to be reunified and made
> a completely independent state. What we are struggling
> for is independence from both Pakistan and India.

In another interview to the Karachi *Herald*, Amanullah
reiterated the demand for independence and said it was
spreading rapidly in Kashmir. Asked how he worked with
groups who wanted Kashmir to accede to Pakistan, he
replied that they were all agreed that Kashmiris should be
given the right to choose among India, Pakistan and
independence. He also reiterated the secular character of
the JKLF and insisted, with little evidence, that some non-
Muslims were sympathetic to the campaign that it was
waging in the valley.

In contrast, the pro-Pakistani groups laid great stress
on creating an Islamic society and threatened those who did
not conform. Many Pandits were dubbed 'informers'. Hindus
felt increasingly threatened and began to leave the valley.
The Allah Tigers, in particular, forced the closure of bars,
video parlours and cinema halls as being anti-Islamic.
Kashmiri women, who are not attached to the *burkha*, were
asked to veil themselves. They were supported by a

fundamentalist women's organisation, the Dukhtaran-e-Millat (Daughters of Islam). Women were even threatened that acid would be thrown on unveiled faces. Even so, many remained unveiled. The JKLF did not approve of such activities, but they attracted the approval of many unhappy with the impact of Westernised culture. Yet it was the JKLF that was put down most firmly by the Indian authorities and much of its cadre eliminated, leaving the field open to its pro-Pakistan rivals.

It was the Centre rather than the State Government that was responsible for giving the JKLF its most publicised boost. On 8 December 1989, Rubaiyah, the daughter of Mufti Mohammed Sayeed, who was the Union Home Minister in the new National Front Government, was kidnapped by a JKLF unit. They demanded the release of five prominent militants in exchange for her freedom. The much-headlined drama continued for five days, with extensive coverage by Doordarshan. Chief Minister Farooq Abdullah, once more abroad in London, flew back. Two Union Cabinet Ministers flew into Srinagar. Intermediaries, including journalists and officials, negotiated terms. The JKLF found that public opinion was turning against it in the valley. Even in sympathetic Islamic countries, holding an unmarried girl as hostage was disapproved.

Farooq insisted that if the Government accepted the terms of the JKLF, the nation would pay a heavy price "as it would open the floodgates for the future and provide a boost to anti-national activities of trying to separate Kashmir from India". The situation developed into a game of nerves; Farooq maintained that Rubaiyah would be released if the Government held out. But an urgent message received from the Union Cabinet Secretary on 13 December asked "the State Government to note that it is their undiluted responsibility to ensure the safe release of the hostage without injury to her and we expect that all actions you will take will be consistent with these requirements".[13]

The Centre had buckled. After Rubaiyah was freed unharmed, the five militants were released and taken out in procession in Srinagar before slipping across the line of control. It was a major, much-publicised boost for the JKLF in particular and militancy in general, as Farooq had predicted, as also for the practice of taking innocent hostages. The militants were encouraged to believe that *azaadi* was around the corner and further stepped up their violent campaign.

The authorities responded to the crisis by flying in para-military personnel from distant places. They did not know the language or the customs of the people and treated them as potentially hostile. The local police were sidelined and treated as unreliable. Consequently, the information needed to identify the militants became scarce. Searches and interrogations became brutal and undiscriminating, creating increased sympathy for the militants and further reducing information about their movements. Finally, by firing from crowded places and provoking the para-military forces to fire back indiscriminately, the militants were able to achieve their primary objective of alienating most of the people of the valley from India.

Panic strengthened the hardliners in New Delhi. The Janata Government depended heavily on its BJP supporters who were keen to curtail Kashmir's autonomy. The pressure of events in 1990 proved to be as momentous for Kashmir as in 1947. But now there was no Sheikh Abdullah to mobilise the valley against Pakistani intervention and stress its secular heritage; nor a Mahatma Gandhi or a Jawaharlal Nehru to create confidence in India. The face of India that they would see was that of Jagmohan, who replaced General Krishna Rao and returned as Governor on 19 January 1990. Farooq promptly resigned, as expected, and Jagmohan was back in full control.

In effect, the attempt to find political solutions to Kashmir's problems was shelved. The realisation that the valley's willing union with India was the biggest tribute to India's democratic and secular character was forgotten. The unstated policy that was emerging was based on repression and on impressing upon the Kashmiris the price of antagonising the Centre. The valley would never be the same again.

Chapter XVII

Vicious Circle

The night and the day after Jagmohan was sworn in again as Governor, 19 January 1990, were the worst that Srinagar had experienced. The Central Reserve Police, a para-military unit, conducted a night search in a locality in which militants were said to be hiding. They were provoked by firing. No casualties were reported among the police but nearly fifty citizens were killed and many more injured. Jagmohan disclaimed responsibility since he was in Jammu and put the blame on verbal instructions from the outgoing Chief Minister, Farooq Abdullah.[1] But the news of Jagmohan's reappointment probably had greater influence with the police. The death toll continued to rise, as did the degree and extent of repression. Apart from firing, extended curfews lasting a week or more became a favourite method of punishing the entire citizenry on the model of the collective fines imposed in colonial times. The entire valley was treated as hostile.

As before, Jagmohan was filled with a sense of historic mission in which critics and opponents became allies of those threatening national integrity. His mood on returning to the Raj Bhavan in Srinagar is best described by himself:

> Obviously, I could not walk barefoot in the Valley full
> of scorpions – the Valley wherein inner and outer forces

of terrorism had conspired to subvert the Union and to seize power. I must equip myself to face all eventualities. I could leave nothing to chance. A slight slip or error would mean a Tienanmen Square or a Blue Star or a formal declaration of a new theocratic state with all its international embarrassment.[2]

This was a reference to information that militants were planning to burn the Indian Tricolour and hoist the flag of a new Islamic republic on Republic Day, 26 January. The plan was said to be for as many as a million people to collect in Srinagar on that day to salute the new flag. The portents were not good. The Kashmir police had nearly mutinied when one of them was killed in firing by the Central Reserve Police and the army had to be called in. Four Indian Air Force officers were killed by militants on the street.

Jagmohan responded by imposing the first of his extended curfews on various towns in the valley from the afternoon of 25 January. His instructions were that curfew be imposed with the utmost strictness. Even the press was incarcerated. There could be no softness in putting down "subversives and their collaborators". Neither he, nor his mentors in the Union Home Ministry, seemed to recognise the political implications of the fact that so many Kashmiris were willing to demonstrate unless forcibly prevented. But the Governor only saw elements of the local police, the hospitals, the municipal services, the lawyers, the press and some other 'malcontents' colluding with the subversives. No effort was made to find common ground. All who thought differently were treated as enemies of the nation. But the nation, too, was seen as weak. Even so, Jagmohan did not falter:

It became increasingly clear to me that, in the current political ethos, with shallowness and superficiality gripping the levers of power, our country could not fully overcome any crisis, much less the crisis of the dimension of Kashmir. Nevertheless, I persuaded myself to believe that I had a national obligation to discharge. With all the frozen turbulence in my mind, with all the millstones round my neck, and with my back badly wounded by the stabs from the rear, I proceeded ahead.[3]

The stabs did not end. As the frequency of firing by the security forces and resultant casualties rose, Farooq Abdullah accused Jagmohan of imposing a reign of terror. So did his friend, Rajiv Gandhi. It was evident that New Delhi was not united behind the Governor. The biggest blow to Jagmohan was the appointment of George Fernandes as Minister for Kashmir Affairs. With a long history of commitment to human rights in and outside the country, Fernandes was the antithesis of Jagmohan. Instead of evolving a clear policy, the V.P. Singh Government was trying to placate both the hardliners and the moderates though it meant causing more confusion. Predictably, the Minister and the Governor did not see eye to eye and put out divergent signals in the valley. One was trying to revive the political process; for the other this threatened law and order.

Jagmohan hit back by dissolving the State Assembly, the last vestige of popular rule. He did so without even informing the Centre, the only Governor in the country with the authority to do so. This was because he used powers derived from the separate Kashmir Constitution (which he otherwise condemned) to impose Governor's rule, originally intended for an elected Sadar-i-Riyasat, not a Central nominee. The Prime Minister, V. P. Singh, was embarrassed and the Home Minister, Mufti Mohammed Sayeed, expressed his unhappiness on hearing the news. Jagmohan has argued that his intention was to show that he wanted to pave the way for elections and a return to popular government. But his letter to the Union Home Minister, on 20 February 1990, indicates that his main target was Farooq. The letter reiterated his right to take the decision to dissolve the Assembly independently, but is otherwise revealing. It was necessary, he wrote, because:

Without dissolution, there was no moral legitimacy for the use of force on an extensive scale. Nor was it possible for me and the advisers to secure the obedience of our orders from local officials who were constantly being fed with the impression that Dr Farooq Abdullah and his colleagues were coming back after the role of "butcher" has been played by the Governor.[4]

Fundamentalist groups among the militants targeted a fear campaign against the Pandit community, which had survived the ups and downs of Kashmir's history for centuries. Some were killed; others threatened or assaulted; and their homes ransacked. Jagmohan facilitated their departure from the valley to refugee camps in Jammu and elsewhere, with the assurance that they would soon be back in their homes. But his measures only alienated the people even more; many Muslims, too, had to flee. The confrontation between people and authority continued, with militants making the most of the opportunity.

On 21 May, Mirwaiz Maulvi Farooq, who had a traditional following in the valley and had criticised the Government without breaking links with it, was shot dead at his residence. He had been conferring with Fernandes. A grieving crowd of his followers was carrying his coffin when they clashed with the Central Reserve Police, who opened fire killing twenty-four persons and even piercing the coffin with bullets. As a result, indignation against the militants, who seemed to be responsible for the assassination, turned into enhanced resentment against the Government. Maulvi Farooq's teenage son, Mohammad Omar, agreed to head an all-party Liberation (Hurriyat) Conference, composed of thirty-two groups, to give political support to the campaign for self-determination.

This was too much even for the indecisive National Front Government. Jagmohan was summoned to New Delhi, where, true to form, he was not dismissed immediately. He got the message from the newspapers, which were briefed that he he would not like to continue in the changed circumstances. This time his tenure was brief. But it marked a quantum jump in the valley's alienation.

A section of the militants began to combine brutality with murder and kidnapping to terrorise opponents and to demonstrate their own fervour. Victims were tortured in the cruellest ways before being left to die. Women were raped. The chief targets were officials, National Conference leaders and other politicians who opposed violence, and prominent Hindus. Extortion was another motive. Official reaction, too, became more brutal. But while terrorism was targeted, reaction was indiscriminate.

Many militants, possibly most, however, avoided brutality. They ranged in age from about fifteen to thirty. They saw themselves as freedom-fighters; some committed to establishing an Islamic state, but not all. Some were committed to joining Pakistan; others to independence. A valuable insight into their thinking and their frustrations is provided by a Pandit politician, Khem Lata Wakhlu in *Kidnapped*. This book gives a detailed account of her kidnapping, along with her husband, by a group of young militants in 1991. They were held for forty-five days. Most of the militants treated the elderly Hindu couple with respect. They were met with consideration in the homes in the valley in which they were hidden with the unwilling assent of the owners.[5]

Some units of the security forces were accused of brutality. Entire villages and localities were emptied of males who were interrogated while their homes were searched for arms. Often they had to stand out in the freezing cold for the whole day. Women could stay indoors, but there were reports of molestation and rape, as well as theft. Suspects were often tortured to provide information. The evidence in the form of scars and broken bones could be seen in hospitals. The number of deaths in custody kept rising.

A human rights team sponsored by the People's Union for Civil Liberties (PUCL), Citizens For Democracy and other volunteer organisations toured Kashmir in March and April 1990. Among the members were two eminent jurists, V.M. Tarkunde and Rajinder Sachar, a well-known educationist and former vice-chancellor, Amrik Singh, and a Jammu-based writer and social activist, Balraj Puri. They condemned both Jagmohan and the militants in their report:

> The fact is that the whole Muslim population of the Kashmir valley is wholly alienated from India and due to the highly repressive policy pursued by the administration in recent months, especially since the advent of Shri Jagmohan in January 1990, their alienation has now turned into bitterness and anger.

And their report on the militants, in the wake of the cruel kidnapping and killing of Kashmir University Vice-Chancellor Mushirul Haque, his secretary, Abdul Ghani, and the General Manager of the Hindustan Machine Tools watch factory near Srinagar, H.L. Khera, stated:

> The militants by their violent activities are not only depriving innocent persons of their civil liberties but also harming the cause of freedom and democracy in the valley. In fact the militants are strengthening the repressive machinery of the state by their activities and are providing a semblance of justification to the government to assume more and more arbitrary powers.

But this was what the militants wanted. They targeted local secular politicians, of whom more than a hundred were killed, and civil servants. Their activities extended to burning public buildings and facilities. Non-Jamaat schools were primary targets. Of the 6000 or more structures burnt in just over two years, over two hundred and thirty were schools. This indicated the gradual ascendancy of the Islamic over the secular militants, a process promoted by the unwillingness of the Indian authorities to distinguish between them and by increasing dependence on Pakistan as more and more weapons and explosives flowed in.

Jagmohan's replacement by a senior intelligence officer, Girish Saxena, made little difference. Possibly he was selected as a counter to Pakistan's Inter-Services Intelligence (ISI), known to be masterminding the guerrilla activities in the valley. But New Delhi overlooked the need for political skills to regain the confidence of the valley people. The 'we or they' approach became firmly embedded in the administration and the security forces despite occasional efforts by the army to improve its image by opening clinics and helping civic works in outlying areas.

Though the Border Security Force replaced the Central Reserve Police in policing activities, its men were not trained for such work and were strained by extended periods of service under conditions of great hardship. When some were killed by snipers, the urge for revenge often proved stronger than discipline. Markets and houses were burnt down and return firing was indiscriminate. The worst such reprisal raid was on the apple town of Sopore on 6 January 1993 in which forty-five people were killed and a large section of the town destroyed. Sopore was a regular target; it was near Pakistan and was a known militant hideout. It was to suffer repeated attacks by both sides.

Earlier, another human rights team, headed by Tarkunde, which visited the valley in May 1992, reported:

> Although the militancy in the valley has been curbed to a noticeable extent, the brutal methods by which this result was brought about have increased the bitterness of the people against the Indian Government as well as the Indian State. There are no processions and slogan-shouting in favour of *azaadi* as in the past, but the people on the whole have become even more sullen and more hostile to the Indian State than what they used to be. The frequent military crackdowns, the inhuman torture of innocent persons, the indiscriminate shooting at people, the frequent thefts, and the occasional rapes

committed by the security forces have increased the disgust and resentment of the people in the valley.[6]

Governments changed in New Delhi, but the Home Ministry remained in control. The biggest symbolic slap to the remaining secular forces in the valley was delivered when the Congress was back in office with Narasimha Rao as Prime Minister. On Republic Day 1992, BJP President Murli Manohar Joshi was flown by helicopter from Jammu to Srinagar. He was anxious to complete his *Ekta Yatra* which sought to build on the Hindu fundamentalist sentiment that his predecessor, Lal Krishna Advani, had aroused with his Somnath-Ayodhya *Rath Yatra* the previous year (with far-reaching consequences for the country).

Srinagar was placed under curfew and Joshi, guarded by an army contingent, raised the Tricolour in an empty Lal Chowk, the square where Jawaharlal Nehru and Sheikh Abdullah had defied the tribal invaders in 1947 and, more recently, Farooq Abdullah had condemned Islamic fundamentalists in 1989 before a large cheering crowd.

Placatory sounds were made in 1993 when Girish Saxena was replaced. His successor was the familiar figure of General Krishna Rao, who was acceptable to Farooq Abdullah but again lacked political experience. Contrary statements emanated from the Home Ministry. Elections were promised but, as militancy continued and casualties rose further, they were hedged by the condition that normal conditions must first return. The military measures taken to restore normality, however, only provoked fresh outbursts of militancy: it was a vicious circle.

Towards the close of 1993, the Hazratbal mosque was the scene of another confrontation, after nearly thirty years. The Indian army beseiged the shrine to capture a group of militants known to be taking shelter there. As in 1963, better sense prevailed over the hotheads in India who wanted the place to be stormed despite the presence of

innocent pilgrims along with the militants. The seige lasted
thirty-two days (17 October to 16 November), after which
the militants surrendered without a shot being fired. Food
had been sent into the shrine, under orders from the
Supreme Court of India, so that the innocents within would
not starve. The image of restraint and care for innocents
at Hazratbal was, however, marred by the firing into a
protest demonstration in the nearby town of Bijbehara
where fifty people were killed. The year ended without any
tangible move to end Kashmir's agony.

A combination of factors, however, gave rise to limited
hopes that 1994 might witness the beginning of the end of
Kashmir's long night. Support for militancy was perceptibly
diminishing after four years of torture, which had yielded
nothing, contrary to the expectations aroused in the late
1980s that *azaadi* was round the corner. More militants
were turning to kidnapping, rape, extortion and other
crimes, thus antagonising their previous supporters. But the
biggest blow to the morale of the militants came from
faraway Geneva when Pakistan's much-publicised campaign
to get the United Nations Human Rights Commission to
censure India for excesses in Kashmir was foiled in March.
Not only was Pakistan forced to withdraw its resolution for
lack of support, but also Iran and China were prominent in
persuading it to do so. Iran's role was particularly
disappointing to fundamentalist militant groups like the
Hizbul Mujahideen because it had upheld Islamic
fundamentalism elsewhere. China's continuing territorial
dispute with India in nearby Ladakh, too, had not persuaded
Beijing to support Pakistan; it was sensitive about its own
human rights problems on Tibet. Hizbul fears that the shift
in public opinion might lead to a political settlement with
New Delhi prompted a wave of terror against National
Conference moderates. Among the victims was former
Speaker of the State Assembly, Wali Mohammad Itoo, who
was gunned down when he emerged after prayers, from a
Jammu mosque on 18 March. Ten years earlier, he had been
pulled out of the Speaker's chair and ejected from the House

when he sought to disqualify the dissidents who brought down Farooq Abdullah's Government and helped instal G.M. Shah in his place.

Farooq Abdullah's return to the valley after the Geneva conference and statements from New Delhi on early steps to restore normalcy reawakened hopes of fresh political initiatives. But ministerial spokesmen did not go beyond holding out the prospect of elections to the State Legislature. Opinion was divided. Projecting Punjab as a model, one group of advisers insisted that elections be held even if many voters did not turn out in the valley. But, as in Punjab, this would revive the process of democratic functioning. The other view was that the situation in the valley was very different to that in Punjab. Factors such as the historical background, Pakistan's claims, the role of the United Nations and the valley's strategic location placed it on a separate footing. So did ethnic and religious factors. No settlement would carry conviction at home and abroad unless there was evidence of popular support. Disillusionment with the militants and with Pakistan should be utilised to win over the people with an offer of effective limits on Central interference, the primary cause of their alienation. Without this, alienation would be further emphasized, providing opportunities for renewed militancy later.

Chapter XVIII

Postscript

*M*any suggestions have been made on ways to solve the festering problem of Kashmir. Ideally, there are precedents in other parts of the world that can serve as models for an agreement in which India and Pakistan can participate. The condominium, or joint control, approach has been favoured by some scholars. For instance: Sudan, when it was under joint Anglo-Egyptian administration; the Free Territory of Trieste, set up by Italy and Yugoslavia on their disputed border; and the four-power administration of Austria after the Second World War. But these were temporary arrangements, with no contending claims to permanent sovereignty. As noted earlier, because Pakistan and India base their claims to the State of Jammu and Kashmir on conflicting principles of nationhood, one religious and the other secular, they find it far more difficult to agree than over disputes that can be resolved without raising unaffordable domestic complications. This was achieved in the Indus Waters Treaty in 1960 and the Rann of Kutch Agreement in 1965. But Pakistan cannot accept a settlement on Kashmir that denies the two-nation theory without destabilising itself; India cannot accept anything confirming the two-nation theory without facing the same consequences.

Another complicating factor is that no comprehensive settlement is feasible for the entire former princely State of Jammu and Kashmir, as carved out by Maharaja Gulab

Singh and his generals more than a century ago. On the Indian side of the line of control, Jammu and Ladakh have distanced themselves from Kashmir's campaign for maximum autonomy or independence. The possibility of their joining Kashmir to form an autonomous condominium or an independent nation is remote. They have nothing in common with the valley, except that they were all exploited by the Dogra rulers. The same is true for most of the area held by Pakistan, except for a small strip of the valley. Gilgit, Hunza, and Baltistan have as little in common with the valley as Ladakh.

One of the proposed suggestions is that India and Pakistan agree to make the line of control that separates their forces in Jammu and Kashmir a soft, porous border. This would enable the divided residents of the State to meet and revive trade and other connections without a formal shift of sovereignty. But neither Government is likely to accept this as long as they do not agree on the future of Kashmir. Both will be suspicious of saboteurs and smugglers crossing over unchecked. That was New Delhi's reason for turning down the Kashmir Resettlement Bill sponsored by Sheikh Abdullah and Farooq Abdullah to enable displaced citizens of the State to return to their homes. A soft border in Jammu and Kashmir is unlikely until the same is achieved all along the Indo-Pakistan border. At present, the hostility and distrust between India and Pakistan are fierce enough to fuel the highest armed conflict in the world, at heights up to 21,000 feet, for control of the Siachen glacier in the remote Karakorams. More casualties have been caused there by the intense cold than by bullets!

The heart of the problem is the valley, where *Kashmiriyat*, Islam and post-accession ties to India are pulling in different directions. This needs to be resolved separately: to await agreement between India and Pakistan means indefinite extension of bloodshed and agony. Since the valley is almost entirely on the Indian side of the line of control, a settlement can be worked out between New Delhi and Srinagar without necessarily involving others.

While the valley's long history and its distinct cultural heritage of *Kashmiriyat* may sustain a case for independence, hard political realities come in the way. Sheikh Abdullah preferred independence, but recognised the hurdles posed by the need for economic viability and national security. But what virtually rules out independence is the fact that no Government in New Delhi can afford to accept the secession of Kashmir. The consequences could disrupt the country's unity. It could touch off similar demands in other ethnic areas. It could reawaken memories of partition massacres in 1947 and reignite communal passions throughout the country. Pakistan, too, does not endorse independence; it has its own ethnic rivalries.

Events have made it clear that the people of Kashmir are alienated from New Delhi and will not accept its domination. They have lost faith in New Delhi's word. At the same time, resentment is growing against the militants, and their Pakistani supporters, for the suffering they have brought without achieving anything.

The foregoing factors narrow the parameters within which a settlement can be negotiated. It must satisfy Kashmir's desire for effective self-government without amounting to secession from India. This was what was attempted under the limited terms of accession signed by Maharaja Hari Singh in October 1947. The powers conceded to the Centre were limited to control over defence, foreign relations and communications. But erosion of the special status promised to the State, and the bitterness and blood-shed that have followed, may make it hard to regain support for a similar arrangement in the valley even if New Delhi is persuaded to consider it. Such an arrangement could gain acceptability, however, if there were adequate guarantees against future erosion. Rival militant groups, with criminals among them, have estranged popular sentiment. The people are also suffering from the havoc caused to the economy. Once the valley is satisfied and is peaceful, the way to an agreement within Pakistan, aimed at converting the line of control into an international border, will be clearer.

Appendix

Instrument of Accession of Jammu and Kashmir State

*T*he following is the text of the actual Instrument of Accession executed by the Ruler of Jammu and Kashmir State on 26 October 1947.

Whereas, the Indian Independence Act, 1947, provides that as from the fifteenth day of August 1947, there shall be set up an independent Dominion known as INDIA, and that the Government of India Act, 1935, shall, with such omissions, additions, adaptations and modifications as the Governor-General may by order specify, be applicable to the Dominion of India;

And whereas the Government of India Act, 1935, as so adapted by the Governor-General provides that an Indian State may accede to the Dominion of India by an Instrument of Accession executed by the Ruler thereof:

Now, therefore, I Shriman Indar Mahandar Rajrajeshwar Maharajadhiraj Shri Hari Singhji, Jammu Kashmir Naresh Tatha Tibbet adi Deshadhipathi, Ruler of JAMMU AND KASHMIR State, in the exercise of my sovereignty in and over my said State do hereby execute this my Instrument of Accession and

1. I hereby declare that I accede to the Dominion of India with the intent that the Governor-General of India, the Dominion Legislature, the Federal Court and any other Dominion authority established for the purposes of the Dominion shall, by virtue of this my Instrument of Accession but subject always to the terms thereof, and for the purposes only of the Dominion, exercise in relation to the State of Jammu and Kashmir (hereinafter referred to as "this State") such functions as may be vested in them by or under the Government of India Act, 1935, as in force in the Dominion of India,

on the 15th day of August 1947 (which Act as so in force is hereafter referred to as "the Act").

2. I hereby assume the obligation of ensuring that due effect is given to the provisions of the Act within this State so far as they are applicable therein by virtue of this my Instrument of Accession.

3. I accept the matters specified in the Schedule hereto as the matters with respect to which the Dominion Legislature may make laws for this State.

4. I hereby declare that I accede to the Dominion of India on the assurance that if an agreement is made between the Governor-General and the Ruler of this State whereby any functions in relation to the administration in this State of any law of the Dominion Legislature shall be exercised by the Ruler of this State, then any such agreement shall be deemed to form part of this Instrument and shall be construed and have effect accordingly.

5. The terms of this my Instrument of Accession shall not be varied by any amendment of the Act or of the Indian Independence Act, 1947, unless such amendment is accepted by me by an Instrument supplementary to this Instrument.

6. Nothing in this Instrument shall empower the Dominion Legislature to make any law for this State authorising the compulsory acquisition of land for any purpose, but I hereby undertake that should the Dominion for the purposes of a Dominion law which applies in this State deem it necessary to acquire any land, I will at their request acquire the land at their expense or if the land belongs to me transfer it to them on such terms as may be agreed, or, in default of agreement, determined by an arbitrator to be appointed by the Chief Justice of India.

7. Nothing in this Instrument shall be deemed to commit me in any way to acceptance of any future constitution of India or to fetter my discretion to enter into arrangements with the Government of India under any such future constitution.

8. Nothing in this Instrument affects the continuance of my sovereignty in and over this state, or, save as provided by or under this Instrument, the exercise of any powers, authority and rights now enjoyed by me as Ruler of this State or the validity of any law at present in force in this State.

9. I hereby declare that I execute this Instrument on behalf of this State and that any reference in this Instrument to me or to the Ruler of the State is to be construed as including a reference to my heirs and successors.

Given under my hand this 26th day of October, nineteen hundred and forty-seven.

(Sd.) Hari Singh
Maharajadhiraj of Jammu and
Kashmir State

Acceptance of Instrument of Accession of Jammu and Kashmir State by the Governor-General of India

I do hereby accept this Instrument of Accession.
Dated this twenty-seventh day of October, nineteen hundred and forty-seven.

(Sd.) Mountbatten of Burma
Governor-General of India

Schedule

The matters with respect to which the Dominion Legislature may make laws for this State

A. *Defence*

1. The naval, military and air forces of the Dominion and any other armed forces raised or maintained by the Dominion; any armed forces, including forces raised or maintained by an acceding State, which are attached to, or operating with, any of the armed forces of the Dominion.

2. Naval, military and air force works, administration of cantonment areas.

3. Arm, fire-arms, ammunition.

4. Explosives.

B. *External Affairs*

1. External affairs; the implementing of treaties and agreements with other countries; extradition, including the surrender of criminals and accused persons to parts of His Majesty's dominions outside India.

2. Admission into, and emigration and expulsion from, India including in relation thereto the regulation of the movements in India of persons who are not British subjects domiciled in India or subjects of any acceding State, pilgrimages to places beyond India.

3. Naturalisation.

C. *Communications*

1. Posts and telegraphs, including telephones, wireless, broadcasting, and other like forms of communication.

2. Federal railways; the regulation of all railways other than minor railways in respect of safety, maximum and minimum rates and fare, station and services terminal charges, interchange of traffic and the responsibility of railway administrations as carriers of goods and passengers; the regulation of minor railways in respect of safety and the responsibility of the administration of such railways as carriers of goods and passengers.

3. Maritime shipping and navigation, including shipping and navigation on tidal waters; Admiralty jurisdiction.

4. Port quarantine.

5. Major ports, that is to say, the declaration and delimitation of such ports, and the constitution and powers of Port Authorities therein.

6. Aircraft and air navigation; the provision and aerodromes; regulation and organisation of air traffic and of aerodromes.

7. Lighthouses, including lightships, beacons and other provisions for the safety of shipping and aircraft.

8. Carriage of passengers and goods by sea or by air.

9. Extension of the powers and jurisdiction of members of the police force belonging to any unit to railway area outside that unit.

D. *Ancillary*

1. Elections to the Dominion Legislature, subject to the provisions of the Act and of any Order made thereunder.

2. Offences against laws with respect to any of the aforesaid matters.

3. Inquiries and statistics for the purposes of any of the aforesaid matters.

4. Jurisdiction and powers of all courts with respect to any of the aforesaid matters but, except with the consent of the Ruler of the Acceding State, not so as to confer any jurisdiction or powers upon any courts other than ordinarily exercising jurisdiction in or in relation to that State.

Notes and References

Chapter I: Introduction

1. Sheikh Abdullah's views were expressed most clearly in his elaborate inaugural address to the Jammu and Kashmir Constituent Assembly on 5 November 1951. It is summarised in Chapter XIII.
2. Kalhana's *Rajatarangini*, First Book, p. 13, translated by M.A. Stein, Motilal Banarsidass, Delhi, 1961. The fruit of over a decade of study, Stein's translation was completed in 1900. It contains not only a flowing translation of *Rajatarangini*, complete with numerous footnotes explaining names and phrases, but also an investigation of Kalhana's sources, authenticity, the dynasties he described and notes on the ancient history and geography of the valley. *Rajatarangini* was written in Sanskrit in A.D. 1148-49.
3. Godfrey Thomas Vigne, *Travels in Kashmir, Ladak, Iskardo and the Himalayas North of Punjab* (two volumes), Henry Colburn, London, 1842. Vigne was one of the many foreign travellers who published highly readable accounts of Kashmir in the 18th century.
4. See Sir Francis Younghusband, *Kashmir*, Adam and Charles Black, London, 1909, p. 179. "The wool [in shawl manufacture] was taxed as it entered Kashmir; the manufacturer was taxed for every workman he employed, and at various stages of the process according to the value of the fabric. Lastly there was the enormous duty of 85 per cent ad valorem. Butchers, bakers, carpenters, boatmen, and even prostitutes were taxed, and coolies who were engaged to carry loads for travellers had to give up half their earnings."
5. Jawaharlal Nehru, *An Autobiography*, Bodley Head, London, 1936; Indian edition 1962, pp. 1 and 37-39. There are many

other descriptions of Kashmir's beauty and history in other writings by Nehru.

6. *Constitutional Relations between Britain and India: The Transfer of Power 1942-47*: HMSO, London, 1982, Vol. XI, Document 229, pp. 442-48. These volumes contain the most comprehensive documentation available on the political negotiations leading to independence and partition. (Further references will be designated *Transfer* with volume, document and page number.)

7. Orient Longman, Madras, p. 170. The relevant paragraph was previously expurgated but published in the 1988 edition:

This was one of the greatest tragedies of Indian history and I have to say with the deepest regret that a large part of the responsibility for this development rests with Jawaharlal. His unfortunate statement that the Congress would be free to modify the Cabinet Mission plan reopened the whole question of political and communal settlement. Mr Jinnah took advantage of his mistake and withdrew from the [Muslim] League's early acceptance of the Cabinet Mission plan.

8. White Paper on Jammu and Kashmir, Government of India, pp. 45-46.

9. Lt. General S.K. Sinha, *Operation Rescue*, Vision Books, New Delhi, 1977, pp. 31-33. Another account of the Kashmir campaign in which the same point is made by Lt. General L.P. Sen, who commanded the advance brigade, is *Slender Was the Thread*, Orient Longman, New Delhi, 1969, pp. 294-95.

10. *Rationale of Hindu State*, Indian Book Gallery, Delhi, 1982, p.72.

11. See Dhananjay Kheer, *Veer Savarkar*, Popular Prakashan, Bombay, 1967, especially pp. 161-62 and 265-68.

12. D.G. Tendulkar, *Mahatma*, Vol. VIII, Publications Division, Government of India, New Delhi, 1963, p. 123.

13. See S. Gopal, *Jawaharlal Nehru: A Biography* (referred to hereafter as *Nehru*) Vol. II, pp. 16-17. Also Rajendra Prasad's letter in *Sardar Patel's Correspondence*, Vol. IV, Navajivan Trust, Ahmedabad, 1972, pp. 337-38.

14. See Rajmohan Gandhi, *Patel: A Life*, Navajivan Trust, Ahmedabad, 1990, pp. 431 and 497; and also S. Gopal, *op. cit.*, p. 16.

15. See Allan Campbell-Johnson's diary entry for 1 December 1947: "There are the symptoms of a Gandhi-Nehru-Abdullah line-up against the Hindu Mahasabha on this issue, and an open

clash between communal and nationalist aspirations inside the Congress. Those in the Congress who want a Hindu State do not want Kashmir," p. 246. Quoted by Sisir Gupta in *Kashmir: A Study in India-Pakistan Relations*, Asia Publishing House, New Delhi, 1966, pp. 125-26.

16. *Looking Back: Autobiography of Mehr Chand Mahajan*, Asia Publishing House, New Delhi, 1963, p. 152.

17. See V.P. Menon, *The Story of the Integration of the Indian States*, Orient Longman, 1956; new edition 1985, p. 149. The entire chapter on the integration of Junagadh, pp. 124-50, merits reading in the context of Kashmir.

18. R.J. Moore, *Escape from Empire: The Attlee Government and the Indian Problem*, Clarendon Press, Oxford, 1983, pp. 332-36.

19. See note from Kashmir Premier Kak to the Viceroy on 14 November 1946 and his response in *Transfers* Vol. IX, Document 37, pp. 71-72. These volumes contain invaluable, comprehensive documentation on developments relating to the withdrawal of British power from the subcontinent.

20. Jawaharlal Nehru, *Independence and After*, Publications Division, Government of India, New Delhi, 1949, pp. 57-58.

21. Tendulkar, *op. cit.*, p 225.

22. See Abdullah's letter to Patel dated 7 October 1948 in *Sardar Patel's Correspondence*, Vol. I, pp. 236-37. Also Abdullah's speech at the UN Security Council on 5 February 1948, *Documents on Kashmir Problem*, Vol. II, Discovery Publishing House, New Delhi, 1991, p. 213.

23. *Sardar Patel's Correspondence*, Vol. I, p. 262, 1971.

24. B.N. Mullik, *My Years with Nehru: Kashmir*, Allied, New Delhi, 1971, pp. 14-17, *passim*. See also Patel's letter to, and concerning, Abdullah and his reply, in *Sardar Patel's Correspondence*, Vol. I, pp. 227-45 and p. 266.

25. See *US Foreign Relations Documents 1948-53*, recording meetings of US diplomats with Abdullah in which he sought reactions to possibility of an independent Kashmir. Also W.R. Crocker, *Nehru: A Contemporary's Estimate*, George Allen and Unwin, London, 1966, p. 95.

26. Professor Riyaz Punjabi of Kashmir University writes in *Perspectives on Kashmir: The Roots of Conflict in South Asia*, Westview Press, USA, 1992:

Thus, within a period of about three decades, a new middle class – mostly urban – emerged on the social scene, reaping the harvest of new found opportunities. The nouveau riche class, which [is] comprised of bureaucrats, businessmen and politicians, successfully manoeuvred the diversion of the benefits of the schemes and programs which were aimed at the amelioration of the general public, towards their *khandans* [families]. The maximum advantages of the appeasement policy were garnered by this tripartite axis of bureaucrats, businessmen and politicians [p. 142].

27. See Kashmir Accord of 13 November 1974, *Documents on Kashmir Problem*, Vol. XV, pp. 177-79.

28. See Farooq Abdullah, *My Dismissal*, Vikas, New Delhi, 1985, especially annexures including text of official press release, pp. 86-90. Also see editorials and news reports in principal newspapers of that period.

Chapter II: Old Kasmira

1. "The name, Kasmira, in its original Sanskrit form, has been used as the sole designation of the country throughout its known history. It has been uniformly applied by its inhabitants and by foreigners. We can trace back its continued use through an unbroken chain of documents for more than twenty-three centuries. The name itself undoubtedly is far more ancient." M. A. Stein, 'Memoir on the Ancient Geography of Kasmir', *Journal of the Asiatic Society of Bengal*, Vol. LXVIII, 1899. Reproduced in Stein's translation of Kalhana's *Rajatarangini: A Chronicle of the Kings of Kashmir*, Archibald Constable, London, 1902; Indian edn. Motilal Banarsidass, Delhi, 1961, Vol. II, p. 386.

2. Stein's note in his translation of *Rajatarangini*, p. 388.

3. *Tuzuk-i-Jahangiri (The Memoirs of Jahangir)*, translated by Alexander Rogers, edited by Henry Beveridge, Royal Asiatic Society, London, 1909; reprinted by Munshiram Manoharlal, Delhi, 1968, pp. 143-44.

4. Francois Bernier, *Travels in the Moghul Empire 1656-1668*, Archibald Constable, London, 1914, pp. 400-01.

5. *Ibid.*, p. 402.

6. Sir Walter Lawrence, *Kashmir and Jammu*, Indian edn., Jay Kay Book House, Jammu, 1985, p. 120.

7. *Travels of Hiouen-Thsang*, translated by Samuel Beall, Trubner, London, 1884, Vol. II, pp. 188-189.

8. Kalhana's *Rajatarangini* translated by M.A. Stein (2 vols).

9. Note by Stein cited by Walter Lawrence in *The Valley of Kashmir*, Oxford University Press (OUP), 1895. Reprinted by Kesar Publishers, Srinagar, 1967, pp. 179-180.

10. R.C. Mazumdar (ed.), *The Vedic Age*, Allen and Unwin, London, p. 49.

11. *Rajatarangini,* Vol. I, verses 57-83.

12. *Ibid.,* p. 104.

13. See P. N. K. Bamzai, *A History of Kashmir,* Metropolitan Book Company, Delhi, 1962, pp. 84-90.

14. *Rajatarangini,* I, pp. 291-293.

15. Prem Nath Bazaz, *The History of the Struggle for Freedom in Kashmir, Cultural and Political, from the Earliest Times to the Present Day,* Pamposh Publications, New Delhi, 1954, p.11.

16. Sir Francis Younghusband, *Kashmir*, Adam and Charles Black, London, 1909.

17. See M.L.Kapur, *Studies in the History and Culture of Kashmir*, Trikuta Publishers, Jammu, 1976, pp. 72-73.

18. Much of the information on the cultural achievements of the pre-Islamic era in Kashmir is taken from Prem Nath Bazaz, *op. cit.*, see especially pp. 20-39. For a detailed exposition of Trikha, see P.N.K. Bamzai, *op. cit.,* pp. 242-55.

Chapter III: Peaceful Conversion

1. Shah Hamdani's extensive travels and repeated visits to Kashmir are detailed in the first volume of G.M.D. Sufi's two-volume history of Kashmir, *Kashmir,* republished by Light & Life Publishers, New Delhi, 1974, pp. 84-92.

2. P.N.K. Bamzai, *A History of Kashmir*, pp. 480-85.

3. P.N. Bazaz, *The History of the Struggle for Freedom in Kashmir*, pp. 83-86. Also M.L. Kapur, *Studies in the History and Culture of Kashmir*, pp. 185-87.

4. *Rajatarangini*, Vol. I, p 130. In a footnote on the same page, Stein provides the historical basis for this conclusion:

The conditions here indicated are illustrated by the frequent references found in Jonaraja's and Srivara's *Chronicles to Brahmans* holding high official posts under the early Sultans. That Sanskrit remained for a considerable period after the end of Hindu rule the medium of official communication and record in Kasmir is shown by the Lokaprakasa. The manifold forms for official documents, reports, etc., which are contained in this remarkable handbook of Kasmirian administrative routine, are drawn up in a curious Sanskrit jargon full of Persian and Arabic words which must have become current in Kasmir soon after the introduction of Islam. The character of these forms leaves no doubt as to their faithfully reproducing in style as well as in contents the actual official correspondence intermediate between the commencement of Muhammadan rule and the adoption of Persian as the official language of the Kasmir administration. The continued popular use of Sanskrit even among the Muhammadans is strikingly proved by the Sanskrit inscription on a tomb in the cemetery of Baha'u-din Sahib at Srinagar, which was put up in the reign of Sultan Muhammad Shah, and which bears a date corresponding to A.D. 1484. Brief Sanskrit inscriptions, without dates, have been found by me on a number of old Muhammadan tombs at Srinagar, near Martand, and elsewhere.

5. Bamzai, *op. cit.,* p. 422.

6. Bazaz, *op. cit.*, pp. 91-92.

7. An anonymous Muslim historian, writing in the seventeenth century, testifies to Zainul Abidin's secular temperament. The valuable Persian manuscript was recently translated into English (from the two copies kept in the British Museum and India Office libraries) by Dr Kashinath Pandit. Judging from the chronicle, the author is an orthodox Muslim who even praises the destruction wrought by the cruel iconoclast Sikandar. His grudging testimony to Zainul Abidin's commitment to *Kashmiriyat*, therefore, cannot but be objective. In his *Baharistan-i-Shahi*, he wrote:

Whereas the Sultan showed considerable favour and regard to the Muslim nobles and their learned men, he also undertook the reconstruction of the monuments of the infidels and the communities of the polytheists. He popularised the practices of the infidels and the heretics and the customs of the idol-worshippers and the people ignorant of faith. All those temples and idol-houses of the infidels, which had been totally destroyed in the rein of Sultan Sikandar, may God bless his soul, were rebuilt and rehabilitated by him. Most of the unbelievers and polytheists, who had fled to the lands of Jammu and Kishtwar because of the overwhelming strength of Islam, were induced by him to return to Kashmir. The sacred books of the infidels and the writings of the unbelievers which had been taken out of this country were brought back, and thus the learning of the unbelievers and the customs of the polytheists were revived by him. He helped the community of the misled idolators to prosper. In every village and town, blasphemous customs connected with spring or temples were revived. He ordered that in every town and locality, celebration of special feasts and festivals by the infidels be revived in accordance with the customs prevalent in the past. He himself attended many of these festivities and distributed gifts among dancers, stage actors, musicians and women singers so that all people, high and low, found themselves happy and satisfied with him.

8. Bazaz, *op. cit.*, p. 61.
9. Although Mirza Haider Dughlat was essentially a military adventurer like Babar, he was a patron of the arts. He was also learned. He wrote several books, among them the *Tarikh-i-Rashidi* while in Kashmir, an autobiographical record of his times.

Chapter IV: Foreign Domination

1. P.N.K. Bamzai, *A History of Kashmir*, p. 359.
2. Thomas Moore, *Lalla Rookh*, George C. Harrap, London, 1846.
3. Quoted in a conversation with Khushwant Singh.
4. The edict reads:

Since all our exalted desire is turned to the contentedness of the people, we gave the order for the repeal of some Acts which in the beautiful country of Kashmir became a cause of distress to the inhabitants of the land. Of the number of those matters, one is that, at the time of collecting the saffron, men used to be impressed for this work without any wages except a little salt, and that the people have suffered much distress. We ordered that no man should, by any means, be molested as to gathering saffron. And as to saffron grown on crown lands, the labourers must be satisfied and receive proper wages. And whatever grows on lands granted in jagir, let the whole saffron in kind be delivered to the jagirdar that he may gather it as he likes. Another grievance is that at the time of the Subadars (viceroys) of Kashmir, they used to levy two dam for wood on each kharwar of rice and during the government of I'tiqad Khan four dam for the same purpose were levied on each kharwar. Since on this account also the people were much distressed, we ruled that the people should be entirely relieved on this tax, and nothing should be taken on account of wood.

Another grievance was that a village whose rental was more than 400 kharwar of shali, was obliged to furnish the authorities of the place two sheep annually. I'tiqad Khan, during his rule, took 66 dam in place of each sheep. Since on this account also the people were very much annoyed, we gave strict order that it should cease; neither should the sheep be taken, nor money in their place; the people should be held excused from paying this impost. Moreover, I'tiqad Khan, during his incumbency, levied a summary poll-tax of 75 dam on each boatman whether young or an old man or a boy, whilst it was the established custom formerly to levy 60 dam on a young man, 12 on an old man, and 36 dam on a boy. We ordered that the former custom should be re-established, that the wrong done by I'tiqad Khan be redressed, and the people not act in accordance with it. Another grievance is that the Subadars, in the fruit season, placed their own men in each garden, large and small, which appeared to contain good fruit, to watch the fruit for themselves and did not allow the owners of those gardens to use the fruit; hence much loss was caused to these people, so that some of these men have destroyed the fruit trees. We ordered that no Subadar should lay an embargo on the fruit of the orchard or garden of anyone. It is proper that noble governors and competent collectors and the officials of this and future times in the province of Kashmir should consider these orders as lasting and eternal, nor should they admit of any change in these regulations. Whoever admits any change or alterations will fall under the curse of God and the anger of the King.

5. Translated from the Persian in G.M.D. Sufi's *Kashmir*, Vol. II, p. 312.

6. William Moorcroft and George Trebeck, *Travels in the Himalayan Provinces of Hindustan and Punjab*, Vol. II, pp. 293-94.

7. G.T. Vigne, *Travels in Kashmir, Ladakh, Iskardo*, Vol. I, p. 308.

8. Baron Erich von Schonberg, *Travels in India and Kashmir*, Hurst and Blacket, London, 1853, pp. 96-97.

Chapter V: Dogra Rule

1. This quote and further quotes from, and references to, Lord Hardinge are taken from Sir Francis Younghusband's *Kashmir*.

As British Resident in the princely State of Jammu and Kashmir, Younghusband had access to official papers.

2. Captain Joseph Davey Cunningham, *History of the Sikhs*, Oxford University Press, London, 1918, p. 319.

3. H.D. Torrens, *Travels in Ladak, Tartary and Kashmir*, Otley, London, 1865, p. 301.

4. Frederic Drew, *The Jummoo and Kashmir Territories*, Edward Stanford, London, 1875, p. 15.

5. The underlying British objective was to take exclusive control of Gilgit, near the Afghan-Russian border. See Bamzai, *A History of Kashmir*, pp. 625-28.

6. Bazaz, *History of the Struggle for Freedom in Kashmir,* p. 129.

7. Lawrence gave further details of the heavy taxes levied by the Dogra rulers in his *The Valley of Kashmir.* Even his Muslim subjects had to pay for the upkeep of temples, including the Maharaja's. Half their crops were taken and every produce was taxed. Officials were empowered to levy their own taxes, on each cow, on fruits, on honey, and on cloth, among other items.

Chapter VI: Mass Awakening

1. An abridged version, translated into English by Khushwant Singh as *Flame of the Chinar*, is to be published by Viking, who have kindly given me a copy of the manuscript (MS). Subsequent references will be to *Flame* and the pages of the MS. The original autobiography was ghost-written in flowery Urdu, corrected and approved by Sheikh Abdullah.

2. *Flame*, p. 58.

3. *Ibid.*, p. 71, *passim*.

4. *Ibid.*, p. 49.

5. *Ibid.*, p. 47, *passim*.

6. *Ibid.*, pp. 40-41.

7. *The Testament of Sheikh Abdullah,* Palit and Palit, Dehra Dun, 1974, p. 67.

8. Bazaz, *History of the Struggle for Freedom in Kashmir*, pp. 153-54.

9. *Ibid.*, p. 168.

10. *The Testament of Sheikh Abdullah*, pp. 72-73.

11. Bazaz, *op. cit.*, p. 212.

12. *Flame*, p. 151.

13. P. L. Lakhanpal, *Essential Documents and Notes on Kashmir Dispute*, International Books, Delhi, 1965, p. 33. The following is an extract from Abdullah's memorandum:

The crux of our contention is that the sale-deed which brought Kashmir under the Dogra House confers no privileges equivalent to those claimed by States governed by the so-called Treaty rights. As such, the case of Kashmir stands on a unique footing, and the people of Kashmir draw attention of the Cabinet Mission to their just claim to freedom on the withdrawal of British Power. We, the people of Kashmir, are determined to mould our destiny....

14. Nehru's statement, penned in journalistic style, also reported:

The whole valley was handed over to military administration. The police, being Kashmiris, were withdrawn. A reign of terrorism and frightfulness then began. Kashmir has been practically cut off from the outside world since then. My information is that far more people than officially admitted have been killed. A much larger number who were wounded were sent to jails instead of hospitals. Srinagar is almost a city of the dead where movement is difficult and large numbers of people are practically interned in their own houses, apart from the many hundreds who have been put in prison. Clashes occur daily and even women have been shot down. But what is worse is the deliberate attempt, reminiscent of the martial law days in Punjab in 1919, to humiliate human beings. I understand that people are made to crawl in some of the streets, that sometimes they are made to take off their turbans to clean the streets and pavements, that they are made to shout at the point of the bayonet 'Maharaj ki jai'. Dead bodies are not handed to the relatives for burial according to religious rites, but are soaked in petrol and burnt. The mosques, including the inner shrines, have been occupied by the military. A wall of the Jama Masjid of Srinagar has been knocked down to make a passage for military lorries. A dangerous feature of the situation is the deliberate attempt to foment communal trouble.

Nehru admitted later that reports of dead bodies being burnt and the breaking of the *masjid* wall were exaggerated.

15. Sonia Gandhi (ed.), *Two Alone: Two Together: Letters between Indira Gandhi and Jawaharlal Nehru (1940-64)*, Hodder & Stoughton, London, 1992, pp. 532-34.

16. *Flame*, pp. 148-49.
17. *Ibid.*, p. 152.
18. *Ibid.*, p. 153.

Chapter VII: Communal Politics

1. See Mushirul Hasan, *Nationalism and Communal Politics in India*, Manohar Books, New Delhi, 1991, especially pp. 25-26. But the author makes the point that the early Muslim reaction to the introduction of the elective principle under British rule was more specific than monolithic.

2. For the principal scholars contributing to India's 'discovery of her past', and their works see K.K. Datta, *Dawn of Renascent India*, Allied, Bombay, 1964, pp. 57-83.

3. K.K. Aziz, *The Making of Pakistan*, Chatto & Windus, London, 1967, pp. 23-29. Recalling the same period, Nirad C. Chaudhuri writes in *The Autobiography of an Unknown Indian*, London, 1951: "A cold dislike for the Muslim settled down in our hearts, putting an end to all real intimacy of relationship."

4. Hasan, *op. cit.*, p. 25.

5. Dhananjay Kheer, *Veer Savarkar*, pp. 263 and 267. The entire chapter entitled Hindu Manifesto, pp. 261-85 merits study. Most of the quotations from Savarkar were collected by Kheer, an ardent admirer and biographer, from his numerous writings and speeches.

6. *Ibid.*, pp. 318-19.

7. M.S. Golwalkar, *We or Our Nation Defined*, Bharat Prakashan, Nagpur, 1947 edn., pp. 55-56.

8. See article by Bhai Mahavir in *The Hindustan Times*, New Delhi, 6 June 1990.

9. Walter Andersen and Shridhar Damle, *The Brotherhood in Saffron*, Westview Press, USA, 1987, p. 49.

10. See *Sardar Patel's Correspondence*, Vol. I, p. 143. Patel's reply on p. 152.

11. Andersen and Damle, *op. cit.*, pp. 55-56.

12. Craig Baxter, *Jana Sangh*, OUP, London, 1971, p. 123.

Chapter VIII: The Last Maharaja

1. Arthur Neve, *Thirty Years in Kashmir*, Edward Arnold, London, 1913.

2. Rani Dhawan Shankardass, *Vallabhbhai Patel: Power and Organisation in Indian Politics*, Orient Longman, New Delhi, 1988, pp. 284-85.

3. State Department Memorandum on Kashmir Dispute, dated 6 February 1950, *Foreign Relations of the USA*, 1950, Vol. V, p. 1381.

4. Karan Singh, *Heir Apparent: An Autobiography*, OUP, New Delhi, 1982; revised edn. 1984. See especially pp. 13 and 37-40.

5. Leonard Mosley, *The Last Days of the British Raj*, Weidenfeld and Nicolson, London, 1962, p. 60. A well-written account which presents entertaining pen-pictures of the principal characters. In essence, Mosley finds Congress fatigue and Mountbatten's haste responsible for partition.

6. Enclosed in a letter to Patel from Kashmir Prime Minister Ram Chandra Kak dated 25 August 1946. *Sardar Patel's Correspondence* (referred to hereafter as *Patel*), Vol. I, pp. 13-15.

7. *Ibid.*, p. 7.

8. *Ibid.*, pp. 12-13.

9. *Ibid.*, pp. 18-20.

10. *Ibid.*, pp. 21-22.

11. *Ibid.*, p. 22.

12. *Transfer,* IX, Document 37, pp. 71-72.

13. *Ibid.,* Document 140, pp. 237-38.

14. Karan Singh, *op. cit.*, p. 48.

15. Alan Campbell-Johnson, *Mission with Mountbatten*, Robert Hale London, 1951, pp. 101-02.

16. *Transfer*, XI, Document 294, pp. 555-56.

17. Alastair Lamb, *Kashmir: A Disputed Legacy*, Roxford Books, UK, 1991, p. 110.

18. *Transfer*, XI, Document 319, pp. 592-93.

19. *Ibid.*, Document 369, pp. 687-88.

20. *Ibid.*, Document 386, pp. 717-19.

21. *Ibid.*, Document 347, pp. 719-20.

22. *Ibid.*, Document 229, pp. 442-48.

23. *Patel, op. cit.,* pp. 32-34.

24. *Transfer,* XI, Document 201, pp. 390-91.

25. *Ibid.,* XII, IV, pp. 3-5.

26. *Ibid.,* XII, Document 129, p. 187.

27. *Ibid.,* XII, Document 149, pp. 211-12.

28. *Ibid.,* XII, Document 249, p. 368.

29. *Ibid.,* XII, Document 259, pp. 379-80.

30. *Ibid.,* XII, Document 260, p. 380.

31. *Ibid.,* XII, Document 280, pp. 410-11.

32. Pyarelal, *Mahatma Gandhi: The Last Phase,* Volume II, Navajivan Trust, Ahmedabad, 1958, p. 363.

33. *Transfer,* XII, Document 269, pp. 397-79.

34. *Ibid.,* XII, Document 302, pp. 449-50.

35. Pyarelal, *op. cit.,* pp. 357-58.

36. *Collected Works of Mahatma Gandhi,* Vol. 89, pp. 5-6. From *Harijan* dated 24 August 1947.

Chapter IX: On the Brink

1. Larry Collins and Dominique Lapierre, *Freedom at Midnight,* Vikas, New Delhi, 1976, p. 282.

2. Leonard Mosley, *The Last Days of the British Raj,* p. 200.

3. *Transfer,* XII, Document 428, pp. 662-63. Ismay wrote to Liaquat:

   ... you surely do not expect the Viceroy to suggest to Sir Cyril Radcliffe that he should make any alteration. Still less can I believe that you intend to imply that the Viceroy has influenced this award. I am well aware that some uninformed sections of public opinion imagine that the award will not be Sir Cyril Radcliffe's but the Viceroy's, but I never for one moment thought that you, who are completely in the know, should ever imagine that he could do such a thing.

4. *Ibid.,* Document 395, pp. 618-20.

5. *Ibid.,* Document 406, p. 639.

6. *Ibid.,* Document 489, p. 769.

7. M.J. Akbar, *Kashmir: Behind the Vale,* Viking, New Delhi, 1991, p. 98.

8. *Patel,* pp. 37-39.

9. *Ibid.,* p. 40.

10. *Ibid.*, pp. 42-43.

11. *Ibid.*, p. 48.

12. *Ibid.*, pp. 48-49.

13. *Pakistan Times*, Lahore, quoted by Josef Korbel, *Danger in Kashmir*, Princeton University Press, Princeton, 1954, pp. 60-61.

14. *Patel, op. cit.*, I, p. 57.

15. *Ibid.*, I, pp. 45-47.

16. *Ibid.*, I, pp. 58-60.

17. *Nehru*, Vol. IV, pp. 1265-66 and 1268-71.

18. *The Hindustan Times*, New Delhi, 14 October 1947. Quoted by Sisir Gupta, *Kashmir: A Study in India-Pakistan Relations*, p. 106.

19. *The Hindustan Times*, 18 October 1947.

20. Josef Korbel (*op. cit.*, pp. 70-71) quotes *People's Age*, Bombay, carrying a report of Abdullah's speech, before a gathering of one lakh, in which he said: "Our first demand is complete transfer of power to the people of Kashmir. Representatives of the people in a democratic Kashmir will then decide whether the State should join India or Pakistan.... We will naturally opt for that Dominion where our own demand for freedom receives recognition and support. We cannot decide to join those who say that the people have no voice in the matter [presumably meaning Jinnah].... The Kashmir Government will not be a government of any one community. It will be a joint government of the Hindus, the Sikhs and the Muslims. That is what I am fighting for."

21. V.P. Menon, *The Story of the Integration of the Indian States*, Orient Longman, New Delhi, 1985 edition, p. 395.

22. Josef Korbel , *op. cit.*, p. 64.

23. H.V. Hodson, *The Great Divide, Britain-India-Pakistan*, Hutchinson, London, 1969, p. 430.

24. Mosley, *op. cit.*, pp. 183 and 186.

25. Quoted by Hodson, *op. cit.*, who had access to the Mountbatten papers, p. 436.

26. V. Shankar, *My Reminiscences of Sardar Patel*, Vol. II, Macmillan, New Delhi, 1974, p. 117.

27. Hodson, *op. cit.*, pp. 430 and 432-33.

28. See Alastair Lamb, *Kashmir: A Disputed Legacy*, p. 122. Also refer to his account of the violence in Poonch pp. 122-25. Lamb generally favours and projects Pakistan's views.

29. *The Statesman* (Calcutta), 4 February 1948. Quoted by Korbel, *op. cit.*, p. 68.

30. Korbel, *op. cit.*, p. 66.

31. Mahajan, *Looking Back*, pp. 141-42.

32. Text of telegrams from P. L. Lakhanpal, *Essential Documents and Notes on Kashmir Dispute*, pp. 50-54.

33. *Patel*, I, pp. 61-63.

Chapter X: Invasion and Accession

1. Campbell-Johnson, *Mission with Mountbatten*, p. 188.

2. See Lt. Gen. L.P. Sen, *Slender Was the Thread*, pp. 294-96.

3. S.K. Sinha, *Operation Rescue: Military Operations in Jammu and Kashmir 1947-49,* p. 115.

4. Hodson, *The Great Divide*, p. 541.

5. *Ibid.*, p. 457.

6. See Josef Korbel, a member of the UN Commission, *Danger in Kashmir,* pp. 138-39.

7. Hodson, *op. cit.*, p. 457, describing the scene when Gracey refused to immediately implement Jinnah's order, writes: "An acrimonious conversation followed, in which General Gracey attributed to Sir Francis Mudie language of undiplomatic tone and imperiousness."

8. Chaudhary Khaliquzzaman, *Pathways to Pakistan*, Orient Longman (Pakistan), Lahore, 1961, p. 292.

9. Hodson, *op. cit.*, p. 447 footnote.

10. Sen, *op. cit.*, p. 36.

11. Mahajan, *Looking Back,* p. 150.

12. B.N. Pandey, *Nehru*, Macmillan, London, 1976, p. 313.

13. Menon, *The Story of the Integration of the Indian States*, p. 398 and pp. 399-400.

14. Mahajan, *op. cit.*, pp. 151-52.

15. *Flame*, p. 195.

16. Government of India White Paper reproduced in *Documents on Kashmir Problem*, Discovery Publishing House, New Delhi, 1991, Vol. XIV, pp. 73-75.

17. Lamb, *Kashmir: A Disputed Legacy,* pp. 135-36. The British historian's anxiety to somehow establish Indian involvement in Kashmir before accession is also seen in the episode of the Patiala battery of guns found sited near Srinagar airfield by

Brig. L.P. Sen, who records the incident on pp. 64-65 of his book. They were of little value because they lacked sights. The Patiala forces had yet to be integrated into the Indian army. Its Maharaja had obviously responded to his fellow-Maharaja's appeal for help. Yet Lamb, p. 131, finds occasion to point a finger at New Delhi.

18. Sinha, *op. cit.*, pp. 11-14.
19. For text of the note signed by the Commanders-in-Chief of the army, air force and navy see Menon, *op. cit.*, pp. 401-02.
20. See Margaret Bourke-White, *Halfway to Freedom*, Simon & Schuster, New York, 1949.
21. Patel, I, p. 68.
22. Sen, *op. cit.*, pp. 114-15.
23. Sinha *op. cit.*, pp. 21-22.
24. *Ibid.*, p. 130.
25. *Flame*, p. 208.

Chapter XI: The Albatross

1. *Documents on Kashmir Problem*, Vol. XIV, pp. 75-76.
2. Hodson, *The Great Divide*, pp. 458-59.
3. *Ibid.*, pp. 460-62, quoting from Mountbatten's report to the King.
4. *Ibid.*, pp. 462-65.
5. Campbell-Johnson, *Mission with Mountbatten*, p. 220.
6. Hodson, *op. cit.*, pp. 466-67.
7. *Selected Works of Jawaharlal Nehru*, Vol. IV, Jawaharlal Nehru Memorial Fund, New Delhi, 1986, pp. 399-403.
8. See Hodson, *op. cit.*, pp. 466-68.
9. *Nehru, IV, op. cit.*, pp. 286-88.
10. *Ibid.*, V, pp. 210-11.
11. *Ibid.*, V, p. 218.
12. Hodson, *op. cit.*, pp. 469-70.
13. *Nehru,* IV, pp. 320d-320e.
14. *Patel* I, pp. 85-87.
15. *Flame*, p. 200.
16. Sen, *Slender Was the Thread*, p. 56.
17. Tendulkar, *Mahatma*, VIII, p. 168.
18. *Ibid.*, pp. 203-04 and 207.
19. *Ibid.*, pp. 222 and 225.

20. *Flame*, pp. 208-09.
21. *Patel*, I, p. 56.
22. *Ibid.*, pp. 113-14.
23. *Ibid.*, 118-24.
24. Shankar, *My Reminiscences of Sardar Patel*, Vol. I, p. 138.
25. *Patel*, VI, pp. 10-11 and 12-13.
26. *Ibid.*, p. 29.

Chapter XII: Rival Loyalties

1. *Nehru*, IV, p. 325.
2. *Documents on Kashmir Problem*, II, pp. 216-17.
3. Walter Crocker, *Nehru: A Contemporary's Estimate*, p. 178. Crocker was High Commissioner for Australia in New Delhi.
4. *Patel*, I, p. 87-88.
5. *Nehru*, IV, p. 351.
6. This extract and the fascinating exchanges involving Nehru, Hari Singh, Abdullah, Mahajan and others described in this chapter are taken from *Patel*, I, pp. 128-44.
7. R.N. Kaul, *Sheikh Mohammad Abdullah: A Political Phoenix*, Sterling, New Delhi, 1985, p. 50. Prof. Kaul, a Pandit and member of the National Conference, describes the wide range of pressures that were brought to bear on Abdullah. For instance: "The Maharaja wanted monarchy to be restored; the Hindu and Muslim jagirdars wanted the feudal pattern of society to last forever; the Hindu extremists, who had acquired wealth in the name of religion, believed that a status quo could be perpetuated by fanning communal flames" (p. 550).
8. *Patel*, I, pp. 134-36.
9. *Ibid.*, pp. 140 and 144.
10. *Ibid.*, pp. 147 and 152.
11. *Ibid.*, pp. 157-65.
12. *Ibid.*, p. 42.
13. *Ibid.*, pp. 174 and 182-83.
14. *Nehru*, V, pp. 268-70.
15. *Patel*, I, p. 193.
16. *Ibid.*, pp. 193 and 197.
17. *Ibid.*, p. 204.
18. *Ibid.*, pp. 212-15.
19. *Ibid.*, pp. 225-26.

20. The letters provoked by Abdullah's press conference are reproduced in *ibid.*, pp. 227-45.
21. *Ibid.*, p. 259.
22. *Nehru*, X, pp. 238-39.
23. Karan Singh, *Heir Apparent*, p. 92.
24. Mahajan, *Looking Back*, p. 162.
25. *Documents on Kashmir Problem*, II, pp. 210-26.
26. *Foreign Relations of the United States 1948*, Washington DC 1975, Vol. V, Part I, p. 292. (Hereafter referred to as *US Foreign Relations*.)
27. *US Foreign Relations 1950*, Vol. V, p. 1381.

Chapter XIII: The Lion Caged

1. *Patel*, I, p. 305.
2. *Ibid.*, pp. 306-10.
3. *Flame*, p. 229.
4. See R.N. Kaul, *Sheikh Mohammad Abdullah: A Political Phoenix*, pp. 55-56.
5. See Karan Singh, *Heir Apparent*, pp. 119-22.
6. *Ibid.*, pp. 131-37.
7. *Ibid.*, p. 145.
8. B.N. Mullik, *My Years with Nehru: Kashmir*, pp. 15-16.
9. Cited by S. Gopal in Vol. II of his biography of Nehru, p. 119.
10. Cited in *ibid.*, p. 120.
11. *Flame*, pp. 246-47.
12. Jawaharlal Nehru, *Letters to Chief Ministers*, Vol. III (1952-54), OUP, New Delhi, 1987, pp. 192, 198 and 230.
13. *US Foreign Relations 1950*, Vol. V, pp. 1433-35.
14. Crocker, *Nehru: A Contemporary's Estimate*, p. 96.
15. *US Foreign Relations 1950*, Vol. XI, pp. 1953-54.
16. Cited by S. Gopal, Vol. II, footnote to p. 131.
17. Cited in *ibid.*, p. 64.
18. Cited in *ibid.*, p. 124.
19. Mir Qasim, *My Life and Times*, Allied, New Delhi, 1992, p. 61. Qasim initially worked with Abdullah and later became Chief Minister of Jammu and Kashmir.
20. Cited in Gopal, *op. cit.*, Vol. II, pp. 130-31.
21. Karan Singh, *op. cit.*, p. 155.

22. Mullik, *op. cit.*, pp. 40-42.
23. Karan Singh, *op. cit.*, p. 161.
24. *Ibid.*, pp. 161 and 163-64.
25. Mullik, *op. cit.*, pp. 44-45.
26. Gopal, *op. cit.*, Vol. II, p. 133.
27. Mullik, *op. cit.*, pp. 44-45.
28. Nehru, *Letters to Chief Ministers*, Vol. III, pp. 364-65.

Chapter XIV: The Bakshi Brothers

1. B.N. Mullik, *My Years with Nehru: Kashmir*, pp. 53, 59, 109-14.
2. Mir Qasim, *My Life and Times*, p. 71.
3. Nehru, *Letters to Chief Ministers*, Vol. III, pp. 395 and 404.
4. Mullik, *op. cit.*, p. 46.
5. Mir Qasim, *op. cit.*, pp. 69-70.
6. Mullik, *op. cit.*, p. 68.
7. *Ibid.*, pp. 72-76.
8. *Ibid.*, p. 102.
9. Y.D. Gundevia, monograph included in *Testament of Sheikh Abdullah*, p. 121.
10. *Ibid.*, p. 116.
11. Cited in S. Gopal, *Nehru*, Vol. II, p. 303.
12. *Flame*, p. 274.
13. Mullik, *op. cit.*, pp. 84-85.
14. Mir Qasim, *op. cit.*, pp. 88-89.
15. Cited in Gopal, *op. cit.*, Vol. II, p. 262 fn.
16. Mir Qasim, *op. cit.*, pp. 94-95.
17. Mullik, *op. cit.*, p. 142.
18. Mir Qasim, *op. cit.*, p. 97.
19. Mullik, *op. cit.*, pp. 155 and 158.
20. Mir Qasim, *op. cit.*, p. 104.
21. Prem Nath Bazaz, *Kashmir in Crucible*, pp. 233-34; a sequel to *A History of the Struggle for Freedom in Kashmir*.
22. Mir Qasim, *op. cit.*, p. 119.
23. *Ibid.*, p. 107.
24. *Ibid.*, pp. 128-29.

Chapter XV: End of an Era

1. *Flame*, pp. 302-03.
2. For the text of the two articles on Kashmir by Jayaprakash Narayan published on 20 April and 15 May 1964 in *The Hindustan Times*, see A.G. Noorani, *The Kashmir Question*, P.C. Manaktalas, Bombay, 1964, appendixes, pp. 110-121.
3. Pakistan's leading paper, *The Dawn*, commented: "Sheikh Abdullah's references to India's so-called secularism have caused a certain amount of disappointment among the public, in general, and the intelligentsia, in particular."
4. Mohammad Ayub Khan, *Friends Not Masters*, OUP, London, p. 128. This is an autobiographical account of his career in the army and as President of Pakistan up to 1965.
5. *Testament of Sheikh Abdullah*, pp. 81-82.
6. *Flame*, p. 307.
7. *Ibid.*, p. 311.
8. *Ibid.*, p. 318.
9. General Mohammad Musa, *My Version*, Wajidalis, Lahore, 1983, pp. 35-37. Earlier, the writer describes his reluctance to get involved in Operation Gibraltar.
10. Lt. Gen. Harbaksh Singh, *War Despatches*, Lancer International, New Delhi, 1991, pp. 25-45.
11. *Flame*, p. 320.
12. *Testament of Sheikh Abdullah*, pp. 41, 45, 68-69.
13. *Ibid.*, p. 142.
14. M.J. Akbar, *Kashmir: Behind the Vale*, Viking, New Delhi, 1991, p. 179.
15. Mir Qasim, *My Life and Times*, pp. 131-32.
16. *Flame*, p. 325.
17. Mir Qasim, *op. cit.*, pp. 142-43.
18. *Flame*, p. 326.
19. *Ibid.*, p. 330.
20. See Akbar, *op. cit.*, p. 192.
21. *Flame*, p. 246.

Chapter XVI: Violence Erupts

1. See Akbar, *Kashmir: Behind the Vale*, p. 186.
2. Mir Qasim, *My Life and Times*, p. 162.

3. Recalled in a conversation with former Governor B.K. Nehru.

4. Jagmohan, *My Frozen Turbulence in Kashmir*, Allied, New Delhi, 1991, pp. 294-95. As Governor of Kashmir, Jagmohan had access to official papers.

5. Recalled in a conversation with B.K. Nehru.

6. See Jagmohan, *op. cit.*, pp. 276-96 and Farooq Abdullah, *My Dismissal.*

7. *The Statesman* (4 July): "It has been clear for many months that Mr Shah's manoeuvres enjoyed the Congress (I)'s active encouragement. The clandestine manner in which Monday's defections took place only strengthens suspicion. What makes matters worse is that Mr Jagmohan seems to have flouted both gubernatorial convention and the State's Constitution in his anxiety to further the Centre's political objectives."

   Economic and Political Weekly (7 July): "The defection of the 12 National Conference MLAs which provided the pretext for Jagmohan to dismiss Farooq Abdullah cannot serve even as the proverbial figleaf. For the defection of the MLAs, the decision of the Congress party in the state assembly to support the government to be formed by G.M. Shah and the dismissal of Farooq Abdullah — all in a matter of a few hours — were part of a scenario worked out during Jagmohan's visit to New Delhi last week.

   Indian Express (10 July): "Mr Jagmohan usurped the reins of government well before the then chief minister, Mr Farooq Abdullah, was dismissed by him...itself an act of dubious propriety.... Idubitably the Governor staged a coup, and he could not have done this with impunity without the knowledge and consent of the Centre.... The implications of Mr Jagmohan's act are many and serious. It establishes a most dangerous and damaging precedent, elevating the Governor to the position of a viceroy.... This is clearly unconstitutional and can only further undermine federal relationships."

8. Article in *The Times of India*, 18 August 1984.

9. Recalled in a conversation with B.K. Nehru.

10. *Sunday*, 14-20 November 1993.

11. Mir Qasim, *My Life and Times*, p. 163.

12. Jagmohan, *op. cit.*, pp. 346-47.

13. Taken from an official note from Dr Farooq Abdullah to Governor Krishna Rao on the Rubaiyah kidnapping.

Chapter XVII: Vicious Circle

1. Jagmohan, *My Frozen Turbulence in Kashmir*, pp. 15-16.
2. *Ibid.*, p. 21.
3. *Ibid.*, p. 34.
4. *Ibid.*, pp. 419-20.
5. Khem Lata Wakhlu and O.N. Wakhlu, *Kidnapped*, Konark, Delhi, 1993. Mrs Wakhlu was a former Minister in the Kashmir Government and her husband principal of the Regional Engineering College, Srinagar. They gave their earlier impressions in *Kashmir: Behind the White Curtain*.
6. *Report on Human Rights Situation in the Kashmir Valley*, 20-25 May 1992, by V.M. Tarkunde, Balraj Puri, Sulochana Shikhre, and N.D. Pancholi, Coordination Committee on Kashmir, Delhi, p. 15.

Select Bibliography

Abdullah, Farooq, *My Dismissal*, Vikas, New Delhi, 1985.

Abdullah, Sheikh Mohammad, *Flames of the Chinar (Aatish-e-Chinar)* (autobiography) translated from Urdu by Khushwant Singh, to be published by Viking, New Delhi.

Abdullah, Sheikh Mohammad, *Testament of Sheikh Abdullah* with a monograph by Y. D. Gundevia, Palit and Palit, Dehra Dun, 1974.

Akbar, M.J., *Kashmir: Behind the Vale*, Viking, London, 1991.

Akbar, M.J., *Nehru: The Making of India*, Viking, London, 1988.

Akbar, M.J., *The Seige Within*, Viking, London, 1985.

Andersen, Walter and Damle, Shridhar, *The Brotherhood in Saffron*, Westview Press, USA, 1987.

Ayub Khan, Mohammad, *Friends Not Masters*, Oxford University Press (OUP), London, 1967.

Azad, Abul Kalam, *India Wins Freedom*, Orient Longman, New Delhi and Madras, 1967 and 1988.

Bamzai, P.N.K., *A History of Kashmir: Political-Social-Cultural from the Earliest Times to the Present Day*, Metropolitan Book Company, Delhi, 1962.

Baxter, Craig, *Jana Sangh*, OUP, London, 1971.

Bazaz, Prem Nath, *The History of the Struggle for Freedom in Kashmir, Cultural and Political, from the Earliest Times to the Present Day*, Pamposh Publications, New Delhi, 1954.

Bazaz, Prem Nath, *Kashmir in Crucible*, Pamposh Publications, New Delhi, 1967.

Beg, Mohd. Afzal, *Sheikh Abdullah Defended*, Srinagar, (other details not available).

Bernier, Francois, *Travels in the Moghul Empire*, Archibald Constable, London, 1914.

Birdwood, Lord, *Two Nations and Kashmir*, Robert Hale, London 1956.

Bourke-White, Margaret, *Halfway to Freedom*, Simon & Schuster, New York, 1949.

Brecher, M., *Nehru: A Political Biography*, OUP, London, 1959.

Brecher, M., *The Struggle for Kashmir*, OUP, New York, 1953.

Burke, S.M., *Pakistan's Foreign Policy*, OUP, London, 1973.

Campbell-Johnson, Alan, *Mission with Mountbatten*, Robert Hale, London, 1951.

Collins, Larry and Lapierre, Dominique, *Freedom at Midnight*, Vikas, New Delhi, 1976.

Crocker, W.R., *Nehru: A Contemporary's Estimate,* George Allen and Unwin, London, 1966.

Cunningham, Joseph Davy, *A History of the Sikhs*, OUP, London, 1918.

Deora, M.S. and Grover, R. *Documents on Kashmir Problem* (15 vols.), Discovery Publishing House, New Delhi, 1991.

Digby, William, *Condemned Unheard*, Indian Political Agency, London, 1890.

Drew, Frederic, *The Jummoo and Kashmir Territories*, Edward Stanford, London, 1875.

Engineer, A.A., *Secular Crown on Fire: The Kashmir Problem*, Ajanta Publications, Delhi, 1991.

Gajendragadkar, P.B., *Kashmir: Retrospect and Prospect,* University of Bombay, Bombay, 1967.

Galbraith, J.K., *Ambassador's Journal*, Hamish Hamilton, London, 1969.

Gandhi, M.K., *Collected Works* (89 vols.), Publications Division, Government of India, New Delhi.

Gandhi, Rajmohan, *Patel: A Life*, Navajivan Trust, Ahmedabad, 1990.

Gandhi, Sonia, *Two Alone: Two Together: Letters between Indira Gandhi and Jawaharlal Nehru (1940-64)*, Hodder & Stoughton, London, 1992.

Gopal, S., *Jawaharlal Nehru: A Biography* (3 vols.), OUP, New Delhi, London,

Gundevia, Y.D., *Outside the Archives*, Sangam Books, Hyderabad, 1984.

Gupta, Sisir, *Kashmir: A Study in India-Pakistan Relations*, Asia Publishing House, New Delhi, 1966.

Hasan, Mushirul, *Nationalism and Communal Politics in India*, Manohar Books, New Delhi, 1991.

Hodson, H.V., *The Great Divide: Britain-India-Pakistan*, Hutchinson, London, 1969.

Jagmohan, *My Frozen Turbulence in Kashmir*, Allied, New Delhi, 1991.

Joshi, D.K., *A New Deal for Kashmir*, Ankur Publishing House, New Delhi, 1978.

Kalhana, *Rajatarangini*, M.A. Stein (trans.) (2 vols.), Archibald Constable, London, 1900; Indian edn. Motilal Banarsidass, Delhi, 1961.

Kapur, M.L., *Studies in the History and Culture of Kashmir*, Trikuta Publishers, Jammu 1976.

Kaul, B.M., *Confrontation with Pakistan*, Barnes and Noble, New York, 1972.

Kaul, R.N., *Sheikh Mohammad Abdullah: A Political Phoenix*, Sterling, New Delhi, 1985.

Khaitan, Rajesh, *The Kashmir Tangle*, Vision Books, New Delhi, 1992.

Khaliquzzaman, Chaudhary, *Pathways to Pakistan*, Orient Longman, Lahore, 1961.

Kheer, Dhananjay, *Veer Savarkar*, Popular Prakashan, Bombay, 1967.

Khosla, G.D., *Stern Reckoning*, Delhi, 1948.

Knight, E.F., *Where Three Empires Meet*, Longmans Green, London 1893.

Korbel, Josef, *Danger in Kashmir*, Princeton University Press, Princeton, 1954.

Lakhanpal, P.L., *Essential Documents and Notes on Kashmir Dispute,* International Books, Delhi, 1965.

Lamb, Alastair, *Crisis in Kashmir: 1947-66*, Routledge and Kegan Paul, London, 1966.

Lamb, Alastair, *Kashmir: A Disputed Legacy*, Roxford Books, UK, 1991.

Lawrence, Walter, *The Valley of Kashmir,* OUP, London, 1895; reprinted by Kesar Publishers, Srinagar, 1967.

Lawrence, Walter, *The India We Served*, Houghton Mifflin, New York, 1928.

Madhok, Balraj, *Kashmir: Centre of New Alignments*, Deepak Prakashan, Delhi, 1987.

Madhok, Balraj, *Rationale of Hindu State*, Indian Book Gallery, Delhi, 1982.

Mahajan, Mehr Chand, *Looking Back: An Autobiography*, Asia Publishing House, New Delhi, 1963.

Mansergh, N. (ed.), *The Transfer of Power 1942-47* (12 vols.), HMSO, London.

Mazumdar, R.C., *The Vedic Age,* Allen and Unwin, London.

Menon, V.P., *The Story of the Integration of the Indian States,* Orient Longman, New Delhi, 1985 edn.

Menon, V.P., *The Transfer of Power in India,* London, 1957.

Mir Qasim, *My Life and Times,* Allied, New Delhi, 1992.

Moon, Penderel, *Divide and Quit,* Chatto and Windus, London, 1964.

Moorcroft, William and Trebeck, George, *Travels in the Himalayan Provinces of Hindustan and the Punjab* (2 vols.), John Murray, London, 1841.

Moore, R.J., *Endgames of Empire,* Clarendon Press, Oxford, 1988.

Moore, R.J., *Escape from Empire: The Attlee Government and the Indian Problem,* Clarendon Press, Oxford, 1983.

Moore, Thomas, *Lalla Rookh,* George C. Harrap, London, 1846.

Mosley, Leonard, *The Last Days of the British Raj,* Weidenfeld and Nicolson, London, 1962.

Mullik, B.N., *My Years with Nehru: Kashmir,* Allied, New Delhi, 1971.

Musa, Mohammad, *My Version,* Wajidalis, Lahore, 1983.

Nehru, Jawaharlal, *An Autobiography,* Bodley Head, London, 1936.

Nehru, Jawaharlal, *Letters to Chief Ministers, 1947-64* (5 vols), OUP, New Delhi.

Nehru, Jawaharlal, *Selected Works,* Jawaharlal Nehru Memorial Fund, New Delhi, 1986.

Neve, Arthur, *Thirty Years in Kashmir,* Edward Arnold, London, 1913.

Noorani, A.G., *The Kashmir Question,* P.C. Manaktalas, Bombay, 1964.

Pandey, B.N., *Nehru,* Macmillan, London, 1976.

Pandit, K.N., *Baharistan-i-Shahi: A Chronicle of Medieval Kashmir,* Firma K.L. Mukhopadhyay, Calcutta, 1991.

Patel, Vallabhbhai, *Sardar Patel's Correspondence,* Durga Das (ed.) (10 vols.) Navajivan Trust, Ahmedabad,

Puri, Balraj, *Jammu and Kashmir: Triumph and Tragedy of Indian Federalisation,* New Delhi, 1981.

Puri, Balraj, *Kashmir: Towards Insurgency,* Orient Longman, New Delhi, 1993.

Rao, Amiya and Rao, B.G., *Six Thousand Days,* Sterling Publishers, New Delhi, 1974.

Rogers, Alexander (trans.), *Tuzuk-i-Jahangiri* (*The Memoirs of*

Jahangir), Royal Asiatic Society, London, 1909; reprinted by Munshiram Manoharlal, Delhi, 1968.

Schonberg, Baron Erich von, *Travels in India and Kashmir* (2 vols), Hurst and Blacket, London, 1853.

Sen, L.P., *Slender Was the Thread: Kashmir Confrontation 1947-48*, Orient Longman, New Delhi, 1969.

Shankar, V., *My Reminiscences of Sardar Patel* (2 vols.), Macmillan, New Delhi, 1974.

Shankardas, Rani Dhawan, *Vallabhbhai Patel: Power and Organisation in Indian Politics*, Orient Longman, New Delhi, 1988.

Sharma, B.L., *Kashmir Awakes*, Vikas, New Delhi, 1977.

Singh, Lt. Gen. Harbaksh, *War Despatches*, Lancer International, New Delhi, 1991.

Singh, Karan, *Heir Apparent: An Autobiography*, OUP, New Delhi, 1982; revised edn. 1984.

Singh, Karan, *Sadar-i-Riyasat*, OUP, New Delhi, 1985.

Singh, Khushwant, *A History of the Sikhs*, Princeton University Press, Princeton, 1963.

Sinha, S.K., *Operation Rescue: Military Operations in Jammu and Kashmir 1947-49*, Vision Books, New Delhi, 1977.

Stein, M.A., *Memoir on the Ancient Geography of Kashmir*, Archibald Constable, London, 1902.

Sufi, G.M.D., *Kashmir* (2 vols.), Light & Life Publishers, New Delhi, 1974.

Tendulkar, D.G., *Mahatma* (8 vols.), Publications Division, Govt. of India, New Delhi, 1954.

Teng, M.K., Bhatt, R.K.K. and Kaul, Santosh, *Kashmir: Constitutional History and Documents*, Light & Life Publishers, New Delhi, 1977.

Teng, M.K. and Kaul, S., *Kashmir's Special Status*, Light & Life Publishers, New Delhi, 1975.

Teng, M.K., *Kashmir: Article 370*, Light & Life Publishers, New Delhi, 1990.

Thomas, Raju G.C., *Perspectives on Kashmir: The Roots of Conflict in South Asia*, Westview, USA, 1992.

Torrens, H.D., *Travels in Ladak, Tartary and Kashmir*, Otley, London, 1863.

Trivedi, Vijaya R., *Facts about Kashmir*, New Delhi, 1990.

United States Government, *Foreign Relations of the US*, Washington DC, 1948-53.

Vashisht, S., *Sheikh Abdullah: Then and Now*, Maulik Satya Prakashan, Delhi, 1968.

Vigne, G.T., *Travels in Kashmir, Ladakh, Iskardo and the Himalayas North of Punjab* (2 vols.), Henry Colburn, London, 1842.

Wakhlu, Khem Lata and Wakhlu, O.N., *Kashmir: Behind the White Curtain*, Konark, Delhi, 1992.

Wakhlu, Khem Lata and Wakhlu, O.N., *Kidnapped*, Konark, Delhi, 1993.

Wolpert, S., *Jinnah of Pakistan*, New York, 1984.

Yasin, Mohd., *History of the Freedom Struggle in Jammu and Kashmir*, New Delhi, 1980.

Younghusband, Sir Francis, *Kashmir*, Adam and Charles Black London, 1909.

Zeigler, P., *Mountbatten: The Official Biography*, Collins, London, 1985.

Index

MY BLEEDING PUNJAB
By Khushwant Singh

"On the 1st of Baisakh, 13th April 1978, celebrated as New Year's day in the Punjabi calendar, Jarnail Singh Bhindranwale exploded like a nuclear bomb. It not only shook overfed Punjabis out of their slumbers but the fall-out continues to plague the rest of the country even today." This indeed is the tragic story of the troubled and terror-torn state of Punjab. Today, the complexities of the problem seem not only to be defying all solutions but at periodic intervals, pose a very real threat to the integrity of the nation. This book, in parts unashamedly emotional, lucidly traces the history of the problem, detailing the grievances and resentments of the Punjabis since Independence and touching upon all the major developments.

What makes this volume special is the author's personal involvement, apparent on every page, and reflecting his views on punjab politics and the mess made by narrow-minded Akali leaders, on the one side, and the deliberately mischievous politics of the central government, on the other. The unfortunate result is there for all to see : all progress in the most progressive state of India is at a standstill, its agricultural and industrial economy lies ruined and its administration and judiciary has been reduced to shambles, what is perhaps more disturbing is the fact that there is still no hope of a solution on the horizon.

This book is a must for anyone who wants an indepth understanding of the present impasse.